Half Moon Series

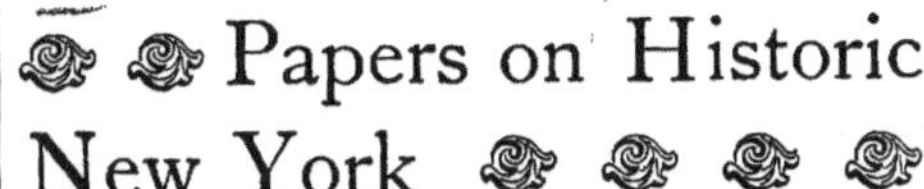

Papers on Historic New York

Edited by Maud Wilder Goodwin :: :: Alice Carrington Royce :: :: Ruth Putnam

First Series

G. P. PUTNAM'S SONS, New York and London The Knickerbocker Press
MDCCCXCVII

Contents

CONTENTS.

Contents.

Half Moon Series

Published in the Interest of the New York City History Club

VOLUME I. NUMBER I

The Stadt Huys of New Amsterdam

BY ALICE MORSE EARLE

THE Stadt Huys of New Amsterdam was, as its name indicates, the first City Hall of the old city that is now New York. It stood on the present site of the warehouses at Numbers 71 and 73 Pearl Street, facing what is now Coenties Slip. It is said a portion of its foundation is still standing; if so, it is the sole relic of Dutch architecture left in New York. To understand fully the exact appearance of this most important and historic building of New Netherland days, we must first know of the condition of the town around it in 1642, when it was built. The shore-line was entirely different from the present one: there were, of course, no slips and wharves; and what are now Water, South, and Front Streets, with intervening lands, were then part of the bay, entirely covered with water by every high tide. There was no street where the Stadt Huys stood; it was simply run up on the "Water Side." It was alone on the strand for some years, with no neighboring houses around; and, as it was twice as high as any of the houses that were built further inland or at its side, it could be plainly and proudly seen by all incoming ships from the anchorage-ground at the foot of Whitehall Street, where Governor Stuyvesant had a "hand-board" set up on the shore, and where all vessels were compelled to anchor until they could be properly supervised.

In front of the Stadt Huys was an uninterrupted view of the cheerful waters of the beautiful river and bay, and eastward across the river lay the green shores of "'t lange Eylandt, the pearel of New Netherland," where, said Hendrick Hudson's men, "the lands were as pleasant with grass and flowers and goodly trees as any they had ever seen, and very sweet smells came therefrom."

Towards the south the distant fruit and nut trees of Nooten Island (now Governor's Island) bounded pleasantly the horizon.

The waters of the bay rolled close to the Stadt Huys, at its very feet; the highest tides rose threateningly near the foundations; and a stone wall was soon put up in front of the building to keep off the encroaching waters. This temporarily protected the building but not the rest of the shore, and often the washing of the tide rendered the vicinity almost impassable.

In 1654 a carpenter named Sybout Claesen, who lived on the shore west of the Stadt Huys, complained to the government (or the director) that he was the only person who made any attempt to protect the shore against the washing of the tide; and that

" inasmuch as the sheet-piling before his house has fallen down during the late high water," he should not repair it unless his neighbors did the same. So it was ordered by the government that from " the gardens at the corner of the ditch" (the foot of Broad Street) to the Stadt Huys, the shore should be planked up and filled in with earth from the hill belonging to Carl Van Brugh, a little elevation near the Stadt Huys. This was the first step of a most important city improvement—a useful water-front; this barrier was known as the Schoeynge, or sheathing of wood. It consisted of planks driven endwise into the mud and filled in behind with solid earth and the city rubbish. This Schoeynge grew from 1654 to 1656, and from Broad Street to Wall Street (not without many threats of fines to negligent neighbors for delinquency in their duty), and on its completion it made a fine dry walk along the shore, which was called *De Waal,* or *Lang de Waal,* which many careless historians (and some great historians) of New York confound with the present Wall Street.

The expense of this Schoeynge was shared by the government and by property owners on the water-side, who were much benefited thereby, for it made good building-lots, and ere long the street grew both populous and popular.

In 1672 this shore highway of wooden supports " between the Stadt Huys and Tryntje Clocks" was so washed away as to be thought " mischievous," and a stone wall was decreed, with two half-moon batteries—one just " before the house where Long Mary lives."

This battery had three demi-culverins. In 1688 it also was "most ruined and washed away by the sea." At the close of the century it had a battery of five guns. In front of the Stadt Huys stood the cage and whipping-post. By Dongan's Charter the city had been granted the shore around the island, from high-water to low-water mark. Soon the tide-lots were divided and sold. By 1692 a regular system of filling-in obtained, and building on reclaimed sites. On the shore south of Whitehall Street was a small street of one block called 't Water, and when the flats were filled in this street was continued and called Water Street.

By the side of the Stadt Huys ran Coenties Lane, which still exists, but no longer green and beautiful as of yore. This lane and Coenties Slip were so called because the land in this vicinity was the property of Conraet Ten Eyck, who was familiarly nicknamed Coentje, or, as we now change the j to i, Coentie. Ten Eyck Slip also was named for him. This name, pronounced coon-ty, was next called coonchy, then quinchy, and is now often called by dock-men quincy.

In the rear of the Stadt Huys was Hoogh Straat, the beginning of the road which led to the ferry-house for the Brooklyn ferry, which was at Peck Slip. From Whitehall to Broad Street Hoogh Straat was called Brouwer Straat. It could be reached directly by persons going from the Stadt Huys by walking through a path in a trim garden which in the early days was cheerful with cabbages and garden flowers, but in its grand and formal position as the Stadt Huys Garden, was waving with grain raised by the burgomaster's secretary. At the end of the path an entrance-gate opened on the street. Hoogh Straat was the favorite location for residences at that time of many of the fashionable folk of New Amsterdam, as these names of its residents show: Loockermans, De Peyster, Van Brugh, Verplanck, Van Couenhouven, Bayard, Duyckinck, and two English gentlemen, John Lawrence and Isaac Bedlow. From its importance and the influence of these solid men Hoogh Straat (and its continuation, Brouwer Straat) was the first street to be paved, which was done with cobblestones in 1657; hence the present name, Stone Street.

Broad Street was, in early days, a canal or inlet of the sea, and was called De Heere Gracht, and extended from the East River to Wall Street; and as far as Exchange Place its water rose and fell with the tide. It was crossed by several foot-bridges, and one broad bridge at Hoogh Straat, which even became a general meeting-place to transact business. And when the burghers and merchants decided to meet at this bridge every Friday morning regularly, they there established the first Exchange in New York City. It is interesting to note that the center of trade has never changed in the city in the lapse of two centuries and a half. The various exchanges still linger in the neighborhood of the early Dutch Exchange, in spite of the miles of city growth.

In 1660 the walks on the banks of the Graft were paved, and soon it was bordered by the dwellings of good citizens; much favored on account of the homelikeness to the Dutchman, so Mr. Janvier suggests, of having a good, strong-smelling canal constantly under one's nose.

Until 1655 the sides of the Heere Graft formed the market-place of the town; it was a landing-place without the expenses of a dock. Here the Indian paddled up in his canoe and bartered his tobacco or maize for blankets or rum. Here the farmer from Long Island or New Harlem, or Bergen Point, brought his fruit and vegetables for exchange for clothing, beer, tools, etc. Here was the annual Kermis, the ten days' fair which began on the Monday after the feast of St. Bartholomew, August 24th. This fair of St. Bartholomew's was also a great festival or fair in England, and one specially observed by the wool-workers and cloth-manufacturers. And when we know the close connection of England and Holland in the manufacture of wool, we can understand the mutual Kermis on St. Bartholomew's Day. At this New Amsterdam Kermis the goods were sold from tents. In 1659 a yearly cattle-market or fair was held on the Bowling Green from October 20th for six weeks. During this fair no visitor could be arrested for debt; and the attendance was large from Connecticut, New Jersey, and up the Hudson. The fish market was on Coenties Slip, in front of the Stadt Huys.

The old Stadt Huys would seem but a poor thing to us to-day, architecturally, as a municipal building; but it was a very satisfactory edifice to the colonists. It was about fifty feet square; three stories high in the walls, and two more good stories in the roof, which afforded some very useful rooms. The little windows high up in the gable ends, and the corbel roof ascending in successive steps, instead of in a regular slope, were suggestive of the architecture of Old Amsterdam. The great court-room within was one of some dignity. On the window-panes were graven the arms of New Amsterdam. Over the justice's bench were the orange, blue, and white colors of the West India Company, and the colors of the Fatherland, and also the painted coat-of-arms for the city, which had been sent over by the Directors in Holland in 1654. On the wall, near the door, hung the fifty leathern buckets, which constituted the chief equipment of the town against fires. The magistrates' seats were invested with dignity and comfort by the stuffed cushions.

This building had not been erected for either town hall or court-house, but had been built originally by Director Keift as a Harberg, or tavern. So many traders and visitors came to New Amsterdam from ships trading between Virginia and New England, and so many had to be entertained at the Fort, that perhaps the Director tired of his enforced and constant hospitality.

Many a merry-making did the old Harberg see when a hostelry, under the jovial reign of mine host Phillip Gerritsen. Many a kan of brandy and anker of wine was sold to the gay visitors and prosperous traders who landed at Manhattan. Occasionally, too, though rarely, a tavern fight took place among half-drunken roysters, in spite of the rigid hand of the law, which was literally the hand of Director Keift or Director Stuyvesant.

The original court of the settlement was composed of the Director and his Council; it was both a legislative and judicial body; and as members of the Council were wholly under the control of the Director, it may be said the court was the Director.

Van der Donck said in his interesting and valuable account of the colony sent to Holland in 1656, that one councilor was wholly overruled by Stuyvesant, another was afraid, that the lieutenant of the soldiers (an Englishman) did not well understand Dutch, and so said yes to everything, while the Fiskaal was kept wholly out of the Council; thus was Stuyvesant monarch of all he surveyed.

In State matters he certainly had unbounded rights; he abolished Indian titles, and no transfers or transactions in real estate were legal without his signature. He incorporated towns, imposed taxes; he borrowed public moneys, and spent them untrammeled and uninspected. He levied fines, established wages, and issued ordinances. In church matters he installed ministers, regulated salaries, enforced church-rates, and banished heretics. In all these doings he was entirely uncontrolled, and for many years entirely unquestioned by any one in the colony.

In 1656, through the persistent efforts of Van der Donck, Bont, Couwenhouven, and other intelligent men in the colony, in well-grounded appeals to the States-General, the West India Company was obliged to resign the form of government by one autocratic and untrammeled Director, and to share the control of New Amsterdam with a board of officers after the manner and name of those of the towns of the Fatherland, viz.: a schout, two burgomasters and five schepens. These officers were by command of the States-General to have been elected by the citizens, but Governor Stuyvesant boldly disregarded orders, and took it upon himself to fill the offices by his own appointments. Naturally, none of the men to whom the reform was due received any office. The appointments were well received and were worthy ones, except that of Van Tienhoven to the office of schout. The early city schout was also schout-fiskaal till 1660, but the proper duties of the schout were really a combination only of these pertaining now to the Mayor, Sheriff, and District Attorney. In the little town one man could readily perform all these duties. He also presided in the court, though to this the burgomasters objected. So it may be plainly seen that an offender could be arrested, prosecuted, and judged by one and the same person, which seems to us scarcely judicious; but the bench of magistrates had one useful power—that of mitigating and altering the sentence demanded by the schout. And we frequently find in the records many changes of the sentences through this power. Often a fine of one hundred guilders would be reduced to twenty-five; often the order for whipping would be set aside, and the command of branding as well. I have not noted any cases where the schout's fine or sentence was increased by the magistrates.

The duties of the burgomasters and schepens were

twofold: they regulated municipal affairs like a board of aldermen, and they sat as a court of justice, both in civil and criminal cases. The annual salary of burgomaster was fixed at one hundred and forty dollars, and that of a schepen at one hundred dollars. As these salaries were to come out of the municipal chest (which was chronically empty) they never were paid. When funds did come in from the excise on taverns and on slaughtered cattle; from the tax on land, the fees on transfers, etc., they always had to be paid out in other ways—for the schoolroom, the Graft, the watchroom, the Stadt Huys, for all kinds of city repairs. It never entered the minds of those guileless New York rulers two centuries ago to pay themselves first and let the other creditors go without; they took their satisfaction in occasionally grumbling, in the dignity of their office, in their grand titles of worshipful lords, high mightiness, etc.; in a separate and exalted pew in church, where they sat in state and comfort on the Stadt Huys cushions, which were brought over for them with some pomp each Sunday to the church by the sexton.

Though municipal powers were accorded to these magistrates, there was considerable curtailing and overriding of their decisions, especially by Stuyvesant; if they ventured mildly to protest, a choleric and overbearing message was his response.

One of the most characteristic examples of Stuyvesant's choler and imperiousness is found in his communication to the burgomasters and schepens in 1654, on the subject of Shrovetide festivities. It had been a custom in the Fatherland as well as in New Netherland to take part on Shrove Tuesday in a sport known as "riding the goose." This cruel Dutch custom consisted in greasing a living goose, hanging it up, and while riding rapidly past it trying to seize it by the head. The Director issued an order forbidding farmers' servants to ride the goose at the feast of Bacchus and Shrovetide. When the burgomasters heard of the putting forth of this order without consultation with their board, they gave expression to some demurs. Whereupon came a fulminating bomb of a message from the Fort insultingly addressed with intent to demean, to the "Little bench of justices." The Director recounted his original order, the burgomasters' objections, and his own reasons for his order, "that it is altogether unprofitable, unnecessary, and criminal for subjects and neighbors to celebrate such popish and pagan feasts; and yet, notwithstanding the same (as the Burgomasters and Schepens sustain) may in some places of the Fatherland be looked at through the fingers." Throughout the entire message the board is often called "the little bench of justices" in such terms as these: "Appreciating their own authority, quality, and commission better than others, the Director and Council hereby make known to the Burgomasters and Schepens that the institution of a little bench of justices under the name of the schout, burgomasters, and schepens, or commissioners, does in no wise diminish aught of the power of the Director-General and Councilors."

All this sort of thing went on till 1658, when the

burgomasters and schepens flatly refused to accept Stuyvesant's appointment of Resolved Waldron as schout; and having conveyed word quietly to Amsterdam by one Pieter Tonneman of Breuckelen, that he was their solid choice, Pieter triumphantly secured his commission, returned with it to New Amsterdam, and took his seat in the Stadt Huys on the bench previously occupied by Schout De Sille.

The court was held once a fortnight, and in times of crowded business once a week. For some years it usually took a winter recess from December 14th to three weeks after Christmas. This long holiday included those Dutch red-letter days, the Feast of Santa Claas, Kerstydt or Christmas, and Nieuw Jaar, or New Year's Day. "Whereas," says the court record, "the winter festivities are at hand, it is found good that between this day and three weeks after Christmas the ordinary meetings of the court shall be dispensed with."

It was very stiff about punctuality and constancy of attendance at board-meetings. In 1663, whoever of its members came half an hour late paid ten stuyvers; an hour late one guilder, and if wholly absent two guilders.

The first lawyer to come to New Netherland was Adriaen Van der Donck. He was a Doctor of both Canon and Civil Laws, and had been educated at the University of Leyden. He made a request of the College of the XIX in Amsterdam in 1653 to be permitted to practice law in New Amsterdam; but with the high sense of justice characteristic in general of the Dutch, he was forbidden to plead, on the ground that, as there was no other lawyer in the colony, there would be no one who would oppose him.

The first notary to come to New Netherland was Dirck van Schelluyne; he arrived in 1641. He was appointed High Bailiff, to levy executions and enforce processes, but he had been a notary at The Hague, and in 1650 was commissioned to practice in New Netherland. He soon protested boldly against Stuyvesant's attacks on the rights of the public, and said he dared prepare no more legal writings under such arbitrary conditions as existed. He finally complained to the States-General, from whom he had received his commission, and it sent across the sea a positive mandamus to Stuyvesant and the Council not to interfere with Schelluyne in his practice. Pelgrum Clocq was another notary, probably not an over skillful or successful one; at any rate, he was at one time suspended for six weeks from his practice as a punishment for his indifference to a law of the subaltern court; and he was also sued for payment of his board.

Another well-known notary and practitioner and pleader in the busy little court held in the Stadt Huys was Solomon La Chair. His manuscript volume of nearly three hundred pages, containing detailed accounts of all the business he transacted in Manhattan, is now in the County Clerk's office in New York. He had a good deal of law business brought to him, for he could speak and write both English and Dutch. He not only conducted lawsuits for others, but he seems to have been in constant legal hot water on his own account. The prohibition, in early New England towns—in Boston and Concord—of lawyers pleading any cases save their own in court might have been placed on Solomon La Chair, and still he would have been reasonably busy.

He was sued for drinking and not paying for a can of sugared wine; and for a half-aam of costly French wine; for the balance of payment for a house he had purchased. He pleaded for more time, and, with an ingenuous guilelessness scarcely characteristic of the law, said in explanation that he had had money gathered at the time for payment, but it had somehow dropped through his fingers. "The court condemned him to pay at once"—not being taken in by any such simplicity. He had to pay a fine of twelve guilders for affronting both fire inspector and court messenger. He insulted the brandt-meester who came to inspect his chimney, and was fined; then he called the bode who came to collect the fine "a little cock, booted and spurred."

He won one important suit for the town of Gravesend, by which the right of that town to the entire region of Coney Island was established; and he received in payment for his legal services therein the munificent sum of twenty-four florins (ten dollars) paid in gray peas. Still poorer was his compensation for legal services to the son of Lady Deborah Moody—"an English book of no use."

He kept a tavern and he had a yacht, *The Pear Tree*, which ran on trading trips to Albany, and there were two or three lawsuits in regard to that. He was also a farmer of the excise on slaughtered cattle; but, in spite of all his variety of profit-bearing employment, he died insolvent in 1664.

The last lawsuit in which Lawyer Solomon had any share was through a posthumous connection: the burgher who furnished an anker of French wine for his funeral claimed a position as preferred creditor to the estate. His widow, Anneke, appeared a few times in court; she pawned a gown and petticoat to Mr. Philipse to support her during her very short widowhood, and after her marriage to William Doeckles received, by permission of the sympathizing court, a portrait of her deceased Solomon, and also, for a fair price, the La Chair family bed.

The notary Walewyn Van der Veen was also frequently in trouble, usually for contempt of court. And I presume "the little bench of justices" was rather trying in its ways to a notary who knew about law. On one occasion, when a case relating to a bill of exchange had been decided against him, Van der Veen spoke of the magistrates as "simpletons and blockheads." This was the scathing sentence of his punishment:

"That Walewyn Van der Veen, for his committed insult, shall here beg forgiveness, with uncovered head, of God, Justice, and the Worshipful Court, and moreover pay as a fine one hundred and ninety guilders."

The contumacious Van der Veen also called the Secretary a rascal; thereat the latter, much aggrieved, demanded "honorable and profitable reparation" for the insult. The schout judged this epithet to be a slander and an affront to the secretary which "affected his honor, being tender," and the honor of the court as well, since the insult was to a member of the court, and the notary paid a fine of fifty guilders as an example to other slanderers, "who for trifles have constantly in their mouths curses and abuses of other honorable people." This seems putting it rather strong, and the honorable bench of High Mightinesses, though so severe on defamatory words of others, did not hesitate to use plain enough language themselves. Poor widow Pierteje Jans had her house sold on an execution, and, exasperated by the proceeding, she called out to the officers, "Ye despoilers, ye bloodsuckers! ye have not sold, but given away, my house." Instead of treating these as the intemperate words of a disappointed woman, the officers promptly ran whining to the Stadt Huys and complained to the court that her words were "a sting which could not be endured." Pierteje was denounced as shameful; her words were termed "foul, villainous, injurious, nay, infamous words," and also called a blasphemy, insult, affront and reproach. She was accused of insulting, defaming, affronting and reproaching the court, and that she was in the highest degree reprimanded, particularly corrected and severely punished; and, after being forbidden to indulge in any more such blasphemies, she was released.

For serious words against the government which could be regarded as treasonable, the punishment, as in all countries and nations at that time, was death.

One Claerbout van ter Goes used such words (unfortunately they are not given in the indictment), and a judgment was recorded from the schout and each burgomaster and schepen as to what punishment would be proper. He was branded, whipped, and banished, and escaped hanging only by the vote of one member of the board.

As the punishments accorded for crimes under the Dutch laws were not severe for the notions of the times, it seems strange to read some fierce ordinances, though there is no record of any executions in accordance with them. For instance, in January, 1659, by the Director-General and Council, with the advice of the burgomasters and schepens, it was enacted that "No person shall strip the fences of posts or rails under penalty, for the first offence, of being whipped and branded; and, for the second, of punishment with the cord until death ensues." Of course, this matter of rail-stealing reached farther than at first appeared; there was a scarcity of grain, and if the fences were stolen the cattle would trample down and destroy the growing crop—hence might come a famine. In 1674 all persons were forbidden to leave the city, except by city-gate, under penalty of death; this also was when war was threatened.

There is one most shocking record of an attempt at capital punishment in 1641, before the Stadt Huys was built. Nine negroes were tried for killing one of their mates. They all pleaded guilty, and this was apparently rather a facer to the magistrates; for to hang nine able-bodied negro slaves belonging to the

Company was a costly operation. The compromising sentence was that the negroes should draw lots to determine who should be "punished with the cord until death"—praying to God to direct that the lot might fall on the guiltiest one. "It fell by God's Providence on Manuel Gerrit, the Giant." Four days later he was brought out to be executed. Mr. Gerard, in his interesting paper on "The Old Stadt Huys," has drawn a striking picture of the scene. The Giant was hanged with two halters, which broke under his great weight. Both men and women pleaded with the Director for his life; the Domine prayed, while the Giant chanted barbaric invocations to his fetich. At last he was pardoned, perhaps because it was so hard to hang him, and led off by his swarthy friends, much sobered and indeed somewhat bereft of his wits by his near view of grim death.

The walls of the Stadt Huys echoed to much talk of trade as well as of law. To it came the welcome news of many an arrival of a trading-ship from Holland, or slaver from "the coast." What pleasure did the news afford the little town! The national flag was proudly hoisted; and the population hastened in boats down the bay to meet the incoming vessel. Think of the excitement to the colonists of an arrival of a ship from Europe in those days, bearing varied stores to add to their personal comfort; bringing information of the intensely thrilling political events which were then in progress in the European states, and, better still, bearing news from friends and relatives in the Fatherland, whom they might never see again! Pleasant to read are the names of the Dutch trading-ships in Dutch days: *Sea Mew, Flower of Guelder, Woodyard, Blue Cock, King Solomon, New Netherlands Fortune, Great Christopher, Black Eagle, Pear Tree,* and others.

The White Horse was a slaver, and *The Herring* was a ship-of-war of two hundred and eighty tons burden, carrying two metal, sixteen iron, and two stone guns, thus making a truly formidable sight. To the Stadt Huys was borne the news of the loss of the ship *Princess*, in 1647, on its way to Holland, with many loved ones on board, eighty in all—the men returning for political purposes. To it came the news of the first shipwreck on our coast of which we have any account—that of the *Prince Mauritz* on Fire Island, and the escape of all on board through the waves and over the ice to a barren shore, "without weeds, grass, or timber of any sort to make a fire;" yet all on board lived through the exposure. The good ship's bones were but the first of many to whiten and splinter and rot on that barren shore. Many yachts or trading-sloops ran up and down the river, bustling into Esopus (now Kingston), and thence to Fort Orange (now Albany). All of the large ships but two were, it is said, owned in Holland, but the coasters and river sloops were usually owned in New Amsterdam. Twenty years after the occupation of the British there were owned in the "Cittie" three barques, three brigantines, twenty-six sloops, forty-six open boats. In the coast trade many vessels from other colonies anchored in front of the Stadt Huys, so it was a pleasant and busy sight when strolling on the strand.

All vessels under fifty tons were obliged to anchor between "Capsey Hook" (the present Battery) and the guide-board set up at the order of Stuyvesant in front of the Stadt Huys, or a trifle below it. Larger vessels were permitted to anchor as far as the second guide-board, which was erected at "Smits Valley" (near present Fulton Ferry).

The walls of the Stadt Huys also heard much queer talk of the Red Sea trade, the Cape traffic, of private ventures to Madagascar—in short, of pirates. It was hard work in those days to be honest on the high seas. That very respectable and upright New York citizen, Captain Kidd, the honored friend of New York's most worthy merchants, the closeted confidant of the Governor, the chosen representative of New York commercial circles, fell sorely from grace when he ventured to sail too close to richly laden galleons in tropical seas, and spent his last days under a serious cloud ere he was hanged. I should not like to affirm that some very shaky transactions in "privateering" were not whispered about and patched up and even hatched out in the Stadt Huys.

The old Stadt Huys saw many of the beginnings of New York's greatness. Within its walls was held, in 1665, the first Court of Admiralty. In 1664 the articles of capitulation, which became the laws of the colony, were signed in the Stadt Huys; and here, too, the surrender of the colony by the English to the Dutch was made; and soon again the English had control. Thus it saw three changes of sovereignty.

The permanent prosperity of the colony of New Netherland did not come with the Dutch rule, but under the English when it beçame New York. This was not at all attributive to nationality, or to any executive inability of the Dutch, or any special excellence of the English, but simply to the conditions by which the Dutch colony was governed. The depressing clogs on commerce, through hampering monopoly of trade, proved the vices and clamps ever attendant on any government controlled solely by a trading-company (as was the Dutch West India Company); "the worst of all governments," says Adam Smith.

In 1652 we learn from a letter of the West India Company to Stuyvesant of another significant day for the Stadt Huys and all it represented—the day when the first public school was held therein. Jan de la Montagne was the teacher; and the walls resounded to the sound of childish catechisms and ciphering in good Holland Dutch, and childish wails also over the stern Dutch discipline. Sometimes there was a sterner scene, a heavier rod. In the presence of the Worshipful Magistrates, a little girl of ten who stole was severely whipped with rods by her mother and Long Anna; poor little Lysbert! bound out to service; and stealing black seawant (as she pleaded with the inconsequence of childhood) because Barbar, the negress, stole a silver bell.

One of the most impressive scenes enacted within

the walls of the Stadt Huys, and one of the last, was the strange and extraordinary midnight funeral of Leisler and Melbourne. Their trial had also taken place in the Stadt Huys. At the time of their execution, in 1691, those victims of political reverses had been buried in a hole at the foot of the gallows. Many of the best citizens finally asked in 1698 that their bodies then receive Christian burial, in the crypt of the old Dutch church. To this the Governor, the Earl of Bellomont, consented, partly "out of a principle of compassion" for the families of the dead men, but chiefly out of respect to an act of Parliament which legitimized Leisler's act. Of course, this decision met much violent opposition, for opinion still was strong on the subject; but the Governor sent a guard of honor of a hundred soldiers to assist in the ceremonies and enforce law. On a bitter night in October, 1698, when "a rank storm blew," at solemn midnight, the poor, dishonored bodies were disinterred; and with a vast concourse of people with lighted torches, to the sound of muffled drums, were borne in coffins to the Stadt Huys, where they lay in state for several days. Truly, this was a weird and gruesome scene—the muffled drums, the fierce winds and rains, the beating of the waves on the shore, and the final repose within the sheltering walls of the old Stadt Huys.

In 1679 the Stadt Huys grew suddenly old. It had been built not two score years and was of stone, and was supposed to be substantial; but an appropriation had to be made for studs and planks to support it in its weakness. For twenty years longer it remained in public life, then was pronounced unsafe by builders. In 1695 it took one hundred and fifty pounds' worth of repairs to make it fit for use four or five years more. In 1697, anticipating a crowded assemblage at a great trial (probably of Bayard and others for treason), the Mayor feared the Stadt Huys would not hold together. So masons and carpenters examined it and again temporarily propped it.

Thus it was honored to the end of the century, and until it had seen the end of the lives of nearly all of its first Dutch friends. Domine Selyns still was living. It was sold with its garden land, at public vendue, to a merchant named Rodman, for nine hundred and twenty pounds. But its bell, the iron work of the prison rooms, and the King's Arms were reserved.

It then entered into a quiet business life. In Revolutionary times such of the building as remained with changes and additions was occupied by a firm named Brinckerhoff and Van Wyck—thus preserving its Dutch character. In 1806 Abraham Brinckerhoff occupied it.

Its successor, of English name and English architecture, City Hall, was built where the Custom House now stands on Wall Street, and it faced Broad Street. It cost £4,000; and in this City Hall Washington was inaugurated President.

The last days of the Stadt Huys "at the turn of the century" saw the city of New York a well-established commercial port. At one time forty square-rigged vessels and sixty-two sloops were entered at the Custom House: so the anchorage-ground was well filled, a cheery sight to the inhabitants. There were four thousand four hundred inhabitants, of whom one-eighth were negroes; when the Stadt Huys was built there were not seven hundred inhabitants. Wall Street was becoming a favorite locality for residences; its uptown popularity was proved by the fact that a lot on the corner of Wall and Broad streets sold for the large sum of eight hundred and fifteen dollars.

The city was practically all south of Wall Street, for the erection of the Cingel, or barricade with gates, on the present line of Wall Street, had formed a strong barrier naturally to the spreading out of the city northward. The universal habit, too, of the day, of aggregation, of crowding together, tended to prevent extension of the city. This would have been natural enough in this new strange world, this sense of clinging together for natural support and neighborliness, even if it had not existed everywhere in the Old World. The habit of city suburbs had nowhere been formed.

Broadway and all the region west of it was really of little account; in the little town it was out of the world. There were a few fine houses near the Bowling Green, but there was no street or road west of Broadway, and not nearly as much land as now; for the tide covered everything in the lower part of the town up to the present line of Greenwich Street. All west of that street is made land.

The upper part of the island was a dense forest, where deer still herded and wolves roamed. Bears, too, were occasional visitors. The English chaplain told of a bear hunt in 1680 in an orchard between Cedar Street and Maiden Lane, which he said gave him great diversion; especially as he did not attack the bear himself, but "prudently despatched a youth after him with a club." The bear was up in the tree, and the youth thumped his paws with the club, and the bear fell grumbling to the ground. And as the clergyman had no weapon, it seems to be doubtful whether in the end the adventurous youth was not despatched by the bear as well as after him.

In spite of the bear in the orchard in Cedar Street, the little, crowded, jostling metropolis had really grown citified, and had many truly urban conveniences for its prosperous citizens. Broad Street was drained with a real sewer; Broadway and some other localities were set out with shade-trees; some streets were lighted at night by a lighted lantern on a pole hung out at every seventh house. A dozen wells had been dug; one was in front of the Stadt Huys. There was a fire department with abundant buckets and ladders and laws. Bradford had introduced printing, and there were New York almanacs. There were five churches: a chapel in the fort, a Dutch Calvinist church, a Dutch Lutheran church, a French church, and the New Trinity church; and there was a Jewish synagogue.

The fine new Dutch Reformed church on Garden Street, now Exchange Place, had been opened in

1693. It had cost $28,000. It was pretty far up town, but as a very suitable piece of land next Mother Drisius's orchard could be obtained, the church had been placed thereon. It was a handsome church, with a brick steeple with a bell. The windows were engraved with the coats-of-arms of people of importance and wealth in the community, the elders and magistrates, and painted escutcheons hung on the walls. Low galleries ran along the sides, and therein sat the men of the congregations on wooden benches. The women sat on benches and chairs on the ground floor. The pulpit, brought from Holland, stood at the end of the middle aisle. The bell-rope hung down in the middle of the church in the central aisle.

Madame Knight's description of the houses in New York at this time is wonderfully clear, as is every account from her graphic pen, but very short:

"The Buildings are Brick Generaly, very stately and high, though not altogether like ours in Boston. The Bricks in some of the Houses are of divers Coullers and laid in Checkers, being glazed, look very agreeable. The inside of them is neat to admiration; the wooden work, for only the walls are plaster'd, and the Sumers and Gist are planed and kept very white scour'd, as so is all the partitions if made of Bords."

There was a regular ferry to Brooklyn, on the Island of Nassau—the ferryman summoned by blast of horn. There was regular mail service to Philadelphia and Boston. The first regular mail started by mounted post from New York for Boston on January 1, 1673. He seems also to have acted as a parcel express, for his "portmantles" were crammed with "small portable goods" and "divers bags," as well as letters. He was "active, stout, indefatigable, and honest." He could not change horses till he reached Hartford. He was ordered to keep an eye out for the best ways through forests and accommodations at fords, ferries, etc., and to watch for all fugitive soldiers and servants. While he was gone a locked box stood in the office of the Colonial Secretary at New York to collect the month's mail. The mail he brought was prepaid, and was carried to the coffee-house, placed on a table to be well-thumbed over by all who cared to examine it, and finally distributed.

There was also in the little town a metropolitan police force, a rattle-watch of twelve men for a night watch, and an imposing uniform of blue with orange list had been adopted for them.

Their wages were twenty-four stuyvers each a night, and the captain collected fifty stuyvers a month from each house as a legalized method of paying expenses. The rules for the watch are amusing. They sometimes slept on duty then as now, and paid a fine of ten stuyvers for each offense. They could not swear, nor fight, nor be "unreasonable."

There was no lack of physicians—half a dozen by 1650. A century later the historian of the province pronounced the town to be swarming with quacks.

Little is known of the early practice of medicine in New York. The doctors made and sold pills, and "Vienna drink" (a terrible dose, in which rhubarb and senna spoiled good port wine), and Dr. Hans Kiersted made Kiersted ointment, and the doctors were licensed to shave. For in Dutch days the starving doctors, to add to their income, petitioned that none but surgeons should be allowed to shave people. This was a weighty matter, and, after profound consideration, the Council gave the following answer:

"That shaving doth not appertain exclusively to *chirugery*, but is only an appanage thereof. That no man can be prevented from operating herein upon *himself*, or doing another this friendly act, provided that it be through *courtesy*, and that he do not receive any money for it, and do not keep an open shop of that sort, which is hereby forbidden, declaring in regard to the last request, this act to belong to *chirugery* and the health of man."

And the surgeons on shore were protected against the ship-barbers who landed, and who made some grave mistakes when trying to doctor as well as shave in the town. In 1658 Doctor Varravanger, somewhat disgusted at the treatment of the sick who had no families and had to trust to the care of strangers, established the first New York Hospital; which was simply a clean and suitable house, with fire and wood, and one good woman to act as matron.

Thus was the little city cared for in sickness and in health; in laws, in morals, and in religion; and the

Stadt Huys was the mill through which all temporal and spiritual matters were ground; all affairs centred and revolved around it. It was, in truth, to paraphrase Dr. Holmes's expression, the hub of New Netherland.

ALICE MORSE EARLE.

HE HALF MOON SERIES OF PAPERS ON HISTORIC NEW YORK WILL BE ISSUED MONTHLY DURING THE COMING YEAR UNDER THE EDITORSHIP OF

MAUD WILDER GOODWIN
ALICE CARRINGTON ROYCE
AND RUTH PUTNAM

AMONG THE SUBJECTS OF THE PAPERS WILL BE THE FOLLOWING

The Stadt Huys of New Amsterdam
By Alice Morse Earle

The Fourteen Miles Round
By Alfred Bishop Mason
and Mary Murdoch Mason

Wall Street
By Oswald Garrison Villard

Anneke Jans' Farm
By Ruth Putnam

The Bowery
By Edward Ringwood Hewitt and Mary Ashley Hewitt

King's College
By John B. Pine

Old Wells and Water-Courses
By George E. Waring, Jr.

Governor's Island
By Blanche Wilder Bellamy

Defences of Old New York
By Frederick D. Grant

Old Greenwich
By Elizabeth Bisland

Tammany Hall
By Talcott Williams

Half Moon Series

Published in the Interest of the New York City History Club

VOLUME I. NUMBER 2

King's College: now Columbia University 1754–1897

BY JOHN B. PINE

IN a letter to the Secretary of the Society for the Propagation of the Gospel in Foreign Parts, written in 1702, during the reign of Queen Anne, Governor Lewis Morris quaintly and prophetically observes:

"The Queen has a Farm of about 32 Acres of Land, wch Rents for £36 p. Ann: Tho the Church Wardens & Vestry have petitioned for it & my Ld four months gave ym a promise of it the proceeding has been so slow that they begin to fear the Success wont answer the expectation. I believe her Maty. would readily grant it to the Society for the asking. N. York is the Center of English America & a Proper Place for a Colledge,—& that Farm in a little time will be of considerable Value, & it's pity such a thing should be lost for want of asking, wch at another time wont be so Easily obtained."

Governor Morris's letter contains one of the earliest references to the "Queen's" or "King's" Farm, as it was generally called, and also offers the first suggestion of founding a college in the province of New York. Some fifty years elapsed before that event occurred. On October 31, 1754, a charter was granted to THE GOVERNORS OF THE COLLEGE OF THE PROVINCE OF NEW YORK IN THE CITY OF NEW YORK IN AMERICA, providing for the establishment of a college, to be known as "King's College," "for the Instruction and Education of Youth in the Learned Languages and in the Liberal Arts and Sciences." The charter named as governors the Archbishop of Canterbury, the governor of the province, and certain officers of the crown, *ex officio*, and twenty-four residents of the city. It also provided that the Rector of Trinity Church and the ministers of the Reformed Dutch, Lutheran, French, and Presbyterian Churches, for the time being, should be *ex-officio* governors; and in this respect, as well as in the prohibition of any religious discrimination, indicated the broad and non-sectarian character of the contemplated college. The delivery of the charter was delayed for some months by the opposition of those who were apprehensive that the institution would be controlled by the Church of England, but their fears must have been allayed by the very first act of the governors, who, on their acceptance of the charter on May 7, 1755, voted unanimously to petition for a supplementary charter permitting the establishment of a professorship of divinity in conformity with the doctrine established by the Synod of Dort. The additional charter was subsequently granted, but the professorship has yet to be established.

On June 3, 1755, was adopted the device for the seal of King's College, which continues to be that of Columbia University, with only the necessary alteration of name. The college is represented by a lady sitting on a throne of state, with several children at her knees to represent the pupils, and a reference to First Peter, indicating the spirit in which they should seek for true wisdom. She holds open a book, the "Living Oracles," and from her mouth proceed the words in Hebrew, "God is my light." At her feet is the motto, IN LUMINE TUO VIDEBIMUS LUMEN.

In anticipation of the granting of the charter, the friends of the college had secured the services of the Rev. Dr. Samuel Johnson, of Stratford, as president. They were singularly fortunate in their choice, as he was a man of broad and sound scholarship and of remarkably liberal and advanced views. He had been much sought after by other institutions of learning, and had resisted the earnest solicitations of Benjamin Franklin to assume the charge of the academy which afterwards developed into the University of Pennsylvania. The first prospectus, issued by Dr. Johnson, May 31, 1754, shows that he aimed to make King's College something more than a training school for the church; he destined it to have a far wider scope than the ordinary college of that day, and the plan of education which he proposed seems almost to contemplate the modern university. After stating that "the chief thing that is aimed at in this College is to teach and engage children to know God and Jesus Christ, and to love and serve him," he goes on to say: "It is further the design of this College to instruct and perfect the Youth in the Learned Languages, and in the Arts of reasoning exactly, of writing correctly and speaking eloquently; and in the Arts of numbering and measuring; of Surveying and Navigation, of Geography and History, of Husbandry, Commerce and Government, and in the Knowledge of all Nature in the Heavens above us, and in the Air, Water and Earth around us and the various kinds of Meteors, Stones, Mines and Minerals, Plants and Animals, and of everything useful for the Comfort, Convenience and Elegance of life, in the chief Manufactures relating to any of these things." The broad lines which Dr. Johnson laid down may be traced through a century and a half, and in the University of Columbia as now constituted, with its college preserving the classic traditions, and its schools of Political Science, or "Government," of "Mines and Minerals," and of Pure Science embracing "the knowledge of all nature," the early prospectus has found a complete and literal fulfilment.

Dr. Johnson was at first the sole instructor, and with a faculty thus constituted the new college began its sessions, July 17, 1754, in the schoolhouse belonging to Trinity Church. The first class consisted of Samuel Verplanck, Rudolph Ritzema, Philip Van

Cortlandt, Robert Bayard, Samuel Provoost, Thomas Martson, Henry Cruger, and Joshua Bloomer.

Trinity Church having in the interval acquired title to the King's Farm, the rector and church wardens forthwith delivered to the governors a lease and release of that portion of the farm lying on the west side of Broadway, between Barclay and Murray Streets, and extending down to the Hudson River, described as being "in the skirts of the City." Steps were at once taken to procure plans for suitable buildings, and to raise money with which to erect them; liberal contributions were received, and on August 23, 1756, the corner-stone of King's College was laid by Sir Charles Hardy, then governor of the province. The occasion is described in the *Weekly Post Boy:* "Our Lieutenant Governor with the Governors of the College and Mr. Cutting the Tutor with the students met at Mr. Willett's and thence proceeded to the House of Mr. Vandenburgh, at the Common, whither his Excellency came in his chariot, and proceeded with them about One O'clock to the College ground, near the River on the Northwest side of the City. . . . . After the stone was laid a Health was drunk to his Majesty and success to his Arms, and to Sir Charles Hardy, and Prosperity to the College." President Johnson delivered a brief address in Latin: "Which being done, the Governors and Pupils laid each his stone, and several other Gentlemen, and then they returned to Mr. Willett's; where there was a very elegant dinner; after which the usual loyal Healths were drunk, and Prosperity to the College; and the whole was conducted with the utmost decency and propriety." The stone, which has fortunately been preserved, bears the following inscription:

HVJVS COLLEGII, REGALIS DICTI, REGIO DIPLOMATE CONSTITVTI IN HONOREM DEI O.M. ATQ: IN ECCLESIÆ REIQ: PVBLICÆ EMOLVMENTVM, PRIMVM HVNC LAPIDEM POSVIT VIR PRÆCEL LENTISSIMVS, CAROLVS HARDY, EQVES AVRATVS, HVJVS PROVINCIÆ PRÆFECTVS DIGNISSIMVS. AVGTI. DIE 23º, AN. DOM. MDCCLVI.

In 1760 the fact is noted in the records that "the College buildings were so far completed that the officers and students began to lodge and mess therein." In honor of George II., and in accordance with the terms of the charter, the building thus completed was designated "King's College," and the original crown which surmounted it remains, a witness to its royal foundation. The Rev. Dr. Burnaby, an English traveller, writes: "The College when finished will be exceedingly handsome. It is to be built on three sides of a quadrangle fronting Hudson's or North River, and will be the most beautifully situated of any College, I believe, in the world"; and the college is described as it existed in 1773 as distant about a hundred and fifty yards "from the Hudson River, which it overlooks, commanding from the eminence on which it stands a most extensive and beautiful prospect." The building was planned to comprise three sides of a quadrangle, facing south. The portion completed at this date included a chapel, a residence for the president, several lecture halls and rooms for a number of students, and a "college hall" where the students dined. The students were required to lodge and diet in college, to wear caps and gowns, and to be within gates at certain hours. Evidently it was true of the social life of the college as of the "plan of education," that it was "copied in the most material parts from Queen's College, Oxford." General Washington entered his stepson John Parke Custis as a student in the college, and from the correspondence with President Cooper we learn that the tuition fee was five pounds per annum, room rent four, and board at the rate of eleven shillings a week.

During the exciting years preceding the Revolution the students seem to have taken an active interest in political affairs. It is related that a number of them participated in the affair with the sailors of the "Asia," and assisted in rescuing cannon and ammunition which were stored on the battery; and Alexander Hamilton had become a conspicuous figure before the end of his sophomore year. Dr. Johnson resigned his office in 1763, and was succeeded by the Rev. Myles Cooper, A.M., a fellow of Queen's College, Oxford. He was a man of much culture and refinement, an able instructor, of a genial disposition, and both a wit and a versifier. He was but twenty-six years of age when elected president, and was earnestly devoted to the college and active in promoting its interests, especially in England, as shown by the numerous gifts received from Oxford. His political opinions, however, rendered him extremely unpopular during the later years of his administration; for he was an ardent Tory, and expressed his views with the utmost freedom. On May 10, 1775, he wrote to a friend, "Whilst I stay in this country of confusion, which for the sake of the College, I am minded to do as long as I can with any degree of prudence"; and on the same night a mob broke into the college grounds intent upon doing him violence. Hamilton and Robert Troup, a fellow student, kept the mob at bay by haranguing them from the steps of the president's house, until Dr. Cooper had time to escape over the back fence in the scantiest of apparel. On the following day he took refuge on the "Kingfisher," an English sloop-of-war, and soon afterwards sailed for England. His Tory principles seem to have had little effect upon his students, some of whom were afterwards among the foremost champions of liberty in the cabinet and on the field —Jay and Livingston, Morris and Benson, Van Cortlandt and Rutgers, Troup and Hamilton; but his extreme partisanship was doubtless reflected upon the college, and tended to render it unpopular for the time being.

In April, 1776, upon the request of the Committee of Safety, the college was prepared for the reception of troops, the students were dispersed, and the library and apparatus were removed to the City Hall. During the Revolution the buildings were used both by the American and British troops as barracks and for hospital purposes.

COLUMBIA COLLEGE

The college exercises, suspended during the pendency of hostilities, were resumed in 1784. On May 1, 1784, an act was passed by the Legislature of the State of New York, entitled AN ACT FOR GRANTING CERTAIN PRIVILEGES TO THE COLLEGE HERETOFORE CALLED KING'S COLLEGE, FOR ALTERING THE NAME AND CHARTER THEREOF, AND ERECTING AN UNIVERSITY WITHIN THE STATE. Under this act the administration of the college passed to the Regents of the University of the State of New York, and the college received the name "Columbia"—"a word and name then for the first time recognized anywhere in law and history"—but which had already gained a patriotic and national significance in a popular song of the Revolution, "Columbia, Columbia, to glory arise."

The Regents met forthwith, and proceeded with commendable energy to reorganize the college and to raise means for its support. They voted to establish four faculties—arts, divinity, medicine, and law: the first to consist of seven professorships; the second, of such professorships as might be established by the different religious denominations; the third to be composed of seven professorships, and the last of three. In addition, there were to be a president, a secretary, and a librarian, and nine extra professors. But in projecting a scheme of such liberality the Regents were far in advance of the times and of their income, which amounted to but twelve hundred pounds. During the brief period of their control they were able to carry the plan into execution only to the extent of establishing a faculty of arts, comprising professors of mathematics, Greek and Latin, geography, natural history, French, German and the Oriental languages, and natural philosophy; and a faculty of medicine, comprising professors of chemistry, anatomy, surgery, midwifery, and the institutes and practice of medicine. The college was opened May 19, 1784, under its new name and government, and DeWitt Clinton entered as its first student.

Experience soon demonstrated that the Regents of the University, as State officers, residing in different parts of the State, were not well constituted for administrative purposes. Accordingly, three years later, the separate identity of the college was restored, and by an act, said to have been drawn by Alexander Hamilton, passed April 13, 1787, its government was transferred to THE TRUSTEES OF COLUMBIA COLLEGE IN THE CITY OF NEW YORK, as the corporation has ever since been known. The trustees found a worthy successor to the first president in his son, William Samuel Johnson, LL.D. He had gained distinction as a special commissioner to England, where he resided for five years; as a judge; and as the representative of Connecticut in the Colonial Congress and in the Constitutional Convention of 1787. He was elected president of Columbia, May 21, 1787, and held that office conjointly with that of Senator from Connecticut while Congress held its sessions in New York.

On the occasion of the first commencement of the college under its new name, held April 10, 1787, the Legislature, upon the motion of Alexander Hamilton, adjourned in order that its members might attend; and in 1789 the commencement was honored by the presence of President Washington and all the principal officers of the Government of the United States.

At the time of Dr. Johnson's accession there were thirty-nine students in the college, a portion of whom lodged and boarded in the college. The income of the college was about £1,330. The faculties of arts and medicine consisted of three professors each. In 1792 the medical faculty was reëstablished on a broader basis, with seven professors, and Dr. Samuel Bard as dean. In the following year James Kent was elected professor of law, and his lectures, afterwards expanded into his "Commentaries on American Law," are said to "have had a deeper and more lasting influence in the formation of national character than any secular book of the century." Under grants from the Legislature, the library, which had been dispersed and almost entirely lost during the Revolution, was enlarged, and a professor of moral philosophy and logic was appointed; but the suspension of legislative assistance after a few years so reduced the income of the college as to retard further progress. This financial condition unhappily prevailed for many years, and rendered it impossible to carry into effect the educational advances projected by the Regents, revived by the trustees in 1810, and again put forward in 1857. Gradual advances were made under the administration of Bishop Moore, who succeeded Dr. Johnson as president; and the fact that the services rendered by the college were fully commensurate with its resources is evidenced by its long list of honorable and distinguished graduates. DeWitt Clinton had opened the Erie Canal; Chancellor Livingston, another graduate, recognizing the genius of Fulton, had supplied the means which led to the development of steam navigation; John Stevens, of the Class of 1768, had introduced the steam railway and the screw propeller; and to all the professions, as well as to church and state, Columbia had contributed her full quota.

In 1810 the course of study in arts was broadened, and the requirements for admission considerably increased. In 1812 the first scholarships were established, and the nomination placed in the gift of the Alumni Association; and within the next twenty years the number of scholarships was largely increased, and the several religious denominations, as well as a number of educational and philanthropic institutions, were given the privilege of appointing scholars.

In 1813 the medical faculty was consolidated with the "College of Physicians and Surgeons," a separate corporation then recently established, and medical instruction ceased to be a part of the curriculum. In 1814 the college received a grant of a tract of land known as the Hosack Botanical Garden, comprising the twenty acres lying between Fifth and Sixth Avenues, Forty-seventh and Forty-ninth Streets, as compensation for lands previously granted to it, but ceded to

New Hampshire on the settlement of the boundary. This tract, which is still owned by the college, and is now one of its principal sources of income, was for a long period a heavy drain upon the slender resources of the institution, and its retention, under all the circumstances, is an evidence of the courage and foresight of the trustees. At the time this grant was made the city scarcely extended above the City Hall, and north of that the island was entirely farming land.

After the Revolution an effort was made to restore the buildings to a condition suitable for educational purposes; but the result was not fully accomplished until 1820, when two wings were added, greatly increasing the capacity and convenience of the buildings. A chapel and a library were also built, and in 1829 a building for a grammar school was erected adjacent to the college. President Moore, in his memorial address, presents a pleasing picture of "the stately sycamores on the Green, the old buildings, the great staircase, the Chapel, with its strange hanging gallery." And Mr. Jay, in his Centennial address, tells us that these venerable trees had an historic interest from the fact, which as a boy he heard from the lips of Judge Benson, that they were carried to the Green and planted by the Judge himself, and by Chief Justice Jay, Chancellor Livingston, and Recorder Harrison, all of whom were alumni.

A member of the Class of '39 gives the following description of the college as it appeared in his day, when it "occupied a plot of ground bounded by Church Street, Murray Street, and College Place.

The building was of brick, covered with stucco, painted light brown, with trimmings of free stone. The front was to the south. At the east and west ends, respectively, were two houses occupied by members of the faculty, which projected considerably beyond the middle buildings; all were three stories high, and there was an old-fashioned belfry in the middle; it was a picturesque old structure, unmistakably academic. In front was a Green of considerable size, bordered by large sycamores. The place had an air of conventual quiet and seclusion, and was delightful in summer when the shadows of the broad leaves rested on the light brown walls and the flagstones of the walk. The middle of the edifice was devoted to the chapel and library. The latter occupied the second floor, and on the floor below were the lecture rooms. The location was about the centre of the fashionable part of the city."

In the midst of these surroundings, under the successive presidencies of the Rev. William Harris, William Alexander Duer, Nathaniel F. Moore, a son of Bishop Moore, and like his father an alumnus, and Charles King, the college continued its work with gradually increasing vigor and usefulness. Most of its offices were filled by alumni—Professors McVickar, Moore, Anthon, Renwick, and Anderson being all graduates, and all men of singular worth and ability. Professor Anderson was a man of exceptional mathematical ability, and a linguist of unusual attainments. Professor Renwick, who occupied the chair of chemistry for thirty-three years, was the author of

"Outlines of Natural Philosophy," the first extended work on the subject published in the United States. Professor McVickar, who occupied the chair of moral and intellectual philosophy and political economy for some forty years, and was afterwards transferred to that of evidences of natural and revealed religion, was a man of wide attainments, as the scope of his professorship would indicate. He gave the first series of lectures on political economy ever delivered in an American college, and in 1825 he published what is probably the earliest work on the subject issued in this country. Professor Anthon's editions of the Greek and Latin authors have carried his name wherever the classics are taught, and made it synonymous with sound scholarship.

The educational work of the college at this time was all that could be desired in quality, and efforts were constantly being made to extend it. In 1830 a scientific and literary course was established, which omitted the classics and offered a wider range of English and the sciences, but it was apparently in advance of the demands of the day. Again in 1857 a very extensive reorganization was determined upon. A statute was adopted making provision for a very liberal undergraduate course and providing for a university course of study, and the establishment of three schools: A School of Letters, including moral and mental philosophy, the Greek and Latin languages and literatures, Oriental and modern languages, comparative philology and ethnology; a School of Science, including mechanics and physics, astronomy, chemistry and mineralogy, geology and palæontology, engineering, mining and metallurgy, natural history and physical geography; a School of Jurisprudence, to include history, political economy, political philosophy, national and international law, and civil and common law. The "university course" so projected was far in advance of anything offered or attempted by any institution in America at that day, and displayed a remarkable degree of foresight and wisdom. It was beyond the means of the college, and evidently was not appreciated by the public, as no considerable demand was evinced for the greatly increased opportunities which it offered, nor was additional support forthcoming. The faculty of arts was enlarged by the addition of several professors, including Francis Lieber, who was appointed to the chair of history and political science, the title of which was afterwards changed to constitutional history and public law, and his lectures were doubtless an inspiration to many of the large number of students who subsequently served their country in the War of the Rebellion. A direct result of the new statute was the establishment of the Law School as now constituted. In 1793 Chancellor Kent was appointed professor of law, as already mentioned, and he then held the position for five years. He was reappointed in 1823 and continued in the office until 1847, and was succeeded by Mr. William Betts, who lectured for several years. In 1858 Professor Theodore W. Dwight was appointed, and the school rapidly assumed its present importance and became a permanent part of the college.

While these educational developments were under consideration, plans for the removal of the college were also occupying the attention of the trustees. The fact that its original site had become unsuitable had long been recognized, though for many years the college green preserved its verdure and tranquillity in the midst of encroaching commerce. By degrees it was intersected with streets: "Chapel Street" and "College Place" for a time marked the site, but even these have now lost their identity in West Broadway. In 1854 the trustees determined upon removal, but the exercises were continued until May 7, 1857, when the last service was held in the old chapel, the ancient corner-stone was disinterred from its long resting-place to be borne to its new home, and the halls which had echoed to the march of history were abandoned forever.

A portion of the Botanical Garden, between Fifth and Sixth Avenues, Forty-ninth and Fiftieth Streets, was selected as the site to which the college should be removed from Murray Street, and Mr. Upjohn was employed to prepare a design for the new buildings. The execution of this project, however, was found to be impracticable, for the time being, on account of the expense involved; and in November, 1856, the trustees purchased of the Institution for the Instruction of the Deaf and Dumb twenty lots situated on Madison Avenue, between Forty-ninth and Fiftieth Streets. The purchase was made upon favorable terms, and the action of the trustees was influenced largely by the fact that the buildings of the institution were available for the immediate use of the college, with but slight alterations. The opening services were held in the chapel of the "New College," as it was called, May 12, 1857. The buildings consisted of a large edifice of brick and brown stucco, standing on the high ground near Fiftieth Street, with adjacent buildings at either end, one of which served as a chapel, and the other as a residence for professors. President King and his family at first occupied rooms in the main building, which also furnished a number of class and lecture rooms. The principal architectural feature of the central building was a lofty portico; and the group of buildings, shaded by a row of fine old trees, on a beautiful lawn sloping southward, presented a pleasing and dignified appearance. "The present location of the College" is described in a contemporary newspaper as "a delightful one, and undesirable only on account of the distance up town. . . . The site is on a commanding eminence, affording an extensive and pleasant view."

Subsequently, the trustees purchased the lots comprising the remainder of the block, including a factory, which was afterwards used for the School of Mines. The buildings continued to be occupied with but little change until 1860, when the president's house was erected. In the same year, by an agreement between the two institutions, the College of Physicians and Surgeons became the medical department of Columbia College. In 1864 the trustees elected to the presidency the Rev. Frederick A. P. Barnard, S.T.D., a profound student of education, in sympathy with all forms of higher development, literary as well as scientific; a man of extraordinarily wide attainments, of an enthusiastic and progressive temperament. Of his influence upon the college, Dean Van Amringe writes: "He gave vitalizing force to the extension and liberalization of the undergraduate course, to the founding of fellowships for the encouragement and assistance in their higher studies of earnest and able young men; to the extension of the library and the liberalization of its management; to the project of a course for the higher study of political and historical subjects, and to the scheme for a broad and liberal system of postgraduate or university instruction, which the college had long but vainly desired."

The School of Mines was at this time in its incipiency, but with his earnest support its faculty were soon able to make it the leading, as it was almost if not quite the first, school of its kind in the country.

The Law School continued to prosper, and in 1880 the School of Political Science was established. Lectures upon political economy had been delivered as early as 1818, and Professor Lieber's course had afforded a brilliant exposition of the principles of international law; but no scheme of systematic independent instruction in these and kindred subjects was provided until the organization of the school. It aimed to give a complete general view of both external and internal polity, from the point of view of law, history, and philosophy. It was a new departure, but it was most timely, and it has exerted a deep and far-reaching influence, as well through the publications of its officers and graduates as by means of the instruction it has afforded its students. Under President Barnard's administration the library was greatly enlarged, and a liberal policy was adopted which rendered it available at all hours to every student, whether connected with the college or not, who desired to avail himself of its resources. In 1883 a collegiate course of study for women was opened, and from this was developed Barnard College, which was established six years later, with the official approval of the trustees, Columbia undertaking to give the instruction and to confer degrees upon such women as should pass the examinations.

At the beginning of Dr. Barnard's administration public attention was absorbed by the great political issues then pending, and the students and graduates of Columbia showed themselves no less patriotic than their predecessors of King's College. Over four hundred of her sons gave themselves to the service of their country in the army and navy; while others filled important offices on the National Defence Committee and the Sanitary Commission. Doubtless the War of the Rebellion somewhat retarded the growth of the college, but during Dr. Barnard's incumbency it began to receive a more adequate return from its real estate, and was in receipt of an income less out of proportion to the needs of a great institution. The president and the trustees were not slow to seize the opportunity to carry into effect their long-projected plans for expansion and development. When Dr. Barnard came to the college there were six hundred and twenty-two students upon the rolls. On his retirement, twenty-five years later, there were seventeen hundred and twelve. During the same period the teaching staff was increased from twenty-three to about one hundred and fifty, and the development of the institution upon the educational side was in like proportion. President Barnard died April 27, 1889, devoting his fortune, as he had his life, to the college. On February 3, 1890, Seth Low, of the Class of 1870, was installed president. The date will always be recognized as the beginning of the new era in the history of the college.

COLUMBIA UNIVERSITY

Great as had been the development of the college under President Barnard, forces had been accumulating tending to still greater expansion, and the time and the man had now come for the realization of Columbia's possibilities as a university. President Low's wide experience and catholic sympathies put him in touch with the city, and his progressive mind at once grasped the requirements and opportunities of the situation. Administrative reform was the first need of the institution, in order that its advantages might be rendered available and a consistent and systematic enlargement of its scope made practicable. Within the first two years of President Low's administration this was accomplished. The college was reorganized on a university basis, with the Schools of Medicine, Law, Mines (since expanded into the Schools of Applied Science, embracing mining, chemistry, engineering, and architecture), Political Science, Philosophy, and Pure Science, under the general guidance of a university council, for the prosecution of professional and advanced study; and its School of Arts, which has since resumed its original title of college, for undergraduate instruction. Courses of study were coördinated and new departments were established. Since 1890 the teaching staff has been increased to two hundred and eighty-eight, and the number of students matriculated during the present year will exceed eighteen hundred. In 1891 the College of Physicians and Surgeons was formally consolidated with Columbia, and became an integral part of the corporation; reciprocal relations were established with the several theological seminaries of the city, and courses of public lectures were instituted; and in the following year the Teachers College became allied to Columbia. A number of fellowships were established for the encouragement of advanced research; and relations were entered into with the Metropolitan Museum of Art and the Museum of Natural History, the collections serving to illustrate the lectures given by the college. Still more recently the undergraduate curriculum has been largely increased in scope and latitude, and so arranged as to afford in logical sequence the preliminary training requisite for admission to any of the professional schools.

In all directions the college and its schools were broadened and strengthened with an almost startling rapidity, but with a sureness and wisdom which have already found ample justification. This extensive growth served to demonstrate the entire inadequacy and unfitness of the present site; and in 1892 the trustees determined upon removal, and contracted for the purchase of four blocks of land on the summit of Morningside Heights. Such an undertaking, involving an original outlay of two million dollars, demanded no small measure of courage and of confidence both in the possibilities of the college and in the liberality of the alumni and of the city of New York; but the generous gifts already received show that that confidence was not misplaced, and the just pride which the city now feels in Columbia gives promise of even more generous support in the future. On May 2, 1896, the new site was dedicated in the presence of the Governor of the State, the Mayor of the City, the trustees and faculties, representatives of other institutions, and about five thousand people; and at about the same date the college fitly assumed the title of university.

The history of the new site dates from 1701, when Jacob deKey purchased his farm from the city; but it was not till September 16, 1776, that the event occurred which renders it memorable, and which can best be described in the words of an eye-witness:

"On Monday morning, about ten o'Clock, a party of the Enemy consisting of Highlanders, Hessians, the Light Infantry, Grenadiers, and English Troops, (Number uncertain), attack'd our advanc'd Party, commanded by Coll. Knowlton at Martje Davits Fly.

They were opposed with spirit, and soon made to retreat to a clear Field, southwest of that about two hundred paces, where they lodged themselves behind a Fence covered with Bushes our People attack'd them in Turn, and caused them to retreat a second Time, leaving five dead on the Spot, we pursued them to a Buckwheat Field on the Top of a high Hill, distance about four hundred paces, where they received a considerable Reinforcement, with several Field Pieces, and there made a Stand a very brisk Action ensued at this Place, which continued about Two Hours our People at length worsted them a third Time, caused them to fall back into an Orchard, from thence across a Hollow, and up another Hill not far distant from their own Lines. . . ."

So wrote General Clinton to the New York Convention describing the Battle of Harlem, which had been fought two days previously, on September 16, 1776. He presents a vivid picture, and we need but follow his description, beginning at "Martje Davits Fly," the meadow lying in the valley between One Hundred and Twenty-fifth and One Hundred and Twenty-ninth Streets, near the Hudson River, across the level ground to the foot of the northerly slope of Morningside Heights, and up the hillside to the "Buckwheat Field on the Top of a high Hill," and we find ourselves upon the field where the battle was fought: the field where Columbia is to stand. What was once the buckwheat field, made memorable by the first battle in which the American troops faced the British and routed them, has become the new site of Columbia;

and where Colonel Knowlton fell the walls of the university are now rising. The college which the traveller of a hundred years ago described as the most beautifully situated in the world, once more looks forth upon the waters of the Hudson, but from a higher vantage ground and with the broader vision of the university. To the natural beauties of the situation, which fit it so preëminently to be the home of learning, is added the element of historic interest, associating the university of to-day still more inseparably with the college of the Revolution.

The land upon which the buildings are to be erected comprises a little more than seventeen acres. It is divided naturally into two levels. The southerly level or plateau, which is one hundred and fifty feet above high water and includes about ten acres, is the higher, and varies in elevation from five to ten feet above the surrounding streets. The buildings in process of erection are being constructed chiefly upon the higher plateau, thus preserving a fine grove of oaks and chestnuts that adorns the northern portion of the grounds, and leaving space for future development. The buildings are arranged in a series of quadrangles, but with spacious openings on the streets and avenues. The library, already partially built, is to form the centre of the group, and its proportions and design will render it one of the most commanding features of Morningside Heights. The main approach to the grounds is from One Hundred and Sixteenth Street, by a broad flight of steps and a court three hundred and seventy-five feet in width by two hundred feet in depth. Another flight of steps will lead to the portico of the library. Purely classic in style, the library, which will be surmounted by a dome, resembles in form a Greek cross. The width of the building will be one hundred and ninety-two feet, and the height of the dome one hundred and thirty-five feet. It will be constructed of Indiana limestone on a basement of Milford granite. The building is a memorial of Abiel Abbot Low, and is given by his son, Seth Low, the president of the university.

To the east and west of the library are to be the chapel and the assembly hall, the latter being intended as a place of meeting for student organizations, such as the literary and debating societies and the glee club, and for public lectures; and generally to serve as a centre for the social life of the students. Opposite each of these buildings will be an entrance from the adjoining avenue.

Schermerhorn Hall, the northeasterly building on the plan, is the gift of Mr. William C. Schermerhorn, the chairman of the trustees, and will be devoted to the natural sciences. The adjoining building is designated the "Physics Building" only until the name of a donor may be substituted. These buildings are also under construction. They are to be built of the over-burned brick of a dull-red color, generally known as Harvard brick, and of Indiana limestone. In style they are in keeping with the library, and represent to some extent a reversion to the best construction of the colonial period: Schermerhorn Hall offers a pleasing reminder of old King's College. Their simple and dignified lines and generous windows fitly express the purpose for which they are to be used, and the intention of the design to subserve the needs of modern scientific education.

Havemeyer Hall, which is to occupy the northwesterly angle of the upper plateau, will be erected as a memorial of Frederick Christian Havemeyer by his sons Henry O., Frederick C., Theodore A., and Thomas J. Havemeyer, his daughters Kate B. Belloni and S. Louisa Jackson, and his nephew Charles H. Senff. It has been especially planned for the study of chemistry, and eventually will be devoted exclusively to that department, but temporarily the upper floor will be used by the students in architecture. The engineering building, as well as the university building, is also in course of construction. The university building will be situated immediately to the north of the library, about two hundred feet distant, and, next to the library, will be the most important and conspicuous building on the grounds. It will include a theatre, a dining-hall, and a gymnasium. The alumni have undertaken to raise a fund for the erection of the dining-hall, to which they propose to give an historic and personal interest by making it the "Alumni Memorial Hall." Here are to be preserved the names and portraits of those sons of King's College who were among the founders of the Republic; of those sons of a later day, Phil Kearney and his brave associates, who gave their lives to preserve the Union; and of all the long line of graduates who, from the time of the Revolution to the present, in the service of the city, the state, and the country, have achieved distinction for themselves and their Alma Mater. Only a portion of the building is to be erected at present, but it will advance as the means are forthcoming, and the design and plans already perfected indicate that it will be one of the most imposing of the entire group.

Of the other buildings for which space has been reserved, the particular uses remain to be determined by the rapidly increasing needs of the university. Possibly some of them may be used as residences for students, as the trustees have recently declared themselves in favor of making provision for this want, but it seems more probable that such buildings will be erected by private capital on land adjacent to the university. A large residence-hall for students, to be known as "Hamilton Court," which has already been projected, bids fair to supply what has long been one of Columbia's greatest deficiencies. The reëstablishment of the student life which existed in King's College will add not only a most attractive feature but an important element of strength to the new life of the university.

To realize to the full the great opportunities afforded by its environment is the duty that now confronts the university. The loftier elevation and greater extent of its new site should find expression in the higher ideals and broader scholarship of the university, in an influence for good more far-reaching and potent. That these results will follow is best assured by the progress that the university has made during the past few years under conditions far less favorable. To the advancement of the highest, and broadest, and soundest learning the university stands pledged, irrevocably; while upon the material side the best professional talent, after the most careful study, has projected the lines of future development. The generosity of Columbia's graduates, officers, and friends has already afforded conspicuous evidence both of their confidence in the work that the university is doing and of their belief in the complete success of her present enterprise.

"Upon the university," said Mayor Hewitt in his address upon the dedication of the new site, "we must build the foundations of our municipal glory and greatness. . . . So far as the city of New York is concerned, the Columbia University must be made the fountain head of knowledge, the centre from which will flow the conservative and recuperative principles of social progress. . . . The city which is its home will feel its influence in every profession, in the walks of business, in its public institutions, in the conduct of its churches, in the execution and administration of the great undertakings which will be demanded by its continued growth. Its citizens will come to its halls for instruction, for guidance, and for inspiration, and as they approach the portal of a higher municipal life, and are confirmed in noble aims, they will feel the force of the prophetic motto of King's College, the mother of Columbia University in the city of New York, IN LUMINE TUO VIDEBIMUS LUMEN."

Half Moon Series

Published in the Interest of the New York City History Club

Volume I. Number III.

ANNETJE JANS' FARM.

WITH SOME TIDINGS OF ITS FIRST POSSESSORS AND THE LATER FRUITS IT BORE.

THERE it lay in the year 1634, a rough strip of half-cleared wood and pasture land. It was a farm but in name, uncultivated and unconscious that future historians would remember its whilom existence *as* a farm, when many of its far more profitable sister "boueries" had long been forgotten in the encroaching city streets of New York. Here is a bare outline of the story of the family who once possessed this property on the Island of Manhattan, outside the walls of the primitive Dutch town, and here, too, is the history of the several names given to the estate before it was lost in the metropolis.

The West India Company had great difficulty in finding settlers for the provinces

Kiliaen van Rensselaer 1620

entrusted to their management. In the early part of the year 1620 there was some talk of asking a "certain English preacher living in Leyden" to emigrate to New Netherland with four hundred families who were, as he assured their High Mightinesses, the States-General and the Worshipful Directors of the new company, willing to brave the perils of the Western Hemisphere if they could be assured of religious freedom. But their High Mightinesses feared lest so large a body of English might prove an entering wedge for English supremacy upon land where Dutch claims were not fully recognized. The suggestion was declined; John Robinson despatched the *Mayflower* to the shores of Plymouth Bay instead of to the banks of the Hudson, and New Amsterdam lost the opportunity of being founded by Pilgrim Fathers "well versed in the Dutch tongue."

Finally, however, a fort was established on Manhattan Island and used as a trading station, but trade did not flourish. Among the founders of the West India Company was a rich Amsterdam jeweller, Kiliaen van Rensselaer. In his youth he had travelled over Europe in the interests of his employer, Wolfert van Bijler, and had used his eyes as he displayed his gems in the various capitals. With this wider experience, gained beyond the limits of the Low Countries, it is little wonder that he

A Scheme of Colonization 1628

showed more enterprise than his brother directors in plans for exploiting the Company's transatlantic territory. He was the only one to see that the desired trade could not be carried on successfully without settlers. "Open up the country with agriculture," he urged; "that must be our first step." Not only would New Netherland be developed to its own good, but Manhattan Island would then be a valuable half-way station, and a source of supplies for ships bound for Brazil and the West Indies. Though himself a merchant in precious stones, living on the Keizersgracht in Amsterdam, Kiliaen van Rensselaer was not ignorant of questions pertaining to the soil. There were family estates in the flat, marshy ground of the Veluwe north of Utrecht near Nijkerk, which were made available by extensive draining operations and careful working, with which methods he was familiar.

Colonists for New Netherland did not offer themselves, and the Company, already losing money, were loath to offer expensive inducements. Finally, however, a scheme of colonization was evolved which threw all responsibility for outlay upon the shoulders of individuals. Large tracts of land in the province, with power to regulate and govern the same, were assigned to those willing to plant colonies at their own expense. Kiliaen received a tract stretching above and below

The Eendracht 1630

Fort Orange on both sides of the Hudson River. It was about twenty-four by forty-eight miles and covered the present sites of Troy and Albany.

Each planter or patroon, as they were called, pledged himself to send out fifty colonists, who were free from all taxes to the Company for the space of three years. Kiliaen van Rensselaer lost no time. He had personal knowledge of many peasants in the neighborhood of Nijkerk, and from them he picked out such as were enterprising enough to make the venture. Wolfert Gerritsz. of Ameersfoort, Brant Peelen of Nijkerk, Rutger and Pieter Hendricks of Soest, all signed their contracts on January 19, 1630. Among the others who went over in the good ship *Eendracht* was Roelof Jansz. of Masterland, with Annetje his wife, and their three children, Sara, Catrina, and Fytje. "Masterland" is probably "Maasland," a little village in the neighborhood of Rotterdam. Jansz. is the contracted form for Janssen; the contraction for the feminine omits the "z," so that Roelof's wife is usually known as Annetje Jans.

They were all humble folks, these brave settlers. Indeed they can hardly be said to have possessed even a patronymic among them. It was Claes the son of Claes, Roelof the son of Jan, and in the next generation Roelof's father was forgotten, and his chil-

The Janssen Family 1630

dren were known but as the offspring of Roelof. There is a vague tradition among some of the descendants of this Roelof and Annetje Jans, that she had the right to claim kindred with the uppermost family of Holland; that her grandfather was no less a person than the founder of the Dutch Republic, William of Nassau, Prince of Orange. A careful search in Holland, both in public archives and in those of the Nassau family, has shown that this tradition is wholly without foundation. Annetje Jans came of a reputable family of village folk; her mother, Tryntje Jonas, was a professional nurse or midwife, who sought and obtained employment in that capacity from the West India Company, and either came to America with Annetje, or followed her shortly afterwards. Annetje's sister, Marritje, was the wife of a carpenter at the time of her emigration. She married twice after his death, and was one of the first ladies in the little town on Manhattan Island before she was gathered to her fathers. Emigration lifted many of the descendants of Tryntje Jonas from the peasant rank of their forebears to the best position that the new world had to offer.

Roelof Janssen was engaged by the patroon as a *bouwmeester* or assistant farm superintendent at one hundred and fifty or one hundred and eighty guilders a year—that is, at a salary

The Patroon's Government 1630

of sixty or seventy-two dollars—for three years, until the farm should prove remunerative. The patroon was responsible for all farm expenses; he supplied cattle, wagons, and tools, and, moreover, paid the wages of the farm hands, who earned forty to ninety guilders annually, and of one farm boy, whose wages ranged from twenty-five to forty guilders annually, with a rise of ten to twenty guilders, and keep. The settlers did all clearing, building, etc.—all, in short, that there was to be done to make the place habitable, with some assistance from the Company's servants. When the farm was once self-supporting, then another arrangement was made. The net profits, after deducting the servants' wages, were divided, year and year about, between patroon and lessee. The former remained owner of the live stock, but the increase and harvest were shared. With the additional animals the patroon was then enabled to stock a new farm.

The craftsmen who went over as colonists earned about as much as the farm overseers, but were subordinate to the latter, and were supported entirely at the patroon's expense. If they did any outside work the patroon had a right to half the profits. Marritje Jans' husband, Tymen the carpenter, came under this head. Thus it is evident that the status and condition of these colonists differed wholly from that of the New Englanders. They were not independent pioneers, but were employés of a paternal landlord.

Difficulties 1633

In 1632, Kiliaen formed a government within his colony by appointing *schout, schepenen,* and *raden.* Roelof Jansz. was one of the latter, so that he was evidently of some weight in the little village. These officers were distinguished by a black hat with a silver band.

The *schepenen* and *raden* took oaths of office to the *schout,* who took his from the Company's Director. The form of the oath was copied from that of Amsterdam, giving, however, due prominence to the patroon, who kept close watch on all the affairs of his "colonie" from his office in Amsterdam. Every possible point was referred to him.

In 1633, Wouter van Twiller was appointed Director of New Netherland. This was a great convenience to Kiliaen, as the new governor was son to his sister Mary. From the patroon's letters it can be seen that he expected his nephew to have an eye to the interests of Rensselaerswijck, and apparently he was not disappointed in his expectations.

The colony had many troubles to work through. In the first year one of the two farm houses was burned down, leaving Roelof, Annetje, and their four little children to seek shelter as best they might until the damage could be repaired. The first harvests, too,

The Patroon's Letter 1634

were not sufficiently abundant to leave any grain for seed, after the colonists' hunger was satisfied. It was so difficult to obtain stock that they did not dare to slaughter any, and depended, for their animal food, on the game brought by the Indians. Indeed they were so well supplied with the latter that they sent some down to Manhattan in exchange for other commodities. Two more children were born to Annetje and Roelof, Jan and another Annetje. Jan took his father's name reversed, as it were, and became Jan Roelofsen.

There is a letter from the patroon to van Twiller dated April 23, 1634, from which we get some idea of the colony. Wonderful indeed is the patroon's knowledge! After commiserating his nephew for the many charges that had been brought against him and his administration, he discusses in detail the condition of his own transatlantic property. He knows that a cow has been bitten by a snake, he knows just how the live stock has increased, and calculates that there is sufficient to stock a third bouwerie, and suggests that if the Director is pleased with Roelof Jansz., that he can promote him to this third farm on the conditions enjoyed by Hendrick Conduit. Elsewhere we find that Hendrick Conduit had half shares.

Roelof's servants, too, are taken into consideration. The four years' service to which

Rensselaerswijck 1634

they had pledged themselves in 1630 had expired, and the patroon suggests keeping them one year more at the same wages, with promise of an increase for the year following. Again, there is a passage that is somewhat obscure. He writes: "I see that Roelof Janssen has been making a fine run on me for provisions,—aye, pretty much all the rations there were in stock. I think that his women, mother and sister and the others, must have been giving away, which must not go on. He complains to me that you have removed him from the bouwerie, and you write me that he wanted to go."

This evidently referred to the farm where Roelof had been superintendent for four years, and Kiliaen's proposition that he should be head of the new farm might have been made in answer to complaints about van Twiller's injustice. At any rate the absentee landlord seems to have some provision for Roelof on his mind, for he makes another suggestion in regard to a "farm at Fort Orange." His proposition is to use Wolfert Gerritsz.' horses there, let Wolfert's son live in the house, and to have Marijn or Roelof, with their wives, guard the house at night and look after the animals.

Such are the scanty records of Roelof's family at Rensselaerswijck. Other allusions to them may lie buried in the church papers at Amsterdam or may exist in the van Rens-

Roelof Janssen 1635

selaer letters. There was one other trace in the region. A noisy little brook, tumbling into the Hudson from the east side, was known as Roelof Janssen's Kill as late as 1680.

In 1635, Roelof was free from obligations to the patroon who had brought him from the tiny village of Maasland to Rensselaerswijck. Once roused to ambition, he was no longer content to live as a subordinate as his peasant forefathers had done for so many generations. We do not know what were the exact conditions that induced him to leave the colony. Possibly the circumstances are recorded in the van Rensselaer family papers, as Kiliaen must have been informed not only of the fact but of the reasons. No detail escaped him and certainly a valuable servant would not have left him without his knowledge, nor probably without his permission.

A sloop took Roelof, Annetje, their five children, and household goods down the river to Manhattan Island. From the reference to the mother and sister in Kiliaen's letter, it is probable that Tryn Jonas and Marritje Jans and family had also spent their first years of American sojourn at Rensselaerswijck and came to Manhattan as a second venture. So quick was the influence of American love of change!

This second voyage was a great contrast to the long passage in the *Eendracht* across the wintry Atlantic. Probably the sloop was re-

Manhattan Island 1635

ceived by the citizens of Manhattan to a man, and if two hundred people had assembled on the wharf, the houses in the settlement would have been left almost empty, in that year of grace 1635. It was a tiny village that the new comers found on the site of this great metropolis. There was the fort, not in very good repair, and a few houses on crooked little streets without its gates. Affairs were not flourishing on the island. Wouter van Twiller was almost at swords' points with the West India Company. The Director was accused of improving nothing in the colony but his own property. It was also said that he was so frequently under the influence of liquor that he often did not know what he was doing. This may be true. It was not a sober age at the best, and there were so many discomforts to be endured by these pioneers, that it is not surprising if some of them indulged in the one pleasure that could be imported. On the other hand, there were complaints that the Company cared for naught but their hoped-for dividends and neglected the true interests of their colonists. Kiliaen was no longer one of the directors in 1634. He says that the Company hated the patroons so bitterly that they would grant no measure beneficial to the former even if it were to be of advantage to themselves at the same time. Thus there was mutual distrust and mutual recrimination.

Farms on the Island 1638

The spiritual, intellectual, and physical needs of the two hundred were looked after by Everardus Bogardus the minister or dominie, Adam Roelantsen the schoolmaster, and Dr. Hans Kierstede the surgeon. The dominie and schoolmaster had come out from the mother-country in the *Soutberg* or *Salt Mountain* with Wouter van Twiller, in 1633. When Tryn Jonas came to Manhattan with her daughters she, too, was employed at a regular salary by the Company and was thus the first medical woman to exercise her profession on Manhattan. She had her own house near that of the Dominie, on Parel or Pearl Street.

Above the settlement there were eight farms or bouweries laid out on the island. The one nearest to the fort on the North River was called the Company's Bouwerie, and was reserved for the use of the Director. The farm north of this, consisting of about sixty-two acres, was given to Roelof Janssen on his arrival from Rensselaerswijck. There are two possible explanations of this gift. One is that the Company were glad to secure a farmer skilled in Dutch methods of agriculture, who had had five years' experience in the new world. The second surmise is this: Kiliaen may have given his superintendent leave to secure this land for the sake of the live stock which the Company were bound to supply, with the condition that, as soon as he could do

The Grant to Roelof Jans3. 1636

so legally, the patroon should have the animals for Rensselaerswijck. It is known that he did this once, and he was quite willing to circumvent the Company if he could do so.

It was a queer irregular tract of land, this Jans' Farm, which attained a reputation undreamed of by its first owner. West of the present line of Broadway there rose a hill called *Kalch Hoek*, or Chalk Hook. Roelof's farm lay around the base of this elevation, somewhat in the form of a badly-made figure eight with rather a long neck between the two circles. The southern boundary was about Warren Street, the northern, Watts or Canal Street, while the strand or river line was at Greenwich Street. There were about sixty-two acres in all, but a portion was marshy, while nearly all was uncleared.

Roelof took possession of his new property, put up a house and had begun to prepare the soil for cultivation when death laid its hand on him and Annetje was left alone with her five children. It is not probable, however, that the helpless family, one little boy being the only masculine protector, were allowed to live on the farm, a mile from the fort.

By the date of Roelof's death, van Twiller had been relieved from the government and Kieft had taken his place, but the ex-director remained in Manhattan and did not neglect the widow's interests. On September 21, 1637,

The Second Marriage 1638

Kiliaen van Rensselaer writes to his nephew by the ship *Harinck:* "I received your brief and hastily written recommendation for the widow of Roelof Janssen, as well as the verbal greeting by Jacob Wolfertsen. I have already arranged about the claims of the said widow."

Annetje did not remain a widow for more than two years. In the spring of 1638, she gave her hand to Dominie Bogardus, who was so much charmed with her that he was ready to assume the care of Roelof's five children. His house, situated on Whitehall Street, was one of the best in the village, boasting of a knocker imported from Holland, and apparently was large enough to hold his newly acquired family. Mrs. Lamb describes Annetje, at the time of her second marriage, as "a small, well-formed woman with delicate features, transparent complexion, and bright, beautiful, dark eyes. She had a well-balanced mind, a sunny disposition, winning manners, and a kind heart." According to the same historian, the Dominie "was large, graceful, sinewy, strong, with a fine, broad, open frank face, high cheek bones, a dark, piercing eye, and mouth expressive of the very electricity of good humor, which was partly hidden by a beard cut in the peculiar fashion prescribed for ecclesiastics during the reign of Henry IV."

The marriage was celebrated in the spring or early summer of 1638. The Dominie at once

A Case of Slander 1642

took charge of his wife's property, for, on August 12th, we find him giving a power of attorney to Wouter van Twiller to collect moneys due Roelof Jansz. The ex-governor was still in America, and was, like many another retired official, devoting himself to law and the care of his property which had flourished only too well during his official career.

Shortly after her marriage, Annetje, now dignified by the title of *Mefvrouw* Bogardus, went to visit one Mrs. van Corlear. Just as she reached the door she heard that one Grietje Reyniers, wife of Anthony Janssen, was within, and she concluded to postpone her call. Both husband and wife were infuriated at this slight. Anthony had already used strong language about the Dominie when asked to pay a just debt, and now Grietje took the opportunity to be very disagreeable about the way in which Mrs. Bogardus displayed her shapely ankles. This came into court. Jacob van Corlear testified that he had been in the blacksmith's shop that very day, when Mrs. Bogardus went by. She had placed her hand on her side and drawn up her petticoat a little, in order not to soil it, as the road was muddy. In those days, the city streets were not above reproach, and the indignant Annetje had no difficulty in proving that her care was to preserve the new clothes of her

The Farm Leased 1639

wedding outfit, not to show her well-turned foot. Grietje was condemned to retract her words publicly and to pay a fine to the poor. Six days after the hearing of this case we find Annetje selling a hog to Cornelis Petersen and buying of him purple cloth sufficient for a petticoat.

The Dominie made no attempt to become a clerical farmer. He too had acquired land in his own right. A large tract was given to him on Long Island, which is often confused with his wife's farm on Manhattan, as the former became known as the Dominie's Hook and the latter as the Dominie's Bouwerie. It is a little doubtful which farm is referred to in the lease of May 17, 1639. This states that the Reverend Everardus Bogardus leased to Richard Brudenell a tobacco house and plantation with a water dog, gun, and powder, at a certain rent payable in tobacco and one third of all the game he shall kill *as long as the powder and ball shall last.* A few years later, Brudenell lived on Long Island without doubt, but the chief proof that this lease refers to the Jans' Farm is that, within a year after its date, Brudenell brought a suit for damages against one Jan Celes, who was addicted to killing hogs on other people's land. Now it is well known that the farm of this Celes, known familiarly as Old Jan, was the northern boundary of Annetje's land. Hence a neigh-

Sara Roelofs' Wedding 1642

borly dispute on the ground of trespassing hogs would have been natural.

The lease of August 14, 1642, is unequivocal. The Dominie leases to Roger (or Rufus) Barton a tract which was undoubtedly the Jans' Farm.

He, Rufus Barton, shall have the land situated on the North River, belonging to him, Bogardus, during five years beginning September 1, 1642, and terminating September 1, 1647, when the harvest shall be brought into the barn; for all of which the tenant shall pay annually two capons as a recognition. Bogardus reserved a pasture for his own cattle and Barton promised to construct a house on a site selected by Bogardus, who should be bound to buy it at an impartial valuation. The preference for future leases was secured to Barton.

Thus Annetje's real estate was provided for for a term of years. It is evident that no rent could be commanded for the farm. The best that the owners could hope for was to find some respectable tenant who would improve the property.

In June, 1642, Sara Roelofs, Annetje's eldest daughter, married Dr. Hans Kierstede. The wedding feast was celebrated with much jollity at the house of the bride's step-father, and Director Kieft made a little plot with the Dominie to turn the festivity to advantage for the community. The first religious exercises

Annetje's Property 1642

on Manhattan were held in the loft of a horse-mill; later, a plain structure was erected and dedicated to divine service, but the good citizens complained that travellers from Boston and Plymouth way called this building nothing better than a barn. In New England the very first action in a new settlement was to erect a church: was it not a shame that New Netherland was so backward? So, at the wedding, according to Captain de Vries, when the third or fourth round of drinking was reached, the Director produced a subscription paper for a fund to erect a new church. Kieft headed the list with his own donation and the convivial guests "each with a light head subscribed at a handsome rate, and, although some heartily repented it when their senses came back, they were obliged to pay. Nothing could avail against it."

Annetje Bogardus was not unmindful of her daughter's interests on this occasion. In 1638, before entrusting herself and her family to the Dominie, Annetje had signed a document making due provision for Roelof's children from their father's property. On June 21, 1642, a week before Sara's marriage, she repeated this declaration with legal formalities, as appears in the records at Albany. It is stated that she settled one thousand guilders on her children and promised to bring them up, with God's help, decently, provide them with necessary clothing and food, and let them learn reading, writing, and a good trade. The original contract was signed and witnessed by Director Kieft, Councillor de la Montaigne and Cornelis van Tienhoven. It is worthy of notice that Sara Roelofs carried her education beyond this stipulated reading and writing. She became so proficient in the Indian tongue that she was employed as interpreter in some of the treaties.

Dominie and Director 1645

The new church was begun within the fort, where alone there was safety for the worshippers to sit quietly as they listened to the Dominie's exhortations. Matters were going very badly. Director Kieft had been unwise in his treatment of the Indians and the result was that they ill-treated the white man whenever opportunity offered. Many settlers returned home in terror. Roger Williams writes at about this time when he sailed from this port for Europe, "Before we weighed anchor mine own eyes saw the flames at their towns and the present removal of all that could for Holland." Shortly, only two farms on the island were worked. Probably one of these was Annetje's as it was fairly near to the fort, but it was not a paying piece of real estate. Undoubtedly the owners considered themselves lucky that it was not utterly abandoned.

It is no wonder that Dominie Bogardus took advantage of having the ears of the com-

The Voyage of the Princess 1647

munity at his command, to utter his opinion about Kieft's administration. He had called van Twiller a "child of the devil" and threatened him with "such a shake from the pulpit as would make him tremble like a bowl full of jelly." Language was not used delicately in those days, and the minister's native Dutch lent itself to strong expressions. Accusations exchanged between Kieft and the Dominie were still more bitter than the above. It was alleged that the Reverend Bogardus was intoxicated in and out of the pulpit, while he did not hesitate to lay all Manhattan's misfortunes to the Director's door. Kieft refused to enter the church and even had a drum beaten during sermon time to drown the preacher's fulminations.

Finally, towards the end of 1646, this quarrel was patched up, Kieft was recalled to Holland, and the Dominie decided to proceed thither too, to lay a few points before the Company, the Classis at Amsterdam and the Worshipful States-General. The two opponents sailed off together in the *Princess*, which was wrecked on the coast of Wales and Dominie and Director perished in the same hour.

So Annetje was again left a widow with four little sons, Willem, Cornelis, Jonas, and Pieter Bogardus in addition to her elder family. Her mother, too, was dead. Before Bogardus

Letter of Megapolensis 1648

sailed, the husband of Marritje Jans gave him a power of attorney to collect the last wages due their mother-in-law, Tryn Jonas, from the West India Company. This paper was, of course, lost in the *Princess*. On August 17, 1649, Annetje and Marritje joined in giving another power of attorney to Cornelis Willemsen Bogaert to receive the sum of two hundred and forty-nine guilders, two stivers, and two pence, due their mother from the West India Company.

It is possible that this Bogaert was brother to the Dominie. The latter had latinized his name according to the pedantic fashion of the day.

When the news arrived that the *Princess* had gone down, Annetje decided to return to the first home she had known in America. Though her two husbands had left a fair amount of real estate, the widow still found it difficult to meet the daily wants of her family. Dominie Megapolensis was now in charge of the church at the Patroon's colony, and he wrote as follows to the Classis of Amsterdam, August 15, 1648: "After the Lord God had been pleased to cut short the thread of life of Dominie Bogardus, late preacher at the Manhattan, by shipwreck, his widow came to Fort Orange in the Colony of Rensselaerswijck to make a living here. She has nine living children, as well from her former

Annetje's Circumstances 1648

husband as from Dominie Bogardus, and besides this she is burdened with considerable debt, to pay which and for her subsistence she has no means nor remedy unless money be paid to her by the West India Company, that is, such sums as are still due for the salary of her late husband, Dominie Bogardus, who always asserted that, before leaving Holland, a higher salary was promised him than he ever received here. In order to explain this, I shall repeat to the best of my recollection what I have heard from him." The upshot of his recollection was, that Bogardus was only paid forty-six guilders a month, and one hundred and fifty guilders for board money, much less than was given to the other preachers in the Company's service. "Annetje," continues Megapolensis, "has therefore requested me to write to the Reverend Classis in her behalf, and request that the Reverend Classis or the deputies might, for the sake of a preacher's widow, petition the Company for the money due her, to be paid to her or her attorney, which would enable her to liquidate her debts and support her family."

It may be inferred that the good Dominie made his picture as touching as possible in his efforts to benefit his late colleague's widow. She was never in straits for the support of *nine* children, as three daughters

The Dominie's Bouwerie 1652

were already married, and shortly after this date Annetje Roelofs died. Mrs. Bogardus was indeed in less narrow circumstances than the major part of the community at Manhattan.

The Reverend Everardus Bogardus was a powerful personality. Every thing he touched bore his impress. So it was with the farm which he had overseen, somewhat, for his wife. It was known as the Dominie's Bouwerie, and the name clung to it through many years. The lease given to R. Barton expired. The next tenant, Egbert Woutersen, kept it for a short time only, and then the farm was again in the market, as no member of the family cared to live upon it. On November 1, 1651, it was let to Evert Pels. The agents who acted for the widow Bogardus on this occasion were Dr. Hans Kierstede, Pieter Hartgers, husband to Fytje Roelofs, and Givert Loockermans, second husband to Marritje Jans. The lease was for six years, May 1, 1652, to May 1, 1658, at a rental of two hundred and twenty-five guilders and thirty pounds of butter. This included two mares, one colt, one stallion, two milch cows, and a calf, taken at joint risk of landlady and tenant. The latter might put up a new house ; if he did not do that, he must put on a new roof to the old one.

Pieter Stuyvesant with his one leg and his autocratic temper had succeeded the unpopu-

Grant of the Farm 1654

lar Kieft as Director for the West India Company. He was desirous of increasing the importance of the little capital where he ruled, and, in 1652, the village of the Manhattoes around Fort Amsterdam was incorporated and the city of New Amsterdam[1] was launched upon its brief existence. In view of these changes in government it was considered wise, by the sons-in-law and advisers of Mrs. Bogardus, for her to make sure of her title to her property. Therefore, on July 4, 1654, Stuyvesant duly confirmed Wouter van Twiller's grant to Roelof Jansz. and recognized Annetje's rights.

Patent.

Petrus Stuyvesant, Director-General of New Netherland, Curaçoa and the Islands thereof, on the behalf of their Noble High Mightinesses the Lords States-General of the United Netherlands and the Honourable Directors of the Incorporated West India Company, together with the Honourable Councillors, declare that We on this day, date underwritten, have given and granted to Annetje Jans, widow of the late Everardus Bogardus, a piece of land situate on the Island of Manhattan on the North River, beginning at the palisades near the house on the Strand it goes north by east up to the partition line of old Jan's land is long 210 rods; from thence along the partition line of said Old Jan's land it extends E. by S. up to the Cripple bush [swamp] it runs S. W long 160 rods from the Cripple bush, to the Strand it runs westerly in breadth 50 rods; the land that lies to the south of the house to the partition line of the Company's

[1] Till 1652 the usual name was *The Manhattoes.*

Records of the Farm 1658

land begins on the east side, from the palisades southward to the posts and rails of the Company's land, without obstruction to the path, it is broad 60 rods; long on the south side along the posts and rails 160 rods; at the east side to the corner of the Kalchhook is broad 30 rods; to the division line of the aforesaid piece of land it goes westerly in length 100 rods; it makes altogether 31 morgens.

The next record of the property of Mrs. Bogardus entered in the court calendar of New Amsterdam may have reference to the farm on Manhattan or possibly to the one left by the minister on Long Island, which was known as Dominie's Hook. On May 6, 1658, Johannes Pietersen Verbrugge [van Brugh] appeared in court as attorney for his mother-in-law, Anna Bogardus [he was Catrina Roelofs' second husband], to sue Lauwrence Duits for the rent of her bouwerie. She had leased it to "Jan van Leiden and Lauwrence Grootschoe stands in his shoes" runs the complaint. The defendant answers that he was not indebted, as the plaintiff's mother-in-law released him from the rent for which he was to pay two hogs, and he hath paid one. The Court decrees that the defendant shall deliver the other hog to the plaintiff.

What had become of Evert Pels, to whom the farm was leased for six years from 1652? Those were years in which the settlers had suffered grievously from the Indians. There is one urgent appeal from the Company ask-

Changes in the City 1658

ing the inhabitants to live closer together like their neighbors of New England, "who do not suffer these horrible massacres." Evert Pels may have been forced to abandon the lonely farm lying a mile from the fort, and Jan van Leiden was the next tenant when times were a little better. There was plenty of room, too, in the safer shelter of the walled village. In January, 1658, the Directors of the Company published a protest about the manner in which land grants were neglected. The recipients of city lots used them as orchards or gardens and the surveyors had discovered several hundred lots within the city walls upon which no building was erected. It was decreed that no houses should be built without the walls until all lots within were taken up.

About this time a market was established to be held "every Saturday at or around the house of Mr. Hans Kierstede, where, after him, every one shall be permitted to buy or sell." The Kierstedes lived on the Strand facing the East River, and here Annetje probably came to visit from time to time. She herself no longer possessed a home within the limits of New Amsterdam. On November 14, 1657, she sold the house on Whitehall, where she and the Dominie had spent the nine years of their married life, to one Wernaer Wessels. "A house and lot opposite

Annetje's Illness 1663

the Five Houses bounded north by Isaac de Foreest and on the south by Robert Boltelaer. Width in front on the street between both houses 25 feet but deducting the drop and in the rear 24 feet and depth the same as the other lots."

In 1663, thirty-three years after the *Eendracht* brought her and her family to the uncleared country, the Dominie's widow felt that her end was approaching and decided to put her worldly affairs in order. On January 29th, Dirck van Schelluyne, the notary public of Beverwijck, was summoned to the little house where the widow Bogardus had lived for sixteen years past. It was about four o'clock in the afternoon when he arrived. Annetje was lying sick abed, but her senses, reason, memory, and understanding were perfectly strong. It was only a consideration of the shortness and frailty of human life, the certainty of death and the uncertainty of the hour thereof, that led her to anticipate the same by a proper disposition of her temporal estate to be left behind. Such is the statement in the preamble of the will which van Schelluyne was called upon to make that afternoon. The testatrix is described as "Annetje Janse, widow of Roelof Janssen of Master Land [Maasland] now lastly widow of the Reverend Everhardus Bogardus, residing in the village of Beverwijck."

Her Will
1663

SHE NAMES AS her sole heirs, her children, Sara Roelofsen, wife of Hans Kierstede; Catrina Roelofsen, wife of Johannes van Brugh; also Jannetje and Rachel Hartgers, the children of her deceased daughter Fijtje Roelofsen, late wife of Pieter Hartgers, representing together their mother's place; also her son, Jan Roelofsen and finally Willem, Cornelis, Jonas and Pieter Bogardus, and to them bequeaths all her real estate, chattels, credits, money, gold and silver both coined and uncoined, jewels, clothes, linen, woollen, household furniture, and all property whatsoever, to be disposed of after her death and divided by them in equal shares, to do with the same their own will and pleasure without any hindrance whatsoever, nevertheless, with this express condition and restriction, that her four first born children first receive their bequest from their father's property, consisting of a farm lying on Manhattan Island on the North River, *the sum of 1000 guilders* out of the receipts or the value of the said Bouwerie before any other division takes place; and as three of these children at the time of their marriage received certain gifts, and as Jan Roelofsen is yet unmarried, he is to receive a bed and milch cow, and to Jonas and Pieter Bogardus she gives a house and lot, situated to the westward of the house of the testatrix in the village of Beverwijck, going in length to the end of a bleaching spot, and in breadth to the room of her, the testatrix, house, besides a bed for each of them and a milch cow to each of them, the above to be an equivalent to what the married children have received; finally, she, the testatrix, gives to Roelof Kierstede, the child of her daughter Sara, a silver mug; to Annetje van Brugh, the child of her daughter Catrina, also a silver mug; and Jannetje and Rachel Hartgers, the children of her daughter Fytje, a silver mug each; and to the child of Willem, named Fytje, a silver mug; all the above gifts to be provided for out of the first moneys received, and afterwards the remainder of the property to be divided and shared as aforesaid. The testatrix declares this document to be her only true will and testament, and desiring that

Birth of New York 1664

after her death, it may supersede all other testaments, codicils, donations or any other instruments whatsoever, and in case any formalities may have been omitted, it is her will and desire that the same benefits may occur as if they actually had been observed ; and she requested me, notary public, to make one or more lawful instruments in the usual form of this, her, testatrix, last will and desire.

Signed, sealed, and delivered at the house of the testatrix in the village of Beverwijck in New Netherland, in the presence of Ruth [Rutger ?] Jacobuse van Schoonderwurt and Evert Wendell, witnesses.

This is the X mark of Annetje Janse
with her own hand.
RUTGER JACOBUS,
EVERT JACOBUS WENDELL.

D. V. SCHELLUYNE, Notary Public.

It is a fair will. All the children are treated equally, according to the good Dutch custom, which did not recognize the sacred rights of primogeniture. Only a few days of life remained to the widow after this testament was made, and death did prove a certainty.

Fate decreed the termination of another existence in New Netherland before the following year passed away. The rule of the Dutch West India Company came to an end, and the province was taken in possession for the English by Colonel Richard Nicolls, in September, 1664. New Amsterdam became New York before it was out of its early childhood as a Dutch city. There were less than sixteen hundred inhabitants at the time of this change

Gov. Nicolls' Grant 1667

in nationality, about the same number of people as are now contained in the group of apartment houses between Seventh and Sixth Avenues, Fifty-eighth Street and Central Park !

The English policy was to keep the Dutch burghers as English subjects, and to assure their enjoyment of all existing legal rights. Johannes van Brugh [his name is often written Verbrugge], Annetje's son-in-law, was one of the first to take the oath of allegiance. He retained his voice in the municipal government, voting in his official capacity of alderman instead of that of *schout.* It was probably through him that application was made to Governor Nicolls for the confirmation of the title of Annetje Jans' heirs to the Manhattan Farm. The grant was given March 27, 1667. It refers to van Twiller's grant to Roelof and Annetje Jans in 1636, and to the patent from Petrus Stuyvesant, late Dutch governor, to the widow Bogardus, July 4, 1634, and then confirms the title to "the children and heirs" of Annetje.

Governor Nicolls' Grant.

WHEREAS there is a certain parcel of land lying on this island, Manhattans, towards the North River, which in the year 1636 was the land and bowery of Anna Bogardus, to whom and her husband, Roelofe Jansen, it was first granted by the then Dutch Governor, Walter van Twiller, at which time the said Roelofe Jansen, first began to manure the said land and to build there-upon ; the limits whereof did then begin from the ffence of the house by the strand side, so running north east to the ffence of Old Jan's land. It's in length two hundred and ten rod ; then going along the ffence of the said Old Jan's land south east, it reacheth to a certain swamp, and is in breadth one hundred rod, and striking along the swamp south west, it's in length one hundred & sixty rod, and from the swamp to the strand going west it's in breadth fifty rod. The land lying on the south side of the house to the ffence of the land belonging to the Company and so to the east side, begins at the ffence & goes south to the posts and rayles of the Company's land, without any hindrance of the path ; it's in breadth sixty rod. In length on the south side along the posts and rayles, one hundred and sixty rod. On the east side to the entrance of the Chalk Hooke, in breadth thirty rod ; and along the said Chalkie Hook on the north side of the land before mentioned, going west is in length one hundred rod ; amounting in all to about sixty-two acres.

Suit for Rent 1666

Before the date of this confirmatory grant Van Brugh had brought a suit in behalf of the estate, against Thomas Wandel for rent due the late Mrs. Bogardus, according to a lease running from April 1, 1657, to April 1, 1665. The rental was one hundred guilders a year, less than half of the rental in the lease to Evert Pels. A verdict was rendered for four hundred and twenty-five guilders ($170).[1]

The thousand guilders left by the widow to her elder family could not be paid until the farm was sold. Finally a purchaser was found

[1] This record appears in English, but the court scribe was evidently Dutch.

Deed to Col. Lovelace 1670

in the person of Colonel Francis Lovelace, the second English governor. It will be remembered that the West India Company reserved the bouwerie on the North River lying nearest the fort, for the use of their Director. It was called the Company's Bouwerie and was the southern boundary of the Dominie's Bouwerie. In 1664, this became the Duke's Farm and was reserved for the English governors. Governor Lovelace bought Annetje's land and added this newly acquired private estate to that which he already enjoyed *ex officio.* The "transport" to Lovelace is as follows. The original is in English.

Deed to Francis Lovelace.

Anno 1670-71. March the 9th.

Have Johannes Van Brugh, in right of Catrina Roelofse his wife, and attorney of Pieter Hartgers, Willem Bogardus for himselfe and his brothers Jan Roelofsen and Jonas Bogardus and Cornelis Borsum, in right of Sarah Roelofs his wife, and by assignment of Pieter Bogardus, all children and Lawful heirs of Annetje Roelofs, later widow of Dominie Bogardus, deceased, for a valluable consideration, transported and made over unto the Right Honble. Collonel Francis Lovelace, his heirs and assigns, their farm a bouwery, commonly called or known by the name of "Dominie's Bouwery," lying and being on Manhattan's Island towards the North River, the quantity of ye land amounting to about sixty-two acres, as in the former ground briefe from Governor Stuyvesant, bearing date the 4th of July, 1651, [1654] and the confirmation there uppon from Governor R. Nicolls, bearing date the 27th of March, 1667, is more particularly

New Orange 1673

set forth—w^{che} transport was signed by them and acknowledged before the Alderman, Mr. Olof Stevensen [Van] Cortland and Mr. John Laurence.

By this time Cornelis Bogardus was dead. He had married the "discreet and modest" Helen Teller of Albany and had one son Cornelis 2nd. It will be noticed that this is the only one of Annetje's descendants whose name does not appear in this document. The probable explanation is that Helen Teller Bogardus, who was already involved in one lawsuit, did not care to be associated with this deed. If the farm did not realize the whole sum of a thousand guilders stipulated by Annetje, it was possible that Roelof's children might claim the difference from the Dominie's sons. Other deeds show that she and her son were duly recognized by the family in the division of the property in which they had part, and that they were all good friends.

In 1673, came the last flash of Dutch rule in the province. Anthony Colve took advantage of open war between England and the Netherlands to capture New Netherlands in the name of the Dutch Republic. For fifteen months New York was New Orange, Lovelace abandoned his gubernatorial chair and his private estate almost without a struggle, and Governor Colve reinstated *burgemeester*, *schout* and *schepenen* in the municipal government. This was a time when Annetje's heirs might have

The King's Farm 1686

asserted their rights to the land they had sold to the fugitive governor. Their chief legal adviser was in authority. Johannes van Brugh, like the Vicar of Bray, held on to office, but he made no use of his official position to reclaim the ownership of the Dominie's Farm in behalf of his wife, when Lovelace fled hastily from the island, leaving property and debts behind him. The ex-governor's tenant, Dirck Sierken or Seckers, remained in peaceful possession of the farm during Governor Colve's short administration. When the colony reverted to the English, in 1674, all of Lovelace's property was confiscated, as the Duke of York claimed that there was a debt of £7000 due him by his late servant. The distinction between the private and official portion of the farm was lost, and the whole was henceforth comprised under one title, which was altered from the "Duke's Farm" to the "King's Farm," and later to the "Queen's Farm," when good Queen Anne began her reign.

Dirck Seckers continued his tenancy through the changes in the ownership of the farm. After his death his widow married George Ryerssen, who was occupant of the farm in 1705, when the next important events in the history of the property took place.

At the end of the eighteenth century Trinity Church Parish was incorporated. Governor

The Church Farm 1705

Fletcher gave the new corporation a lease of the whole farm for seven years at an annual rental of sixty bushels of wheat, but the former tenants remained as sub-tenants. There was some objection to this action by his successor, Governor Bellemont, who felt that Fletcher had no right to grant privileges beyond his own occupancy.

In 1705, came the final disposition of the land. The Queen's Farm was granted by Anne to Trinity Church, forever. The Companie's Bouwerie and Dominie's Bouwerie disappeared together into the boundaries of the Church Farm, and not one of Annetje Jans' descendants made the slightest suggestion that they had any further interest in the one portion of this united property which they had transferred with all the legal formalities deemed needful at the time, to Governor Lovelace, for a "valluable consideration." The families were well known in that little old New York. They bought and sold land, they appeared in various suits, they married and they died, and all is duly recorded. There is every evidence, moreover, that they unhesitatingly claimed all the good things of this world to which they fancied they were entitled, but no one of the van Brughs, the Rombouts, the Bogarduses, or the others, ever asserted that they had the slightest claim on any portion of the Dominie's Bouwerie,

Claims of the "Heirs" 1738-1893

which they saw in the peaceful possession of Trinity Church. Sixty-eight years after the sale to Lovelace, and thirty-one years after Queen Anne's grant, the descendants of Cornelis Bogardus began to protest against the occupancy of Trinity Church. There was a confused notion then as to what they could claim, and this confusion has increased in the minds of the "heirs" during two hundred years. The history of the repeated suits is long and involved. No court has sustained the claims of the "heirs" for a minute, and yet, with every generation, new claimants appear, though every possible right has long since been outlawed. Mr. Schuyler says in his *Colonial New York:* "In view of the repeated decisions of the highest judicial tribunals and of their publicity, any lawyer who can now advise or encourage the descendants of Annetje Jans to waste their money in any proceedings to recover this property must be considered as playing on the ignorance of simple people, and as guilty of conscious fraud, and of an attempt to obtain money under false pretences." Mr. Schuyler made a close study of the subject, and is himself a distinguished descendant of Roelof and Annetje Jans.

It is evident that this historic farm never became part of New Amsterdam nor, indeed, of Old New York. In 1755, Maerschalck's map

City Streets 1820

shows a line of palisades just north of Warren Street, the southern boundary of the Dominie's Bouwerie. The early growth of the city northward was on the east side. There, land could be bought in fee, while church land was, in the main, sold on leases. Another reason why houses were not built between Warren and Canal Streets was that the swamp at the base of *Kalch Hoek* or Chalkie Hook was a breeding-place for fevers until the region was improved by Anthony Rutgers, who drained the swamp in return for the land. This new district was known as Lispenard's Meadows from Rutgers' daughter, Mrs. Lispenard.

At the time of Washington's first administration, Ranelagh and Vauxhall gardens, both situated on or near the farm, were famous places of resort. Just above the boundary, on Old Jan Celes' land, was Richmond Hill, the residence rented by Aaron Burr. For a quarter of a century after the Revolution, the farm remained debatable ground between the city and Greenwich. In 1803, all the streets from Warren to Canal, covering the site, were laid out and the land ceded to the city. St. John's Chapel was build in Varick Street in the same year, but the region was still desolate. Several other churches were erected. Among them was the First Unitarian Church in New York, built for Mr. Ware, in 1821,

The Last Bit of the Farm 1897

on the corner of Chambers and Church Streets. In that same year St. John's Park was laid out between Hudson and Varick, Laight and Beach Streets. This was a beautiful spot and invited fashion to settle there. She came and for about twenty years the quarter was in high reputation. But there was a gradual change and when the Hudson River Railroad planted a freight station on the green grass of the park, fashion fled hastily and has never been heard of since in the region. Tall warehouses overshadow the modern brick and wooden structures still scattered through the quiet streets, while the turf on the little enclosed triangle at Duane Street is the last memorial of the green sward of the Jans' Farm.

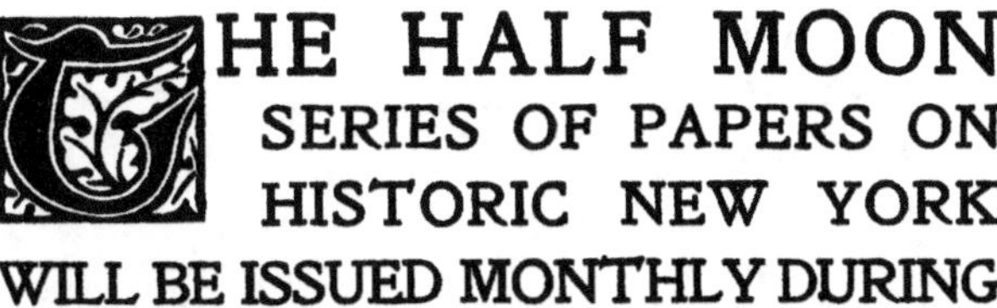

THE HALF MOON SERIES OF PAPERS ON HISTORIC NEW YORK WILL BE ISSUED MONTHLY DURING THE COMING YEAR UNDER THE EDITORSHIP OF

MAUD WILDER GOODWIN
ALICE CARRINGTON ROYCE
AND RUTH PUTNAM

AMONG THE SUBJECTS OF THE PAPERS WILL BE THE FOLLOWING

The Stadt Huys of New Amsterdam
By Alice Morse Earle

The Fourteen Miles Round
By Alfred Bishop Mason
and Mary Murdoch Mason

Wall Street
By Oswald Garrison Villard

Annetje Jans' Farm
By Ruth Putnam

The Bowery
By Edward Ringwood Hewitt
and Mary Ashley Hewitt

King's College
By John B. Pine

Old Wells and Water-Courses
By George E. Waring, Jr.

Governor's Island
By Blanche Wilder Bellamy

Defences of Old New York
By Frederick D. Grant

Old Greenwich
By Elizabeth Bisland

Tammany Hall
By Talcott Williams

Barnard College

343 MADISON AVENUE

COURSES IN AMERICAN HISTORY

For Undergraduates. General course, reading, recitations and lectures.—Three hours a week: H. A. Cushing, A.M.

For Graduates. Political History of the Colonies and of the American Revolution.—This investigation course, extending through two years, deals in the first year with the settlement of the Colonies and their development in the seventeenth century, and in the second year with the growth of the system of colonial administration, the conflict with the French, and the revolt of the Colonies. The work of the students consists chiefly in the study of topics from the original sources, with a formal account of the results of such study.—Two hours a week for two years: Professor Herbert L. Osgood, Ph.D.

These courses are open not only to candidates for degrees, but to special students who can show ability to read French and German, and can satisfy the Dean and Faculty of their general competence.

Half Moon Series

Published in the Interest of the New York City History Club.

Volume I. Number IV.

THE EARLY HISTORY OF WALL STREET. 1653–1789.

By OSWALD GARRISON VILLARD, A.M.

THE small town of New Amsterdam, whose quaint little Dutch houses nestled so lovingly about the high-walled fort at the extreme southerly end of the island of Manhattan, was neither contented, nor happy, nor prosperous, in the year 1644. "Our fields lie fallow and waste," said a communication from the eight leading burghers to their home government in Holland, "our dwellings and other buildings are burnt. We are burdened with heavy families; have no means to provide necessaries any longer for our wives and children. . . . We have left our fatherland and had not the Lord our God been our comfort, must have perished in our wretchedness."[1] To so earnest an appeal for aid even New Amsterdam 1644

Peter Stuyvesant 1647

the slow-moving States-General could not turn deaf ears. Recognizing that the situation called for a stronger hand than any which had thus far held the reins of government over the distant and struggling colony, they sent, in 1647, Peter Stuyvesant to take command of it.

If the early history of this able man is not altogether as clearly known to us as could be wished, it is at least certain that he had won the reputation, which led to his being considered worthy of so trying a post, in the Dutch West Indies, where he had lost his right leg in battle. Whether he had been maimed while fighting creditably was even doubted by some of his contemporaries. But chosen he was, with the result that he proved himself by no means unfit for the position, and even if he had other faults besides arbitrariness, his motives were excellent, the colony improved steadily under his guidance, and much was accomplished that was good and lasting.

Arriving in New Amsterdam on the 27th of May, 1647, Stuyvesant began his administration—the first of the many reform governments the island of Manhattan has seen—by a number of vigorous ordinances and regulations. All nuisances were ordered removed from the streets, the proprietors of vacant lots were given nine months in which to improve

Stuyvesant's Reforms 1647

them, under penalty of forfeiture, and non-observance of the Sabbath, as well as drunkenness and street disorder, was forbidden. The walls of the fort were repaired, the little church within it completed, embankments built along the rivers, and a revenue tax put on wine and beer. Not content with caring for the moral and religious behaviour of the burghers, Stuyvesant gave constant attention to the foreign affairs of his little domain. He at once strictly forbade the selling of liquor to the Indians, who often wandered in from the upper part of the island; he repaired the buildings burned in the wars with them and, by resettling the outlying bouweries, or farms, encouraged trade with these native neighbors.

Five years after Stuyvesant's arrival, in 1652, war broke out between England and Holland, and the news created consternation in New Amsterdam which was exposed to attacks from the English settlers in New England and Virginia. Knowing how impossible it would be for his weak colony to resist these more powerful settlements, Stuyvesant at once sent messages to them assuring them of his unaltered peaceable disposition. But at the same time he began to make all the preparations for defence that lay in his power. On the 13th of March, 1653, a general meeting of the Director-General and Council of New Netherlands was held, with the Burgomasters and

Preparations for Defence 1653

Schepens* of the town attending, at which it was decreed that all the burghers of the city should keep watch by night at designated places, and the fort of New Amsterdam should be repaired and made sufficiently strong to stand a hostile attack. "Thirdly," the record says, "taking into consideration that the Fort of New Amsterdam could not contain all the inhabitants, and to protect the houses and habitations of this city, it is deemed essentially necessary to enclose the greater part of the city with upright palisades and a small breastwork, so that, in case of necessity all the inhabitants may retire therein and, as far as practicable, defend themselves and their property against attack." [1]

This action, which determined that New York should be a walled city, and have a *wall* street, was confirmed two days later when Peter Wolfersen Van Couwenhoven and Wilhelmus Beeckman were chosen as commissioners and authorized, with De la Montagne, Stuyvesant's representative, to offer proposals, invite bids, make the contract for, and supervise the construction of the works. At the same time it was determined that the treasury should be supplied with from four to five thousand guilders to defray the cost, the money to be raised by a tax "levied on those interested in New Netherlands accord-

* The magistrates of the city.

The Wall Completed May, 1653

ing to the value of their estates," and the property of the burghers was divided into four classes for the purposes of taxation. Work on the wall was at once begun, the contract price for this part of the defences being three thousand one hundred and sixty-six guilders, and it was entirely completed on the first day of May, 1653.[1]

According to the conditions of the contract, the wall was solidly constructed. Round palisades twelve feet in length, eighteen inches in girth and sharpened at the top were placed in a line, interrupted at intervals of a rod by posts twenty-one inches in circumference, to which split rails were nailed two feet below the top of the palisades. A sloping breastwork three feet wide at the top and four at the bottom and four feet in height was then thrown up inside the palisades and against them, the dirt for which was to be thrown up from a ditch two feet deep and three and one-half broad located two and one-half feet within the breastwork. The length of the wall was about 180 rods and it ran along the East River for a short distance before extending straight across the island to the North River, skirting, as it passed, the end of De Heere Gracht, an inlet of the sea where Broad Street now is. The North River side of New Amsterdam was left defenceless because of a pretty steep bluff along it, long since

Description of Wall 1653

levelled, while the East River received the slight protection afforded by the Schoeynge, a barrier of planks driven into the mud like the modern system of piling. It must be noticed, too, that in those days the Island of Manhattan did not have the breadth many years of filling in of mud flats have since given it, for the ground covered now by Water, South, and Front Streets was then a part of the bay and river. In its location the wall was about on the line of a primitive fence built by Stuyvesant's predecessor, Governor Kieft, to keep the cattle from wandering out of their joint pasture lands and falling a prey to the wild animals that roved over the upper part of the island.

Three years later there were two substantial gates built in the wall; one, known as "*T' Water Poort*" or Water Gate, stood at the junction of the present Pearl and Wall Streets, being designed by a Captain Conwick, an educated officer in Stuyvesant's service.[4] The other gate, known as the Land Gate, was at the corner of Broadway and Wall Streets and was the means of ingress and egress of the dwellers on the bouweries near the present City Hall Park, then known as *De Vlacke*, or Flat, and used as the common pasture land. It is interesting to note in these days of currency discussion that the contractor, Tomas Bacxter, was paid in "seawant" money made

The Burghers as Soldiers 1653

from shells, which was for many years practically the sole medium of exchange in New Amsterdam.

As the days went by and nothing was heard of any hostile movement of the English, the enthusiasm of the burghers waned rapidly under the fatigue and trials of military life. When, on the 28th of July, Stuyvesant reminded the Burgomasters and Schepens of their promise to help the company finish its fortress, they declined on the ground "that the citizens at this time are so exhausted and worn out by their former general work."[5] Two weeks later the city authorities were more compliant, for when the governor complained that the hogs were doing great damage to the newly erected works, the court messenger was sent to notify the burghers with all the haste possible for so dignified an official, that the hogs must be kept shut up, until the works could be properly protected from them by fencing. Even this action did not avail much towards the preservation of the works, for they deteriorated so, that, on the 13th of March following, Stuyvesant appealed to and obtained aid from the outlying villages of Breukelen, Midwout (Flatbush), and Amersfoort (Flatlands), which supplied palisades for the wall and the East River water front to replace those destroyed by the severity of the winter.[6]

News from Boston 1654

In the following June the citizens again exerted themselves on receiving the news of the arrival in Boston of several vessels with troops and war supplies and of the raising of soldiers in Plymouth and New Haven. They prosecuted the work with great zeal, until, on July 16, 1654, the welcome news of a treaty of peace between England and Holland reached them and had a magic effect in stopping all work.

To prepare for war in time of peace was not a maxim of those quiet-loving burghers, and so they neglected their defences until the danger was at hand. Thus, in 1655, the short war with the Swedish settlements on the Delaware or South River and the Indian attacks on Hoboken, Pavonia, and Staten Island led first to a tinkering at the wall and then to a decided strengthening of the palisades, by nailing boards to the height of at least ten or twelve feet above the pointed tops of the palisades, so as to prevent the "*overloopen*" (jumping over) of the savages.[1] Despite all these dangers and others threatened before the city finally outgrew its protection, the wall was never called upon to show its strength and never became the scene of strife or bloodshed.

The matter of paying for the wall and the other fortifications, as well as for the constant repairs to them, soon became a burning question in the little community and led to a seri-

Stuyvesant Quarrels with the Schepens 1653

ous breach between the West India Company and the city authorities. Stuyvesant wished the city to bear the original cost of the wall and of the first repairs to the fort, but the burgomasters and schepens held that it was the company's duty to defend the city. Being upheld by the burghers, they said that if the director-general would abandon his excise on wine and beer and transfer the money received to the city, they would find the means needed. Stuyvesant held out for some time but finally yielded, and turned over to the city this obnoxious tax, thus giving it the first revenue it ever received. The money for the fortifications was then promptly raised by the aid of "divers honorable merchants."

When, in 1655, the plank curtain was built on to the wall and the fort again strengthened, a joint meeting of the governor and his council and the burgomasters and schepens called for voluntary subscriptions to defray this new expense and decreed, October 11, 1655, that in case of opposition or refusal by "disaffected or evil-minded" such should be assessed according to their state and condition, a reasonable contribution exacted from them and execution levied at once. The result was the sum of six thousand three hundred and five guilders, mostly made up of voluntary subscriptions largely in excess of what would have been exacted of the givers.[8]

Stuyvesant again Asks for Help 1656

A year later Stuyvesant again appealed to the burghers for money, complaining that as far as the fortifications were concerned, "what has already been done is wholly in ruins." After some deliberation the city authorities replied that, in view of the "low and sober condition and circumstances of the Inhabitants of this City" whereby they were so "reduced that many scarcely see where they are to get the means, and others have in consequence gone away," the city must refuse to raise money in any way except by creating and farming, if their lordships of the council saw fit to grant them permission, some imposts least burdensome to the city.[9] In 1658, despite Stuyvesant's opposition, the imposts were placed upon taverns, land-transfers and slaughtered cattle, but they neither properly filled the city treasury, nor settled the vexed question of payments for the fortifications, for as late as 1692 the city declined to pay for new repairs on the ground that this duty in no way belonged to it.[10]

When, in 1664, Stuyvesant's worst fears were realized and the dreaded English actually obtained possession of New Amsterdam, the inhabitants of the open space adjoining the wall then known as "*De Singel ofte Stadt Waal*" (the circuit or city wall) were few in number and dwelt in very humble structures. Jacob Jansen Moesman was the most dis-

Directory of Wall Street 1664

tinguished one, by virtue of the fact that he kept a general store in the best building along the wall. His neighbors were Dirck de Wolspinner (woolspinner); Gridtje, the chimney sweep; Jan Jansen Van Langendyck, a tapster; Jan Teunizen, a miller; Abram Kerner, Barent Eghberzen, Jan Videt, Pieter Jansen, and Dirck Van Clyf, all of whose buildings were one hundred feet within the wall and facing it.[11] Originally a common pasture, Stuyvesant had granted to Domine Drissius, the officiating clergyman of the Dutch Church, the land which now lies between New and William Streets, south of Wall Street, and his property bounded upon the farm of Jan Jansen Damen which ran parallel with, and a few feet north of, the present line of the street between Broadway and William Streets. South of the street and west of New Street, the original grantee of the land was Cornelis Groesens, one of the early settlers, while Jacob Hendrick Vorravanger had a grant near what was afterwards the Water Gate.[12] We also find in the old records the complaint of Jan Vinje, asking for compensation for the damage his property sustained, and for that part of it taken away because of the construction of the wall.[13]

In 1673, the good burghers of New Amsterdam were released from British domination by the recapture of the city by two Dutch mari-

Anthony Colve Takes Possession 1673

ners, Cornelis Everts and Jacob Binckes. Captain Anthony Colve landed with six hundred men, and met with no resistance. After the ships had fired a few broadsides, they at once took possession of the city and reorganized the government, Colve remaining as military head and chief officer of the administration. He immediately set about repairing the fortifications, tore down several buildings erected north of the wall, in which an enemy might find shelter, stationed sentinels along the wall, and ordered that the gates should be closed from sunset until sunrise. Anyone leaving or entering the city except by means of the gates was to be punished with death—a penalty never inflicted.[14] Despite all his energetic efforts Colve was forced to see New Netherland again pass into the hands of the English the very next year, by virtue of the joint restoration of conquests agreed upon in the Treaty of Westminster between England and Holland.

As the English soldiers again guarded the gates or leisurely patrolled the wall, they had time to observe that the street had improved somewhat during their absence, as it then consisted of an irregular line of some seventeen houses of a better appearance. There was one rated as first-class, being valued at about $2000, one of the second-class, seven of the third, and seven or eight of the fourth. But

Wall Street in 1674

they were often separated by vacant lots, and one of these was "Patorson's cornor by y^e wall 28 foot front to y^e wall." Another was "the other cornor old house and ground front to wall 22 foot to ye street 26," and a third that of "Mother Drissius 150 foot front along ye wall fitt for to build." Jan Jansen Van Langendyck now appears on the list in the anglicized form of John Johnson Langdyke, which helps to explain how some of the old Dutch names either disappeared or came down to us in a mutilated form. Samuoll Wilson appears as the owner of the first pretentious dwelling of which the street could boast, and in consequence paid the heaviest taxes for 1677.[16]

The old wall again underwent considerable strengthening before terminating its usefulness as one of the defences of New York, and Governor Andros for a time in 1682 forced the early closing and morning opening of the gates as Colve had before him, Andros' punishment for violations of the rules being however only a fine of ten guilders. Some repairs were proposed in 1683, but five years later, when Governor Dongan ordered a survey made, from which it appeared that most of the palisades between the water gate and the artillery mount (which had been constructed at what is now the corner of Wall and William Streets) were nearly all down; the Water Gate itself—now called, according to the nar-

Building the Bastions 1692

rative of Chaplain John Miller, the "fly block house"—was in a complete state of decay. The rest of the wall and the Broadway gate were in a similar state ; but, strange as it seems, the French war of 1692 led to a serious effort to reconstruct the defences.[16] On April 4th of that year, because of "the danger wee by in from the Enemy," the Common Council ordered that "each respective Inhabitant from fifteen years and upwards not listed in the trane bands, as also each servant and negroe upon notice from the Capt of each respective Ward doe appear . . . and afford their labour with shovels, pickax, wheelbarrow and other needful instruments towards the repairing and mending the fortifications of this Citty."[17] Two large stone bastions were built, one on the site of the artillery mount at William Street, and the other on Broadway.[18]

Although by the next year most of the wall was gone and the street laid out upon new lines by Governor Dongan, there was still a final tinkering at the defences, as all the freemen of the city were ordered to work upon the different fortifications on the 6th of July, 1695. Probably those in Wall Street received but little of the £500 expended for this purpose after being raised by a special tax.[19] By 1699 the end came, and that part of the wall not already levelled was removed at the request of the citizens, expressed in a petition

Leo Beckwith's Survey 1685

to the Common Council, which, in view of the fact that the fortifications were decayed and a new city hall was about to be built, prayed "his Excellency that the said fortifications be demolished and the stones of the bastions be appropriated to building said City Hall."[20] Thereafter the street name, destined to become the most famous in all the great metropolis, alone served as a reminder of Stuyvesant's active desire to preserve for his employers the colony entrusted to him, until it became associated with an entirely new train of ideas.

As early as 1685 the northern side of Wall Street was carefully surveyed "by vartue of a Warrant from the honble Coll Tho. Dungan Gouarnor Generall of his Majesties Coll of New Yorke" by Leo Beckwith, whose ability to spell does not seem to have corresponded to his skill as a surveyor. He ran his line from "ye Westernmost cornor of ye Bucthers Pen" at "an angle of 313°, or northwest by west nine degrees fifteen minutes" four hundred and twenty-three feet to the farthest corner of Smyth's Street (originally Smee's, now William Street); thence by an angle of 323° four hundred and thirty-one feet to the farthest corner of the Gracht Street (Broad Street), and from here at an angle of 319° the line ran one hundred and fifty-one feet to the farthest corner of "Stoutenberg's garden,

Governor Dongan's Example 1686

which is right Opposite to the South East Corner of ye New Street, the saide street being laide out thirty six foote, in bredth, Performed this 16 day of Decemb. 1685. Py Mee. Leo Beckwith, Dept. Surveior."[21]

On the wall's being taken down, Governor Dongan considered that the one hundred feet of land left between the wall and the houses that there might be room for the movement of troops, was altogether too much space for a street to occupy and, cutting off at least forty feet within the ramparts, seems to have sold the land thus gained and applied the earnings to his own purposes.[22] This action of his has forced and forces every day many thousands of people to walk in the street, because street and sidewalks are far too narrow to accommodate the vast numbers which daily pass through, and he thereby set a bad example of misconduct to the succeeding city authorities, which has been followed down to the very latest times. He was probably also instrumental in bringing about the first pavement laid in Wall Street in 1693, which, instead of extending from one side to the other, covered a width of only ten feet in front of each row of houses from the gate at Broadway to Broad Street.[23]

From this time on Wall Street grew steadily, not only in the numbers of its inhabitants and their dwellings, but in their quality as well. In 1694 John Theobald and Peter Adolf built

City Hall Begun 1699

a wharf on it near Pearl Street which facilitated the approach to it by water,[24] and while lots sold at about $30 in 1682, one on the southeast corner of Wall and Broad Streets brought $815 in 1700.[25]

But these are minor events compared with the already mentioned fact that the site chosen for the new City Hall was at the head of Broad Street on Wall, a piece of land ever since devoted to public buildings, for the presence of this structure made Wall Street the centre of city affairs and later drew to it, or near it, men whose names will ever be household words in America. Trinity Church also helped to improve the new street, for it had stood opposite to it on Broadway since 1696, and from 1698 on contained an official pew in which the mayor, recorder, aldermen, and assistants of the city listened to an annual sermon preached for their benefit.[26]

The foundation of the new City Hall was laid on August 9, 1699, and by aid of the stones from the bastions, the sale of the old City Hall, and by appropriating the ferry revenues to it for seven years, as well as by appropriating sums outright, sufficient means were raised to construct what was for that time a notable building.[27] The estimated cost was £3000, but it finally called for the expenditure of £4000 before being finished, and as the Governor, Earl of Bellomont, had greatly en-

Governor Bellomont's Arms 1701

couraged the undertaking, the architect, James Evetts, was ordered to build into the wall the arms of Bellomont and of his Lieutenant Governor, Captain Naufon.[28] But such is the mutability of men's minds, that we find it recorded but two years later that the Marshal was ordered to forthwith pull the arms down and break them, Bellomont having fallen into disfavor with the good citizens.[29]

The first floor of the new building was half taken up by a large corridor which ran through from front to rear, the entrance being by means of a flight of steps. In one room, after a time, was kept the city fire engine and there was a dungeon in the rear for all prisoners except debtors, who had special quarters in the garret, there being no separate prison in New York until 1759. On the second floor were the court-room, the jury-room and the Common Council room, with which arrangement of rooms the building stood down to 1763, except for the removal of the prisoners.[30] On the opposite side of and in the street stood the cage, pillory, stocks, and whipping-post so characteristic of this period, and, to make the street more impressive, it was repaved in 1701, and from Broadway to Smith Street in 1704.[31]

Governor Dongan in the course of his land scheme had sold the frontage on the northerly side of the street to Messrs. De Peyster and Bayard, who in turn disposed of a lot at the

The Bayards in Wall Street 1701

corner of William and Wall Streets in 1701 to Gabriel Thompson, an innkeeper, for the sum of £120.[32] About 1713 they decided that they were entitled to the land upon which stood the City Hall, and brought a suit of ejectment against the Corporation which seems to have been successfully defended by the Recorder.[33] In 1718 these same men sold to the trustees of the First Presbyterian Church, whose congregation had for some time been worshipping in the City Hall, a lot west of the City Hall, with a frontage of 88 feet and a depth of 124, upon which the first church building was erected in 1719. This church, enlarged in 1748, was rebuilt in 1810 and later removed brick by brick to Jersey City, where it now stands. It was therefore long one of the landmarks and sights of the fast growing city together with its older rival Trinity, then still the small, square building with a very tall spire, in which Rev. William Vesey had preached the first sermon on the 6th of February, 1697.

Close to the City Hall the Bayards erected in 1729 a large building in which they introduced into New York what they termed "the mystery of sugar refining," which structure marked their close connection with early Wall Street for the rest of the century, and which was turned into a tobacco factory in 1773.[34]

Meal Market 1726

But even before the Bayards thus set their stamp upon the street, a building had been erected in 1709 which made the street the centre of a good deal of trade and of a peculiar kind of traffic one does not expect to find in New York. On the 4th of October of that year the inhabitants of the East Ward received permission to erect a market house at the east end of Wall Street at their own charge. They built it near the site of the old tavern much patronized by Long Islanders on their trips to New York and which was founded by Daniel Litschoë. After his death in 1660 it was carried on by his wife, who late in life sold it to a Jewish butcher, Asser Levy, who in turn used it for the purposes of his business.[35] By 1720, repairs of such a serious nature were required, that it was decided to move the market higher up into the street, and six years later it was ordered that the Wall Street market be the public market place for the sale of all sorts of corn, grain, and meal, which should thereafter be sold in no other market in the city.[36] This action gave it the name of the "Meal Market," by which it was commonly known, and cut meat was not permitted to be on sale there until 1740, when Isaac Varian and Charies Denison leased the first two regular butcher stands. At the same time arrangements were made for storing in the market the unsold meal and grain which

Ordinance of 1731

had hitherto been kept over night in neighboring stores. One of these was that of John Briggs, who advertised in *Bradford's Gazette* that in his shop at the corner of the Meal Market all sorts of drugs and medicines could be bought at wholesale.[87]

It was in 1731 that this market received its unusual feature by an ordinance of November 18th, which said that "All negroes and Indian slaves that are let out to hire within this city do take up their standing, in order to be hired in the Market house at the Wall Street Slip, until such time as they are hired, whereby all persons may know where to hire slaves as their occasion shall require and all Masters discover where their slaves are so hired." But slaves were bought and sold as well as hired there, and that the law had no compassion for these poor ignorant bondmen can be seen all too clearly from the punishment of one transgressor.

Mr. Jacob Rignier's man Mars, having been convicted of wounding Ephraim Pierson, a constable of the watch, it was ordered that he "be stripped from the middle upwards and tyed to the tail of a cart, at the City Hall, and be drawn from thence to Broadway and from thence to the Custom House, thence to Wall Street and from thence to the City Hall again; and that he be whipped upon the naked back, ten lashes at the corner of every street he shall

The Meal Market 1762

pass and that he afterwards be discharged from his imprisonment, paying his fees, etc." It will hardly be maintained that the sight of this bleeding wretch could have been a profitable one, either to the city fathers on their way to the City Hall, or to the school boys, who doubtless followed the cart with jeers and jokes, unless fortunately in school during the period of punishment.[28]

From 1750 onward the business of the Market began to fail and the building to decay, if we may judge by the increased bills for repairs, which figure largely in the records from 1720 down, £43, 5*d.* being expended for that purpose in 1760.[29] It is not surprising, therefore, that the city government ordered its removal in May, 1762, after having received a strong petition from various people residing nearby, who said that "they conceive the building called the Meal Market is of no real use or advantage, either to the community in general or with the inhabitants living near thereto. . . . That the said building greatly obstructs the agreeable prospect of the East River, which those that live in Wall Street would otherwise enjoy, occasioning a dirty street, offensive to the inhabitants on each side, and disagreeable to those who pass and repass to and from the Coffee House, a place of great resort." The alderman and "common councillman" of the ward supervised

Wall Street 1731

the removal and had the few butchers' stands still in use transferred to the Oswego, or Broadway, Market.[40]

By the time the slave market was established, Wall Street showed signs of considerable growth and of development along those lines which made it before the end of the century the leading street of the city socially and politically, if not commercially. The south side of the street grew naturally more rapidly than did the north side, upon which there stood in 1728, between Broadway and William Streets, only the Sugar House, City Hall, and Presbyterian Church. But beyond William Street there were numerous smaller buildings, so that the east end had a built-up aspect on both sides of the street. From the City Hall to Broadway the street had at that time a width of forty-one feet. The presence of the Meal Market and the Long Island ferry, which had existed from an early day, gave a commercial aspect to the lower part of the street which it has never lost, while the two churches and the City Hall drew to the upper end more and more people of means, so that even before Revolutionary times it was the most fashionable residence street, a growth best indicated by the increase in value of the land. In 1706 a lot 25 by 166 feet on the north side cost $580; a lot on the south side, 42 by 108 feet, with the modest

Sale of Land 1793

house which stood upon it, brought in 1793 $12,000. This was the property of Alexander Hamilton, and a similar house with a lot only 44 by 51 feet of land, sold for $12,550 a year later.

The City Hall in those days attracted to itself some of the ablest citizens, and was the scene of so many interesting and exciting events that its history is also that of the city and state, and later on of the new nation itself. Immediately after the death of Lord Bellomont, the Mayor, Thomas Noell, refused to sit with some newly-elected aldermen, on the ground that they should have been sworn in by him and not by the retiring Mayor, so that excitement ran high until the Supreme Court adjusted the matter.[41] It was also the scene in 1735 of the famous trial of the editor Zenger. Brought on by free criticism of the officers of the city, it soon became a question as to the liberty of the press, and so intense was the popular excitement that the court-room was crowded and hundreds awaited the verdict in the street. When the news was brought out that Andrew Hamilton, the learned lawyer of Philadelphia and friend of Franklin, had obtained a verdict of "not guilty" for the prisoner, on all the charges of false, scandalous, malicious, and seditious libel, extraordinary demonstrations resulted. The entire populace seemed to be in the celebration and paid Mr.

Stephen DeLancey

Hamilton such honors that the freedom of the city was given him, and the Mayor felt himself moved to bestow a gold snuff-box upon the eloquent Philadelphian.[42]

Naturally the men of those times took a pride in a building about which the entire city life revolved, and in 1715 Stephen De Lancey, a member of the Assembly—which also sat there *—showed his appreciation of and love for the building by purchasing, with the £50 check he had received for his service as assemblyman, a cupola for it. This cupola contained a clock, with four large dials, and it was exactly rebuilt in January, 1738, when it was discovered to be entirely decayed.[43]

The city records contain many items of interest, from year to year, about the changes and repairs to this historic building, such as the fitting up of one room for another "strong and useful prison" in 1727, and of another room in 1732 for the use of the speaker and committees of the Assembly, while the fire engines received theirs in 1731. The Assembly chamber was "ornamentally repaired" in 1758, the prisoners all removed in 1759, and the City Hall entirely repaired and somewhat altered in 1763. To cover the expenses of this undertaking, these three sums were raised by a

* The State Assembly met in New York until 1797; in the City Hall until the Revolution.

Rev. John Millington's Gift 1730

lottery on April 12th of that year: £958, 14*s.* 8*d.*; £490, 14*s.*, 4*d.*; £1239, 7*s.*, and thus encouraged, a committee was appointed to write to Bristol, England, for copper with which to cover the roof. Later it was determined to "raise the building a story higher," which resulted in the city's borrowing the sum of £500 as an addition to the lottery moneys, and in 1764 the grim whipping-post, stocks, cage, and pillory were at last removed from Wall Street and moved to the new gaol."

Still another fact which must not be overlooked, now that New York is to build a splendid and united library, is that the first library in the city was housed in this old City Hall in a room directly opposite that of the Common Council. There were 1642 volumes, the bequest of the Rev. John Millington of Newington, England, to the Venerable Society for Propagating the Gospel in Foreign Parts, which did so much for religion in the early colonies, and which sent this gift at once to New York. "We are truly sensible," said the Common Council, "of the great advantages which may arise from so generous and seasonable a present and we are zealously disposed to receive the same." Before the arrival of the books in 1730, the Common Council proclaimed their decision that "the Clergy and Gentlemen of this Government and Jersey, Pensilvania and Connecticut might borrow Books to read upon giving security to Return them within a Limited Time. . . ." To these books Rev. John Sharp added his own collection (he had been chaplain to Lord Bellomont), and opened the library to the public as the "Corporation Library."

Rev. John Sharp's Gift 1730

The interest in the library seems to have died out shortly after and did not revive until 1754, when some public-spirited citizens, who had founded the "Society Library," got permission to deposit theirs also in the City Hall. When the latter was rebuilt, provision was made for a new library room, "to be finished in as cheap a manner as possible," and as soon as it was ready Mr. Thomas Jackson was appointed librarian on August 23, 1765, and ordered to be in the room "on Mondays and Thursdays from one half after Eleven o'Clock in the Morning until one to let out the Books." A Folio cost "two shillings, a Quarto one shilling and an Octavo or Lesser Volume Sixpence, per month." Mr. Jackson was required to keep a strict account of the income therefrom and to catalogue the Library, for all of which he received the magnificent salary of twenty dollars per annum! In 1772 King George III. granted it a charter under the name of the New York Society Library, and after having been thoroughly vandalized by British soldiers in the Revolution and probably by the patriots also, finally became the Mercantile

Pitt's Statue Erected 1770

Library.[45] Judge Jones states that he himself saw many valuable books sold by soldiers for drink.[46]

Wall Street received its first ornamentation when the white marble pedestrian statue of William Pitt was erected on September 7, 1770, near the intersection of Wall and William Streets and in front of the residences of John Thurman and Evert Bancker. The work of the then celebrated artist Wilton, of London, the statue represented Pitt in a Roman habit in the attitude of an orator, holding a scroll in his right hand, the left being extended. It was voted at a town meeting held June 23, 1766, as a token of the gratitude of the colony of New York for Pitt's eminent services to America, particularly for his aiding the repeal of the Stamp Act, the news of which had just reached the city. In the midst of the angry passions aroused by the Revolution, the statue was too conspicuous a mark to go unscathed, and so suffered the indignity of having its head cut off. It stood in this condition for some years and was then removed by city ordinance as an obstruction to the city. Part of it is still to be seen in the rooms of the New York Historical Society.[47]

During the series of events which led to the actual outbreak of the Revolutionary War, Wall Street was always the centre of the popular outbursts of feeling or passion, and re-

Tea Meeting 1773

mained as such and as the abiding place of the military authorities until the restoration of peace and a civilian government. From 1765 on the trouble began, one of its most dramatic events being a great tea meeting in the City Hall in 1773, when General Lamb read the Act of Parliament placing a duty on tea and received an overwhelming vote of No, when he asked whether it should be paid. Another event was the appearance in Wall Street of one hundred and fifty armed men, who marched into Trinity Church in a vain attempt to make the rector, Rev. Charles Inglis, forego his prayers for the king and the royal family, a fact which shows how rife the revolutionary spirit was and how ready the citizens were to receive with cheers the reading in Wall Street, on July 18, 1776, of the Declaration of Independence.[48]

The citizens paid dearly, however, for these demonstrations, and for the privilege of having for a short time Washington's headquarters and the presence of the Provincial Committee, which sat in the City Hall, undisturbed by renewed rail-riding of loyalists through the adjoining streets, of which acts it disapproved by a weak resolution passed June 17, 1776.[49]

The long years of English occupation told heavily upon the city, and Wall Street echoed and re-echoed to the tramp of the occupying army, and soon began to show signs of the

Presbyterian Church Reopened 1785

suffering ever attendant upon an appeal to arms. The great fire which destroyed four hundred and ninety-two houses, about one-eighth of the city, September 21, 1776, mercifully deprived Wall Street of Trinity Church alone—a severe loss in itself, however. The Presbyterian Church, in which Whitefield had spoken with that stirring eloquence which moved all who heard to tears, became a hospital and harbored the wounded and their unskilled nurses and surgeons throughout the war, not being re-opened for religious purposes until 1785.[50]

As for the City Hall, it became the main guard-house and military headquarters of the Americans and British. The latter's soldiers roamed through it at will and paid no more respect to its fittings and dignity than they did to its library, which is what must be expected of every invading army. General Knyphausen was one of the English officers who lived in a large house on Wall Street, and Benedict Arnold is also said to have lived in a house on the street after his flight to the British. Many of the younger officers boarded in or near it, beguiling their days of inactivity by paying attentions to the young American loyalists of the opposite sex, who still remained in the city. Doubtless there were many gay sleighing parties and entertainments even in that bitter cold winter of 1779–

End of War 1782

80, when the snow was so deep and fuel so scarce, that the beautiful trees, which added so much to the attractiveness of Wall Street, were, one by one, felled to furnish the kindling so greatly needed.[51]

So the street looked very shabby and battered when the end came and General Henry Knox entered New York at the head of the American army, marching through the Bowery to Wall Street, and then going back to the Bowery to receive his commander, George Washington, to whom he was always so devoted, as soon as the English troops and loyalists had withdrawn. In the evening of the same day, Washington and his general officers were given a public dinner at the tavern on the corner of Wall and Nassau Streets, then the most fashionable one in the city, of which John Simmons, a man of immense size, was the proprietor. After the dinner the French officers with Washington superintended a display of fireworks in Bowling Green, as their part of the celebration over New York's release from the incubus of an English garrison.[52]

The city at once began to recover rapidly, trade commenced again, those who had fled from the city because of the presence of the English returned, and the blessings of peace made themselves felt on every hand. The next year saw the establishment of the First

The City Revives 1786

Bank of New York,[53] the leading men of the nation came to the city, and in 1786 a directory of the city was published, which gives us a clear insight into the flourishing Wall Street of that period. From this first city directory we learn that, according to their business or trades, the street contained one apothecary, three auctioneers, one grocer, six merchants, two tailors, one clockmaker, one printer and bookseller, one snuff and tobacco manufacturer, one owner of a vendue and commission store, one tavern-keeper, one owner of a "porter house," one milliner, one school-teacher, one upholsterer, one owner of an intelligence office, one quartermaster-general (William Denning), and six residents who have no occupation set after their names. We also find in Mr. Kelby's compilation of the newspapers of that year a number of interesting items.

Francis Childs announces on February 27th that he "has removed his printing-office from 189 Water Street to the corner of Wall and Water Streets, opposite the Coffee House bridge, where the *Daily Advertiser* will be published as usual."

On April 15th the greater part of the proprietors of Wall, as well as of Green and Water Streets, requested the Corporation to order all sea-going vessels out of Wall Street Slip, except the coasters and wood boats, thus giving them back privileges of which they had been deprived for twenty years.

On May 28th, Richard Varick, Recorder of the city, and for many years connected with the city government, moved into 52 Wall Street, a house previously occupied by Colonel W. S. Livingston, while a week later Edward Fogarty announced that the hours of attendance at his school, 46 Wall Street, were from 9 to 12 A.M. and 2 until 5 P.M. each day.

That the contents of the street were a temptation to wrong-doers even at this time, we learn from the fact that on June 19th there was an "attempted robbery of Montgomery, the watch-maker in Wall Street. The villains got only five or six lead watches that hung in the window by way of ornament. Mr. Montgomery offers a reward of twenty dollars for the arrest of the villains." Doubtless the thieves would have secured a greater booty had they tried the store at 116 Wall Street, where Nicolas Low offered for sale looking-glasses from London, Carolina indigo, glassware, French brandy, rums, and best James River tobacco. The lower end of Wall Street was in this year again greatly in need of repairs, a state of affairs which crops up regularly in the records from 1700 down. This time the auctioneers, who lived there, are particularly urged to subscribe to the list started at the Coffee House.

Coffee House 1786

This Coffee House, like the tavern at the corner of Nassau Street, was a much frequented place, being the rendezvous of the merchants and therefore also a political headquarters. It stood on the corner of Wall and Water Streets, and when the new "Tontine Coffee House" was built in the years 1792–94, it lost ground and was known as the Old Coffee House. Its tontine rival was built by an association of merchants and cost $43,000.

William Duer, for many years President of Columbia College, in describing the fashionable end of Wall Street as it was about this time, says that a large three-story double house of brick, which stood on the northwest corner of Broadway, was the family mansion of the Marstons, but was at this time occupied by Mynheer Van Berckle, Minister from the States-General of Holland. Opposite to it lived William Edgar, and next to him lived Colonel William Lamb, Collector of the Port of New York under the State government, and a veteran of the Revolutionary struggle. On the same side lived people with the familiar names of the Cuylers, Dennings, Smiths, and Stebbins. On the northerly side were the Whites, Goulds, Buchanans, and Van Hornes, as well as Mrs. Daubigny, who kept a very fashionable bachelor lodging house, and "the more notorious bachelor homestead of Daniel McCormick, upon whose stoop

Wall Street's Prosperity 1788

were seated for several hours every fair day, himself, his cronies, and his toadies, the latter of whom generally stayed to dinner."[54]

This was truly the flourishing time of Wall Street, the beginning of its most fashionable period, when its sidewalks resounded to the steps not only of the leaders of fashion, but of the leaders of the government of the United States. Washington and his cabinet, the foreign ambassadors, the first Congress under the new Constitution, and all the leading lawyers of the day, such men as John Jay, Duane, and Livingston, came to swell the throng of well-dressed and distinguished men and women, in whose daily walk Wall Street was ever included, making a gathering of high-minded, able patriots, whose fame increases as we become further removed from their day.

How to receive and house the new government properly became the question of the hour in 1788, until the Common Council resolved, on September 17th, to appropriate the whole of the City Hall to the use of the Federal Government, and the work of completely altering it was begun in the next month. The city wisely employed Major L'Enfant, the French engineer to whom we owe the laying out of the city of Washington. At a cost of $65,000, the building, which had previously been raised upon arches, under which passed

Representative Chamber 1788

the pedestrians on Wall and Nassau Streets, upon whose lines it encroached, was completely remodelled and enlarged. Some new walls were built, and the interior was decorated and fitted up with an elegance unequalled in the new republic. The Representative chamber had an arched ceiling 46 feet in height in the centre, and had an octangular shape. Its other dimensions were 62 and 58 feet, and it contained two galleries, a Speaker's platform, quaint fire-places under each window, and a separate chair and desk for each representative.

The ceiling of the Senate chamber, naturally a smaller room, was painted a light blue, and decorated in the centre with a sun and thirteen stars. The Senators sat in semicircles, and the Vice-President's chair, elevated three feet above the floor, was under a crimson damask canopy. On the Wall Street side were the three windows and the famous balcony, twelve feet deep, upon which took place the swearing in of the first President of the United States.[66]

It is sad to have to relate that in 1801, when Major L'Enfant's pecuniary condition was such that he felt compelled to ask the city to reimburse him for these services, which he had intended to be gratuitous, the Corporation of the city awarded him but $750, which he declined. In 1789, when the build-

Washington's Arrival 1789

ing was finished, Major L'Enfant was offered ten acres of land near Provost's Street, a pecuniary compensation, the thanks of the corporation, and the freedom of the city, accepting only the last two rewards.[66]

In 1789 came the inauguration of President Washington, and an ending of the troublesome times passed under the government provided by the Articles of Confederation. Escorted by the leading functionaries of the latter government, Washington crossed from Elizabethtown to the foot of Wall Street in the great rowboat steered by Commodore Nicholson, and manned by thirteen shipmasters or pilots, General Knox, John Jay, and many others being in the accompanying boats. Welcomed at the foot of Wall Street by Chancellor Livingston, Richard Varick, the recorder of New York, the Mayor, Aldermen, and other officials, Washington proceeded, amid the firing of cannon, to the residence of Governor Clinton in Queen Street, escorted by the militia, the Cincinnati and other societies, and everywhere enthusiastically greeted by the dense masses of people who crowded the wharves and every available inch of the streets through which the hero passed.

At sunrise of the next morning, the 30th of April, a salute was fired from the Battery, and in the services which were held in all the churches, the various congregations im-

Washington's Inauguration 1789

plored "the blessings of heaven upon their new government, its favor and protection to the President, and success and acceptance to this administration." [67]

Congress assembled at noon in the City Hall, now called Federal Hall, the procession formed in Wall Street and went to Washington's house, 3 Cherry Street, to which he had gone from Clinton's during the previous evening, and where he found Mrs. Washington attended by many ladies. On its return, the procession, with Washington between the committee of the Senate and the committee of Representatives, passed through Queen and Great Dock (Pearl) Streets into Broad and up the latter to Wall Street, the latter being particularly well decorated.[68]

When Washington, attended by Livingston and the Senators' and Representatives' committee, appeared upon the balcony in full view of the dense throngs in Wall and Broad Streets, as well as in every window and on every roof from which a view of the proceedings could be obtained, his entrance was greeted with universal shouts of joy and welcome. According to Mrs. Josiah Quincy, an eye-witness, "his appearance was most solemn and dignified. Advancing to the front of the balcony, he laid his hand upon his heart, bowed several times, and then retired to an arm-chair near the table. The populace seemed

Washington Takes the Oath 1789

to understand that the scene had overcome him and were at once hushed in profound silence.

"After a few moments Washington arose and came forward. Chancellor Livingston read the oath of office according to the form prescribed by the Constitution, and Washington repeated it, resting his hand upon the Bible. Mr. Otis, the Secretary of the Senate, then took the Bible to raise it to the lips of Washington, who stooped and kissed the book. At this moment a signal was given, by raising a flag upon the cupola of the Hall, for a general discharge of the artillery of the Battery. All the bells in the city rang out a peal of joy, and the assembled multitude sent forth a universal shout."[59] "Such thundering peals," says another eye-witness, "went up from the crowds as seemed to shake the foundations of the city, and long and loud were they repeated, as if their echoes were never to cease."[60]

Such was Wall Street's most historic event and the beginning of its short but brilliant period as the seat of the government of the nation.

If it is to-day no longer the haunt of statesmen, or the lounging-place of fashion, its fame has in no wise decreased, for it contains now the commercial leaders of the republic as it did the political leaders one hundred years ago.

Wall Street 1897

If there is much in its life to-day which calls for the deepest censure and regret, it is still the pulse which records the heart-beats of the nation, and still the wall, the bulwark, to which the people look for the means of defence of the city, the state, and the nation in times of financial danger and national peril.

REFERENCES.

1. BAYARD TUCKERMAN'S *Stuyvesant*, p. 51.
2. *Records of the Burgomasters and Schepens* (translation), i., p. 150.
3. *Ibid.*, i., pp. 153–4.
4. D. T. VALENTINE, *Manual of the Common Council*, p. 537.
5. *Records*, i., pp. 216, 229.
6. *Ibid.*, i., pp. 418, 427.
7. *Ibid.*, ii., p. 211.
8. *Ibid.*, ii., pp. 215–16.
9. *Ibid.*, ii., pp. 551–56.
10. *English Records of the Common Council*, ii., p. 35.
11. VALENTINE, p. 541.
12. *Ibid.*, p. 537.
13. *English Records*, ii., p. 23 (5th October, 1654).
14. VALENTINE, p. 538. W. L. STONE, *History of New York City*, pp. 67–68.
15. *English Records*, i., p. 99 ; VALENTINE, p. 324.
16. *English Records*, i., pp. 17, 211.
17. *Ibid.*, ii., p. 44.
18. VALENTINE, p. 542.
19. *English Records*, ii., pp. 182, 228.
20. VALENTINE, p. 546.
21. *Documentary History of New York*, iii., p. 244.
22. VALENTINE, pp. 541–42.
23. MARTHA J. LAMB, *Story of Wall Street*, p. 23 ; *English Records*, ii., p. 98.
24. *Ibid.*, ii., p. 357.
25. TUCKERMAN, p. 149.
26. *English Records*, *Ibid.*, ii., p. 298.
27. *Ibid.*, ii., p. 357.
28. *English Records*, ii., pp. 363–4, 422.
29. *Ibid.*, ii., p. 516, Dec. 1st, 1702.
30. VALENTINE, p. 551.
31. *English Records*, ii., p. 358 ; VALENTINE, p. 551 ; *Records*, ii., p. 431.

32. Valentine, p. 56.
33. *English Records,* iii., pp. 269, 272.
34. John A. Stevens, *The Progress of New York,* ii., p. 27.
35. Thomas F. De Voe, *The Market Book,* p. 242.
36. *English Records,* ii., p. 508; Stevens, ii., p. 27.
37. De Voe, pp. 242, 247; *English Records,* v., p.33.
38. De Voe, p. 244; *English Records,* iv., p. 237.
39. De Voe, p. 251.
40. *English Records,* vi., p. 159; De Voe, pp. 251-52.
41. Lamb, p. 26.
42. *Ibid.*, p. 29.
43. *Ibid.*, p. 30.
44. *English Records,* iv., pp. 121, 261, 284, 476; vi., pp. 12, 63, 190, 193-94, 197, 219, and 224.
45. *English Records,* iv., pp. 175–76, 192, 195; vi., pp. 270, 278; Mary L. Booth, *History of the City of New York,* pp. 319–20.
46. Thomas Jones, *New York in the Revolution,* p. 136.
47. *English Records,* vii., p. 44; Stevens, pp. 13–15; W. A. Duer, *Reminiscences of an Old Yorker,* p. 4; J. F. Watson, *New York City and State in the Olden Time,* p. 202.
48. Lamb, p. 36 *ff.*
49. Jones, i., p. 101.
50. A. T. Goodrich, *The Picture of New York and Stranger's Guide,* p. 364; Thomas E. V. Smith, *The City of New York in the Year of Washington's Inauguration,* p. 148.
51. Booth, p. 511; Lamb, p. 44.
52. Goodrich, pp. 67-68; Smith, p. 121.
53. Stevens, ii., p. 40.
54. Duer, p. 5.
55. Lamb, p. 57.
56. Duer, p. 67; Smith, pp. 217, 219.
57. *Gazette of the United States,* May 2, 1789.
58. Duer, pp. 67, 69.
59. Smith, pp. 231-32.
60. Duer, p. 68.

HE HALF MOON SERIES OF PAPERS ON HISTORIC NEW YORK WILL BE ISSUED MONTHLY DURING THE COMING YEAR UNDER THE EDITORSHIP OF

MAUD WILDER GOODWIN
ALICE CARRINGTON ROYCE
AND RUTH PUTNAM

AMONG THE SUBJECTS OF THE PAPERS WILL BE THE FOLLOWING

The Stadt Huys of New Amsterdam
By Alice Morse Earle

The Fourteen Miles Round
By Alfred Bishop Mason
and Mary Murdoch Mason

Wall Street
By Oswald Garrison Villard

Annetje Jans' Farm
By Ruth Putnam

The Bowery

By Edward Ringwood Hewitt
and Mary Ashley Hewitt

King's College

By John B. Pine

Old Wells and Water-Courses

By George E. Waring, Jr.

Governor's Island

By Blanche Wilder Bellamy

Defences of Old New York

By Frederick D. Grant

Old Greenwich

By Elizabeth Bisland

Tammany Hall

By Talcott Williams

Barnard College

343 MADISON AVENUE

COURSES IN AMERICAN HISTORY

For Undergraduates. General course, reading, recitations and lectures.—Three hours a week: H. A. Cushing, A.M.

For Graduates. Political History of the Colonies and of the American Revolution.—This investigation course, extending through two years, deals in the first year with the settlement of the Colonies and their development in the seventeenth century, and in the second year with the growth of the system of colonial administration, the conflict with the French, and the revolt of the Colonies. The work of the students consists chiefly in the study of topics from the original sources, with a formal account of the results of such study.—Two hours a week for two years: Professor Herbert L. Osgood, Ph.D.

These courses are open not only to candidates for degrees, but to special students who can show ability to read French and German, and can satisfy the Dean and Faculty of their general competence.

Half Moon Series

Published in the Interest of the New York City History Club.

Volume I. Number V.

GOVERNOR'S ISLAND.

By BLANCHE WILDER BELLAMY.

The Purchase 1637

GOVERNOR'S ISLAND makes its modest but official entry into the records of "Historic New York" on a Summer's day, the 16th of June, 1637.

The new little Fort at the Bowling Green, with its earthworks and bastions, has been recently completed by the Dutch West India Company, under its colors of orange, white, and blue, with the lettering "G. W. C.," *Geoctroyeerde West-Indische Compagnie.*

In the fort sits Wouter Van Twiller, second director sent by this "Privileged West India Company" to the Province of New Netherland. With him are Jacobus Corler, Andries Hudde, Jacus Boutyn, and Claes Van Elslant. All of them, under a variety of spellings, are men of note in the colony, and all sign themselves as members of the Director's Council.

The Purchase 1637

Two Indians, Cakapeteijno and Pehiwas, are also present. They have appeared and presented themselves and declared that, voluntarily and deliberately, and with the approbation of the community, for and in consideration of certain parcels of goods which they acknowledge to their full and grateful satisfaction to have received, they do "transport, cede, give over and convey to Wouter Van Twiller, Director General of New Netherland, the Nooten Island, in the Indian tongue called Pagganck, situate over against the Island Manahatas between the North and East Rivers of New Netherland."

In a word, to dispense further with the formalities of the Roman-Dutch law, Van Twiller has bought the Island, now known as Governor's Island, from the Indians. He gives them in exchange an axe-head or two, a string of beads, a few nails. We cannot fix exactly the contents or value of these "certain parcels of goods," yet the bargain we may be sure is a shrewd one and notable, too, for one cause other than its shrewdness. No record has been found of any other sale of Pagganck, Nooten, Governor's Island, in the subsequent two hundred and sixty years of its history. Granted, captured, granted, leased, ceded, it has but once been made the subject of so plebeian a matter as exchange and barter.

Court Record Endorsed Copy of What Witnesses Say

When the Director cast his acquisitive eye on Nooten or Nutten or Noten or Nut Island, it lay close beside and was almost a part of Long Island. Marabie Bevoise testified in court a century later that she "heard Jeromus Remsen's mother say that there was only a small creek between Nutten Island and the shoar, and that a squah carried her sister over it in a tub"; and Jeromus Remsen added that he had "heard his mother say . . . that it was all Sedge and Meadow, only a Creek between Nutten and Long Island."

This Creek, now Buttermilk Channel, a deep arm of the sea thrown around the island, was at low tide a shallow ford. The little Huguenot who was first ferried over it in a wash-tub was Sara, the daughter of Katalyntie Trico and Joris Jansen de Rapalye, "the first born Christian daughter in New Netherland." She was not the first European visitor to the island. The proud boast is even made that it was the first place of settlement in the harbor. This rests on a precarious support, an equivocal entry in the journal of the Labadist travellers, Dankers and Sluyter in 1679: "In its (the river's) mouth, before the city and between the city and Red Hoeck on Long Island lies Noten Island opposite the fort, *the first place the Hollanders ever occupied in this bay!*"

It is certain that the cattle of the settlers who came in 1625, bringing horses, cows,

The First Building 1638

sheep, and hogs, were landed on Nutten Island, and remained there a day or two, but "there being no means of pasturing them there they were shipped in sloops and boats to the Manhates, right opposite said Island."

Having escaped these intruders, the Island was left to its owners, the Indians, "who sometimes manifested themselves with arrows," in undisturbed verdure and beauty until Van Twiller possessed himself of it, and began to put up the first building. This we learn from the fact that when his greedy rule ended in 1638, and an inventory of his property was made, he had "On Nooten Island the frame of a house and 21 pairs of goats." A saw-mill was also built at the Company's expense. In 1639 it was leased by "the Honorable, wise and right Prudent Mr. William Kieft" to Evert Bischop, Sibout Claesen, and Harman Bastiansen, who "acknowledged to have amiably agreed and covenanted for the hire of it." They were to pay five hundred merchantable or sound planks yearly, one half pine and the other half oak; to keep the mill in repair; to deliver it in as good order as they received it, and "to saw not less than 65 to the bulk." They also undoubtedly supplied to the thrifty Dutch housewives those excellent hickory logs which they soon learned to appreciate "both for fire on their hearths and coals for their footstoves, because they

Act of the Xth Year of William

last longer than others and are not buried in ashes."

After Van Twiller, "full of curses and of Council dinners," had departed from office, his so-called purchases were claimed by the Government. The fact that he, the Governor, was the first and only private owner of the Island, however, still links his memory to it, though it does not owe its present name directly to him. During the Dutch period, and generally throughout the English Colonial period, it was called Nutten Island, from the groves of nut trees, hickory and chestnut, which covered it.

But in 1698 it was set aside by the Assembly as being "part of the Denizen of his Majestie's Fort at New York, for the benefit and accommodation of his Majestie's Governours and Commanders-in-Cheif for the time being," and thence came to be familiarly called "The Governor's Island."

Another link with the memory of Van Twiller is the fact that when he came over in *De Zoutberg* in 1633 he brought with him one hundred and four soldiers, the first military force sent to the province. He was therefore its first official military head, a fact which properly associates his memory with the "Forteresse" now occupying his peaceful plantation. This "plantation," on which, by the way, Van Twiller did not, himself, plant,

Bill for Breaking Extravagant Grants of Land 1699

became in time a pleasant "Withdrawing place" for the Governors, but it proved a snare to one at least of the Royal Colonials who were its temporary possessors, and whose residence in the fort at the Battery was "only a gun-shotte away."

These Governors were, many of them, no less greedy and grasping than their Dutch forerunner, Van Twiller. In 1638 he was chastened for having taken to himself, among other trifles, Nooten Island, Red Hook, the two Islands at Hellegat, and for "Stretching out a hand toward two fflats on Long Island."

But in 1699 Lord Bellomont, then Governor of the Province, received instructions from the Lords Chief Justices of England whereby he was directed "to use all legall meanes for the breaking of Extravagant grants of Lands." The Council decreed that Mr. Attorney General should prepare a decree vacating the aforesaid grants, and his Excellency moved "That there bee a clause inserted in the Body of the Bill to prevent the Governor or Commander-in-Cheif of this Province for the time being from alienating Nutten Island, the King's Farm, the King's Garden, and the Swamp and Ffresh water as being the Demesne belonging to the Kings Governour for the time being."

The fact was that Bellomont's predecessor, Colonel Fletcher, had been rapidly disposing of all the lands within reach (on a strictly paying basis, of course), "Making immense grants in parcels of upwards of a hundred thousand acres to one man." He offered a peculiar outrage to his successor by proposing to lease Nutten Island, "Where the Governor kept a parcel of sheepe," to a footman!

Petition of Lessee in 1770

The later Governors did in fact lease the Island for their own profit. We have a pious petition from Richard Deane to Lord Dunmore in 1770 begging for a continuance of his lease.

"The petition of Richard Deane," he says, "Most humbly Sheweth

"That Your Lordship's Petitioner having Rented an Island call'd the Governor's Island from his Honour the Lieut Governor For the space of two years from the First of March last which Island is now your Lordship's.

"Your Lordship's Petitioner has been at a great expence cultivating said Island which he knew he must lose very considerably by; and which would greatly distress him and his large family, if it was not continued to him the time he agreed for, and as it allways has been customary when the Island has been lett and a change in Government to happen the Tenant in being to be continued at least for the time he had taken it; And it was on expectation of the same kindness that your Lordship's Petitioner was induced to go to that Expence, therefore

"Your Lordship's Petitioner Most Humbly submits his hopes to your Lordship's great goodness, not doubting to find that tender Benevolence for which your Lordship is so justly esteem'd; and obtain your Lordship's Permission to continue and proceed on in his business as the season is so far advanced, which will the better enable him to pay your Lordship's Rent.

"That your Lordship's petitioner has been led by the

Character of Cornbury 1702

Ruleing hand of kind Providence to the honour of being your Lordship's first Tenant in America. In which situation he is determined to Merit your Lordship's attention by a strict adherence to every duty incumbent on him which he humbly hopes will meet your Lordship's aprobation.

"And your petitioner as in duty bound will not only forever pray; *but will pay your Lordship's Rent very punctualy!*"

This cheerful assurance would certainly have appealed to Fletcher and still more to Bellomont's successor. This was Lord Cornbury, Queen Anne's cousin, who made a fine stir in the province, and a fine scandal for his pecuniary dealings with the Governor's Island.

In the Rutherford MSS. is a paper inscribed with the warning, "Felix quem faciunt aliena Pericula Cautum."

It contains a portrait not too flattering of Lord Cornbury.

"*He was Farre from being the slave of his word,* nor had the sence of honour or of shame the least influence upon his conduct. Farre from having any deep designes all his thoughts were employed on the then present moment and like a sharper in low life scrupled not at any means of aquiring money which he spent as profusely as he basely got. . . . . .

"In short he was a fine companion and with a great deal of good manners, almost the worst representative of a King that this quiet, easie, good-natur'd, giving people ever had."

Smith, in his history of 1757, also pays his compliments to Cornbury:

The Tax for Fortifying The Narrows 1703

"We never had a Governor ſo universally deteſted nor one who ſo richly deſerved the Publick Abhorence. In ſpite of his noble deſcent his behaviour was trifling, mean and extravagant. It was not uncommon for him to dreſs himſelf in a woman's habit and then to patrole the Fort in which he reſided. Such freaks of low humor expoſed him to the universal contempt of the people, but their indignation was kindled by his despotic rule, ſavage Bigotry, inſatiable Avarice and Injustice not only to the Publick but even his private Creditors."

This was the Governor who came into possession of the Island in 1702. One of the oft recurring "French Scares" coming on at about that time he called "a Councill in Fort Anne, the eighth day of Aprill, 1703," announced that he had private information of a proposed attack by the French and urged an appropriation with the Design to "erect two Batteries of Guns at the Narrows, one on each side." The Assembly voted £1500 for the purpose, to be raised in the following way:

Resolved, That the ſaid Fifteen Hundred Pounds be raiſed by a Poll Tax, and other ways in manner following, to wit:

That every perſon having the Honour to be of her Majeſty's Council of this Province shall pay Forty shillings.

Every Representative in the General Assembly Twenty Shillings.

Every Practitioner in the Law, Twenty Shillings.

The Tax for Fortifying The Narrows 1703

Every Perſon that Wares a Periwig, Five Shillings and Six pence.

Every Bachelor above the Age of 25 years, Two Shillings and Three Pence.

Every other Freeman from 16 years to 60, Nine pence.

The Masters or Mistreſſes of Every ſlave or ſlaves, for each ſlave from 16 to 60 years of Age, One Shilling.

And every gallon of ſpirits distilled in this Province from anything but Grain to pay Three pence per Gallon until the 25th day of March next.

The sum resulting from this amusing tax on bachelors, periwigs, etc., was made over to the Governor, but nothing more was heard of the fortifications. "The money," writes Cadwallader Colden, "Lord Cornbury applied to building a pleasure house on Nutten Island for himself and succeeding Governors to retire to, when he inclined to free himself from business!"

Cornbury boldly denied the charge that he had appropriated this sum, but we do not forget that he was "Farre from being the slave of his word." That he expended it all upon Governor's Island is another question. It is fair to state that no trace of the "pleasure house" remains, and that in 1703, "The time of the Great Sickness," Lord Cornbury re-

Sale of Governor Montgomerie's Barge 1732

moved himself and his Court not to the Island, but to Jamaica, "a pleasant village" twelve miles out of harm's way. That he wished a convenient "With drawing place" at hand is altogether probable. We find in *Parker's Post-Boy* the following advertisement:

"On Monday, the 2nd of October next will be exposed for Sale at Publick Vendue a large fine barge with Awning and Damask Curtains. Two setts of oars, sails and everything that is necessary for her. She now lies in the Dock and did belong to the late Governor Montgomerie."

In such a "large fine barge" we can imagine an early Governor and his lady embarking on a summer evening to enjoy the cooling breezes of his "Demesne" on the Governor's Island. But the records do not justify the belief that it ever served the purposes of elegant villegiatura, and I think the high-sounding word "Demesne" has been misleading, as applied to the island. It was, as Bellomont wrote, "Useful for the grazing of a few coach horses and cows for the Governor's Family." There was a house on it, where Governor Tryon "kept out of the way" in the early days of the Revolution, when the Liberty Boys threatened his safety; and where, when the few British troops at the fort were removed to the *Asia,* that they also might be out of the way of the rising wrath, the women and children of the regiment were permitted to stay. It was certainly a cool and pleasant

The First Quarantine Station of the Province 1710

spot where a Governor might "Smoke his Canaster and tipple his ale in the shade." But the theory that Cornbury made it a country seat of any pretension is not tenable, as is shown by its use a very few years later, when, in 1710, it became of public importance. The island then served, in fact though not in name, as the first quarantine station of the Province.

This distinction it owes to the magnificent barbarity of Louis XIV. and to the pathetic plight and flight of the Palatines.

In 1689 Louis, under the pretext of hunting down the Huguenots, swept the Protestant Palatinate clean with fire and sword. The exiled wretches who had been its peaceable and prosperous inhabitants drifted about Europe for several years. In 1708 a small company of them found their way to England. They were headed by a Lutheran pastor, Joshua Kockerthal, and petitioned Queen Anne to send them to her American Colonies. The petition was favored by the "Lords Comm^rs. of Trade and Plantations." They at first thought of sending the Palatines to Jamaica or "Antego," where there was a great want of white people; but, "in regard that the climate of those Islands was hotter than that of Germany, they feared it might not be agreeable to their Constitutions." So they wrote to the Queen's most Excellent Maj^tie:

The Coming of the Palatines

"We humbly propose that they (the Palatines) be sent to settle upon Hudson's River in the Province of New York where they may be usefull to this Kingdom particularly in the production of Naval Stores *and as a frontier against the Ffrench and their Indians.*"

The Queen graciously inclined her ear, and informed Lord Lovelace, the departing Governor, that "She was pleased to send Fifty-two German Protestants to New York and settle 'em there at her own Expenses." They were to "Goe with Lord Lovelace in the Man of War and Transport Ship." The Queen promised to subsist 'em for a year, at 9*d.* a day a head, with tools and implements, with a special gift of a glebe to their leader Kockerthal. They had some struggles with hunger, hard work, and greedy middle men, diversified by the pleasurable excitements of a religious controversy. Nineteen of their number became Quietists, and their countrymen suggested that it would be well to deprive them of their share of the Queen's allowance. It is pleasing to relate that Messieurs Van Dam, Barbarie, Provost, and Du Bois, appointed "to make an inquire into the dispute," reported that "no aligations were proved," whereupon Colonel Wenham was requested to "Victuall 'em in like manner with the other Germans till the aligations be maid out!"

Arrival of the "Lyon" 1710

A grant of land was made them and they were at length settled on Quasek Creek, now Chambers' Creek, in a locality called the Danskamer near the site of the present City of Newburgh.

In 1710 a large body of Palatines was sent over with Governor Hunter, followed at intervals by others until they numbered several thousands.

They were despatched through "the piety and bounty of the Queen of Great Britain," who "pincht herself to give them a subsistence," with a shrewd enough provision for repayment in the future.

On the 13th day of June, 1710, the Council in session was informed that the first of the vessels bringing the immigrants, the ship *Lyon*, was in the harbor with many Palatines on board. The Mayor and the Corporation "prayed that they might not come within the Citty as there was just cause to believe that there were many contagious distempers among them which might endanger the Health of the Inhabitants of the Citty."

This was certainly the case, for the Chyrurgeon, Thomas Benson, affirmed that he had administered aid and medicines to above 330 P'sons all sick at one time in the said passage and none but himselfe to assist them; that he had not, with a covetous mind, made it his Bussynesse to heep up riches to himselfe,

Shelter for the Palatines 1710

and that, for the preservation of their severall healths he had expended medicines of his owne to the amount of £8, 6d.

It was promptly decided that Nutten Island was "the properest place to put them," from which the "properest" inference seems to be that it was not in use as a Governor's seat.

It was further decreed that huts should be put up for the Palatines. It was ordered that "chiefe justice Mr. Barberie, and Mr. Bickley, commissionated to execute ye Office of Attorney Generall Draw uppe a Scheme for ye Ordering, Ruleing and Government of ye Palatines." Doctors Law, Moore, and Garran were sent to the ships to report "on the state and condition of Health," while two carpenters, Johannes Hebon and Peter Williamse, were ordered "to wait on the President to Nutten Island at two in the afternoon with respect to the Building the aforesaid huts."

The other Palatine ships (except the *Bercley Castle* left at Portsmouth, and the *Herbert Frigat* cast ashore off Long Island) soon arrived, and the Island swarmed with its new colony.

Governor Hunter immediately established special courts of Judicature, appointing Justices of the Peace for the Island, "because the said Island called Nutten Island lyeth not within the body of any County of this Province, and

Legislative Acts 1691

in noe wise subject to the Jurisdiction of any of the Courts that are established within the same."

I think it interesting to notice here the legislative acts which had gone before and made this necessary.

On Saturday, the 26th of September, 1691, the Assembly of the Province read for a third time a bill "to divide this Province and Dependencies into Shires and Countyes." The first clause reads: "The city and county of New York to contain all the Island commonly called Manhatans Island, Manning's Island, the two Barren Islands, and the three Oyster Islands. Manhatans Island to be called the City of New York, and the rest of the Islands the County." The bill, with one "for the raising and paying 150 men for the defence of Albany" passed the Assembly and their journal has this record :

> "It was ordered that Alderman Merrett, Mr. Cortlandt, Mr. Beekman, Mr. Renssalaer, do carry up the two bills (ut supra) to the Commander in Cheif and Council for their Assent.
>
> "The gentlemen returned from the Fort, say they delivered the two Bills (ut supra) and the Commander in Cheif and Council say it is very well, they will make all the speed imaginable."

We note that the Journal of the Legislative Council has this entry :

Charter of 1730 Act of 1788

"At a Councill held at Fort William Henry the 26th of September, 1691. . .

"The bill for dividing the Province into Shires and Countyes, read the third time, is consented unto by this Board with the following amendments, vizt.,

"*Nutten Island* and the three Oyster Islands to be added to the County of New York."

Returning to the Journal of the Assembly again we find that Colonel Cortlandt and Chidley Brook Esqs. brought back the bill to the Assembly on the 28th of September, and that "Upon reading the amendments of the Bill for dividing the Province &c., this House has agreed to all the amendments and corrected them in the Bill accordingly except *Nutten Island* which belongs to his Majesty's Fort and Garrison and ought not to be comprehended in the County."

This decision was sent up again to the Fort, this time "by Mr. Pell & Mr. Duckfberry," and assented to by the Governor and his Council. Then the bill was sent to England for the approval of the King, and in "Baskett's Laws" we at last find it marked "confirmed May 2, 1708," without the amendment.

Nutten Island was made a part of the City of New York by the Montgomery Charter of 1730. By an act of March 7, 1788, it was finally included in the County of New York, but it was Governor Hunter's ordinance which gave it the necessary jurisdiction "For ye order-

Special Jurisdiction 1710

ing of ye Palatines!" Under this jurisdiction they spent the summer on the Governor's Island and in the fall were placed upon lands purchased for them on Livingston Manor. They had agreed to settle on the lands which were assigned to them; not to leave them without permission and not to manufacture woollen goods. They were to make tar and turpentine to be sold for the benefit of the government until all the money advanced had been repaid. When the debt was wiped out each was to have forty acres of land, free of taxes for seven years.

Their leaders had hoped to secure "The sunny lands of Schoharie," but they were forced (it is said "by early ring-rule in Albany") to take up the gloomy pine forests of the Livingston Manor, disposed of at a neat profit by their owner who also got the contract "to subsist 'em" and a salary as their chief inspector; while a part of them were settled near Saugerties, then called the West Camp, on the other side of the river.

Their struggles and sufferings are a sorry page in the Colonial records, brightened by the fact that some of them had the courage to break away from their miserable bondage and to finally establish themselves in the place of their own choice.

The Governor's Island entertained one angel unawares when it harbored the Palatines.

The Trial of Zenger 1735

In the list of those left in New York after the removal to Livingston Manor, we find

Johanna Zangarin Wid. 33.
John Peter 13.
Johannes, 7.
Anna Katharine, 10.

This little "John Peter 13" was the famous Zenger. Apprenticed to William Bradford the Printer, he became in 1733 the proprietor and publisher of the *New York Weekly Journal.* In this paper he defended popular rights and the popular party with such boldness and power that like Wilkes, thirty years later, he had the good fortune to be martyrized.

Nos. 7, 47, 48, & 49 of his Journal were ordered to be burned by the hands of the common hangman or whipper, near the pillory, between the hours of eleven and twelve, as containing in them many things tending to sedition and faction. He himself was imprisoned in the City Hall in Wall Street and sued for false, scandalous, malicious and seditious libel. His trial is famous in early Court records of the Province. Andrew Hamilton of Philadelphia made a brilliant defense on the ground that the charges made by Zenger in his paper were true; putting to open confusion the claim of the judges that "no testimony as to the truth of the facts could be admitted" and that "a libel was all the more dangerous for being true."

The First Encampment 1755

The verdict was "Not Guilty." Hamilton departed for Philadelphia with colors flying, cannon saluting, Aldermen dining and the corporation offering him its crowning glory, the freedom of the City in a gold box.

Zenger, the obscure little immigrant from the Governor's Island, remained with the lasting honor of being the first Citizen of New York to assert, and to vindicate the freedom of the Press.

The year 1755 was the first to see the Governor's Island fulfilling its manifest destiny as a peaceful abode for the men and munitions of war. Sir William Pepperell, the hero of Louisburg, after distinguishing himself on Cape Breton Island, was ordered in 1755 to take part in the triple expedition against Canada, and to proceed to Niagara under the command of General Shirley. Upon reaching New York he received from England his appointment as Major General. This rank gave claim to a higher command than that of one regiment, and he returned to New England, where Shirley appointed him to the command of the Eastern Frontier. While in New York, beside being much honored and entertained he was occupied in filling his regiment, and in the New York Archives I find this bill :

"New York, June the 3rd, 1755.

"Rec'd of the Honble. James De Lancey Esq. &c., the

The First Encampment, 1755

sum of Three Pounds, fourteen shillings and nine pence for five cords and three quarters of Oak wood for the use of Sr. Wm. Pepperel's Regiment encamped on Nutten Island in full pr. me ben hildreth."

The Treasury warrants of April 26th, 1755, give an order for the payment to Oliver De Lancey, Esq., or his order of

"Two thousand pounds to be by him applyed in the furnishing Six months provisions and providing for the transportation and other necessarys for the two Companies of Sir William Pepperell's Regiment and a Detachment of all the effective men belonging to the two Independent Companies of his Majesty's Troops in this Province now ordered to Oswego."

On August 23d, 1755, this bill was sent in:

"James Delansea Esq.,
To Cornelius Tiebout.

Aug. 23, 1755.

To 322 bunches Straw for Gene'l Peppari's Redgement. } a *4d.* £5.7.4"

In these scanty records I can find no proof that Sir William was present in person on the Island. He may have put his regiment there for safe-keeping (since it is not so easy to desert from an island, and its ranks were then thin), while the Livingstons were offering him colonial hospitality in the town. But it is safe to believe, at least, that he often set sail in Governor Delancey's barge to visit and in-

The First Fortification 1776

spect his men encamped on the Governor's Island.

1755 saw the first military encampment. 1776 saw the first fortification. There had been unending talk about fortifying the Island. The Governors wrote about it but did not do it although, in 1774, an "Estimate of the Expence of a Fortress on Nutten Island" was carefully made, and called for £17,536. 4*s*. 7*d*. Smith says,

> "About 6 Furlongs South Eaft of the Fort lies Nooten Ifland, containing about 100 or 120 acres, referved by an act of affembly as a sort of Demefne for the Governors, upon which it is propofed to erect a strong caftle, becaufe an enemy might from thence eafily bombard the city without being annoyed either by our battery or the Fort."

But the "strong castle" was not erected, nor were any defenses undertaken until, in 1776, the storm centre of the Revolution moved from Boston to New York.

In the spring of '76, all the familiar story of the hasty preparations for defense was being enacted in New York. The *Phœnix* and the *Asia* were "bullying the town," "everybody turned to with great spirit and industry," and the works were well under way when General Putnam arrived, on April 4th, preceding Washington by ten days. On the 7th of April, 1776, he wrote to the President of Congress: "After getting the works in such for-

The First Fortification 1776

wardness as will be prudent to leave I propose immediately to take possession of Governor's Island which I think a very important post."

On the 9th, Colonel Silliman, of Connecticut, wrote to his wife:

"Last evening draughts were made from a number of Regiments here, mine among the rest, to the amount of 1000 men. With these and a proper number of Officers Gen'l Putnam at Candle lighting embarked on Board of a number of Vessels with a large Number of intrenching tools and went directly on the Island a little below the City called Nutten Island where they have been intrenching all night and are now at work and have got a good Breast work there raised which will cover them from the fire of the Ships. . . ."

The *New York Gazette* says: "Monday night 1000 Continental troops stationed here went over and took possession of Governor's Island and began to fortify it. . . ." A citadel and outworks were begun, and the general orders of April 16th read: "Colonel Prescott's Regiment is to encamp on Governor's Island as soon as the weather clears. They are to give every assistance in their power to the works erecting thereon."

This was the famous Bunker Hill regiment, the 7th Continental Infantry, the first after Pepperell's to occupy the Island. Later they were joined by the 4th Continental Infantry, Colonel Nixon. In May, Washington wrote to Lee: "In a fortnight more I think the City will be in a very respectable position of de-

Escape of the Garrison 1776

fence. Governor's Island has a large and strong work erected and a regiment encamped there. In August, a few days before the battle of Long Island, Lord Stirling wrote, in answer to a request for more men on the Island : "The General bids me say, that in our present situation Governor's Island is more strong and better guarded than any other post of the Army."

On the 27th day of August, 1776, came the battle, the defeat, and the escape of Long Island. Neither Washington nor Nixon seems to have given any especial account of the Governor's Island garrison, but the Tory, Thomas Jones, Justice of the Peace for the Province, does his best to supply the omission. He says :

"The rebels in their hurry and consternation upon abandoning Long Island left the garrison upon Nutten Island (which they had strongly fortified) consisting of 2,000 men, 40 pieces of heavy cannon, military stores and provisions in abundance without the least means of quitting the Island. The British army was at Brookland, the distance from thence to Nutten Island not more than a mile, the distance from Long Island opposite to it not more than a quarter of a mile. The royal army consisted of near 30,000 men, in high spirits and flushed with victory, yet no steps were taken to make prisoners of the garrison and get possession of the forts, stores, artillery, and provisions there deposited. In the evening of the same day (unaccountable as it is) a detachment of the rebel army went from New York to Nutten Island with a number of boats, and carried off the troops, the stores, artillery, and provisions without the least inter-

Fortifications Repaired 1779

ruption whatever, though General Howe's whole army lay within a mile of the place, and his brother, the Admiral, with his fleet, covered the Bay at a little distance below the island. It is a circumstance somewhat remarkable that while General Howe was engaging the rebel army upon Long Island, the Admiral lay still at Staten Island. Indeed he sent up four ships, which anchored about two miles below Nutten Island, and kept up a most tremendous fire against the rebel fortifications there. But the distance was so great it made no impression, did no injury, and might as well have been directed at the moon as at Nutten Island, for the good it did. The rapidity of the tide between Staten Island and New York is such that the whole fleet might with ease have reached the East River with the flood in two hours, had the wind even been ahead. Had this been done on the day of the action upon Long Island, and the river lined from Nutten Island to Hellgate (and the ships he had under his command were more than sufficient for the purpose) not a rebel would have escaped from Long Island; all must have submitted. The whole rebel grand army, with Washington at their head, would have been prisoners, rebellion at an end, the heroes immortalized, and the 27th day of August, 1776, recorded in the annals of Britain as a day, not less glorious than those on which the famous battles of Ramillies and Blenheim were fought and celebrated victories obtained, by the heroic Duke of Marlborough. But this was not done, and why it was not, let the brothers Howe tell."

"The brothers Howe" were able at least to secure the cage after the birds had flown. They occupied and held Governor's Island until the Evacuation of New York.

In 1779, when D'Estaing's fleet was looked for, General Pattison, the British Commandant, writes to Lord Townshend that he is busy "repairing the ruined fortifications and bat-

Supplies for the Workmen 1779

teries erected by the rebels on Governor's Island." "I called a meeting of the principal Inhabitants," he says, "and stated to them the expediency of the Citizens taking up Spade and Pick axe to defend and secure their own property against a Foreign enemy. They most readily and obligingly met my wishes and the next morning 500 Citizens were at work throwing up Earth, &c., &c., on Governor's Island. They still continue their work with great good humor and cheerfulness. A great many of the most Capital Merchants and Shop-keepers pique themselves upon working with the rest and will receive no pay or reward. The lower class are paid at the expense of the City at the rate of ten shillings currency per day, and their rations of provisions from the Government."

These laborers did not lack substantial comforts. "Sir," says an order of September 29, 1779, "I am directed by Major Gen'l Pattison to desire that you will be so good as to order the usual allowance of provisions, Rum and Spruce Beer to be issued to 300 laborers who are to be employed on the King's works at Governor's Island, and to commence to-morrow the 30th Instant." A second order calls for tents, blankets, camp kettles, fuel, and boats, all to be ready at six o'clock in the morning at White Hall.

But their labors were in vain. The Union

Jack ran down for the last time from its staff at the fort, and the British bade a lasting goodby to New York. How and when they left Governor's Island we know definitely from two letters found in the Clinton MSS.

Evacuation of the British 1783

"GOVERNOR'S ISLAND Dec. 3rd, 1783, 7 A.M.

"SIR:

"Having received orders from Rear Admiral Digby to withdraw the Guard together with the whole naval Hospital from this Island, I beg to acquaint your Excellency, that at the hour of Eleven A.M. this day the Guard together with the Naval Hospital will be withdrawn from the Island; Lieutenant Graham of the Navy only excepted who will remain a certain time in order to deliver up the keys of the different buildings &c. to whom you shall think proper to send and take charge of them. . . .

"I am also desired to inform your Excellency, that the only property disposed of belonging to Government on Governor Island are the hulls of two Brigantine's hauled up on each side of the wharf, formerly occupied as store hulks for naval provisions, and sold some time ago by John Delafons Esqr. Agent Victualler in consequence of orders to him given by Rear Admiral Digby to a Mr. Jos. Mercereau of Staten Island.

"I shall do myself the honor to inclose for your Excellency's better information a description List of the different buildings regularly numbered with the Keys, to the person you shall think fit to take charge of them from Lieutenant Graham, who will have the honor of delivering this and will answer such questions respecting the present state of the Island as your Excellency may be desirous of knowing.

"I have the honor to be your Excellency's

"Most obedt & Most humble Servt.,

"JAMES DUNCAN,

"Capt in the Navy &c.

"To His Excellency

"Governor CLINTON, &c., &c.,

"State of New York."

The Buildings 1783-1841

"*Centurion*, OFF NEW YORK, Dec. 3, 1783, 11 A.M.

"SIR:

"Agreeable to my letter of this morning's date, I do myself the honor of inclosing your Excellency a description List of the different buildings &c. on Governor's Island, and have order'd the Keys to be label'd with numbers corresponding to the different houses &c. I have the honor to be your Excellency's most obedt. & most humble servant.

"JAMES DUNCAN."

A DESCRIPTION LIST OF THE BUILDINGS &C., ON GOVERNOR'S ISLAND, DEC. 3.

1. No. 1. The Wharf.
2. A well 18 feet deep with pump &c.
3. Captain's Kitchen.
4. ditto Cellar.
5. A Barn for Cattle.
6. Gardner's House.
7. Hospital Kitchen.
8. Do Well.
9. Captain's Well.
10. Guard House.
11. Convalescents Hospital.
12. Captain's Barrack.
13. Lieutenant's do.
14. Do Kitchen.
15. Summer House.

A child who lived and played on the Island in 1841 remembered the "Old Summer House" on the western side, and "Rotten Row," which must have been a barrack. It was a series of tumble-down rooms one story high, of wood on a stone foundation, and each room had a trap-door!

Survey Ordered 1788

There were also stone ruins called the "Old Guard House." These have all disappeared, but the wharf, it is thought, stands on the site of the one first built, and a "well with a pump" between the wharf and the South Battery, on the eastern side, is still pointed out as the "Old Well."

In 1784 colonial governors were things of the past, but their successors in the State were at once confirmed in one of their privileges, "Governor's or Nutten Island" being assigned for their use by the Legislature until otherwise ordered.

There is a tradition, often repeated, that Governor Clinton leased the Island for a race-course, and that races were run upon it in 1784–85. No such lease can be found among Governor Clinton's papers, nor any allusion to the races in the newspapers of the day. The evidence seems to be hearsay only, and of corresponding value. But the tenure of the Governors was brief. In 1788 the Surveyor-General was ordered by the Legislature to survey the Island (which had been done, by the way, by Captain Montressor in 1766); to lay it out in lots not exceeding two acres each, with such lanes or streets as were deemed proper, and to sell these lots after the manner prescribed for unappropriated lands. The commissioners of the Land Office were given power to reserve any part they thought neces-

Grant to the Regents 1790

sary for fortifications. The survey may have been made; but I have not found the sale of any lot recorded, though there is an allusion made to some small claim of Morgan Lewis.

But the Legislature soon bethought itself of a new use for the Island. The Regents of the University, Alexander Hamilton's pet institution, represented that *Columbia College* and the various academies under their rule "labored under impediments because of a deficiency of funds." To assist them in these sadly familiar circumstances, the Legislature in 1790 empowered them to take seizin and possession of certain lands belonging to the State, among them "a certain Island called and known by the name of Governor's Island;" to lease, grant, and demise it from time to time "so that no more than two dwelling-houses shall at any time be erected on the said Island;" and to use the rents, issues and profits for the benefit of the said college and academies.

They reserved the right to claim any part of it, however, if it were needed for public defence.

Let us hope that it was gratitude for this generosity which brought the entire faculty and students of Columbia College, tradition says, with spades and pick-axes in their academic hands to labor at earthworks on the Island when the "French scare" of 1797 again called loudly for harbor defence.

The Federal Salute 1794

The Regents at once arranged to lease the Island "so as no lease should be for a longer term than twenty-one years, and so as that said Island should not be leased in more than two parcels." Their first and only tenant was John Price, who rented the Island for twenty-one years for an annual rent of £93, without any deduction for taxes.

But Columbia College cannot have waxed rich on its share of this sum.

In 1794, an old act of 1758, the first quarantine act of the Province, "to prevent the bringing in and spreading of Infectious diftempers in this Colony," was revived with a change! That act compelled infected vessels to "make their quarantine" at Bedlow's Island. Now, the Governor was authorized to appropriate Governor's Island for the purpose.

To what extent the act was operative in its new form is a question.

In 1794 and 1795 Governor's Island was certainly a military post. On the 11th of October, 1794, a commanding officer on the Island, stronger in military etiquette than in the civilian commonplaces of spelling, writes:

"GOVERNEURE ISLAND, October 11th, 1794.

"SIR:

"Yesterday morning Admiral Murra Sent a Lieut. to this Island to inform me as a commanding officer weather it would be proper or weather it had been Customary to Selute the Flag of the United States at such a Distance and what number of guns would be given. In answer to his

Salute of the Semillante 1794

Selute I informed the Lieut. that the Admiral Lay at such a Distance I thought it Improper to Selute but should it so Happen that the Admiral, did Come Up within one mile in a Southerly Direction of this Island according to Your Excellencies orders I should Return his Selute But as to Stipulate for the Number of Guns it was out of my power But that our National Selute was thirteen at present.

"Agreeable to your Excellencies order Sometime ago I shall attend to Returning the Selute Should the Admiral Come Up. Your Excellence will please to understand that Admiral Murra lays at the watering plase so caled nere Staten Island.

"I am Sir Your Excellencies
"Most obedt & Humbl Servt.,
"CORNS R. SEDAM,
"Capt N Sub Legion."

In this year also the Ferry was established "at 3d a head but *all fatigue parties* to pass gratis."

Again on the eighteenth day of November, 1794, the Secretary of War, Knox, informs "the Officer Commanding upon Governor's Island" that the Minister of the French Republic has made representations to him! The French frigate *Semillante* had fired a salute of fifteen guns. The fort had not replied. The returning of a salute was "a respect justly due to a Nation with which we are connected by sentiments and Treaties of Friendship and Alliance." The President of the United States wished the commanding officer immediately to fix a time when he would fire the Federal salute of fifteen guns!

Fort Columbus and Castle William

And once more on the 19th of April, 1795, "Alex. Thompson, Capt. Corps Artillerists and Engineers," writes to Governor Clinton that the French vessels of war have left the North River, and that at this time the fifteen-gun salute was duly delivered from the Battery, on the island where he commands.

But, in spite of these extremely civil salutes, our relations with France became unpleasantly strained. Great fears were felt of a French attack, and New York City begged for protection. New York State was in debt to the general government, however, and could get no appropriation until Congress permitted it to spend money on its fortifications, which should be credited against its debt; the fortifications with their improvements to belong to the United States Government.

Great exertions were at once made, and continued for several years, resulting at length in those beautiful and peaceful ornaments of the harbor known as Fort Columbus and Castle William.

For close upon a century they have smiled upon the city, and been ready to frown upon a foe, and undoubtedly they would have fired a hostile gun had any enemy appeared within reach to justify such an incivility. All the authorities agreed that they were necessities, however, during the uncertainties of the years from 1794 to the close of the War of 1812.

Vincent's Observations 1794

The State had already appropriated £30,000 for fortifications at or near the city and port of New York, and £20,000 to be used only on Governor's, Bedloe's, and Oyster Islands, when in 1794 a committee reported to Congress that $3,727.52 were needed for the defences on Governor's Island. At this time M. Vincent made a report on the needs of the harbor, when the always expected, never arriving enemy's fleet should appear. "Arrived at the entrance of Sandy-Hook," he says, "the hostile Ships will have yet twenty miles to run before they can annoy the City and the Vessels in the Harbor!" "If they should arrive to the narrows," he adds, "Governor's Island will be most important because its happy position can secure crossing fires with the points taken on the right hand shore and also with the city, at the mouth of the East River." . . . This point will be consequently the object of the nicest attention. It will be occupied by at least twenty pieces of the largest caliber and four mortars, the whole distributed with cautious knowledge."

To know what was really done upon the Island for the next twenty years, we must take the American State Papers for military affairs, and note the reports of committees and of the Secretary of War. In 1794 Knox reports through *Vincent's Observations*, that there is "on Governor's Island one bastioned

Fort Jay 1797-1806

square commanding two low batteries, quite finished." "It is to be observed nevertheless that, being only sodded it will not stand a very long time."

In 1796 the Report dignifies the works with the name of a Fort:

"Governor's Island has been fortified with a Fort made of earth and two batteries under its protection partly lined with brick masonry, two air furnaces, a large powder magazine, and a barrack for the garrison." In the next year, 1797, John Adams wrote: "Although I think the moment a dangerous one I am not scared!" This was not true of New York. It was badly scared! The French crisis seemed at hand, work began with energy, supported by an appropriation of thirty thousand one hundred and seventeen dollars, and the Fort received the added distinction of a name, Fort Jay. From 1794 to 1806 something over a hundred and ten thousand dollars was devoted to the works on the Island. But the Fort was not so lasting as the honor of its name. In 1806 it disappeared, pulled down in disgrace, pronounced by no less a dignitary than Thomas Jefferson, as "rubbish." "All except the walled Counterscarp, the Gate, the Sally-port, Magazine and two barracks." "On the site of the old fort," continues President Jefferson's report of 1809, "A new one, Fort Columbus, has been erected, of the same

Fort Columbus 1809 Castle William 1811

shape on three of its sides as the former, with the addition of fourteen feet on each side. On the North side a ravelin has been added, with two retired, casemated flanks. The new Fort with two new brick barracks is now nearly completed and has fifty cannon mounted. On a point of rocks at the Western Extremity of Governor's Island a circular castle of durable Mason work, to be connected with Fort Columbus by a zig-zag covered way has been commenced and completed to the second floor and is now ready to receive its first tier of guns, which are mounted and ready to be placed. The exterior diameter of this Castle is two hundred and ten feet, and when finished will mount two hundred pieces of heavy ordnance."

This "circular castle," named for General William of the New York Militia, was completed in 1811. And now the Island was in fine trim for defence, if only it had been attacked; but it never was! A century of peace with France began. The War of 1812 came and went. Troops were on the Island. Four companies of artillery, three of the First Regiment and one of the Third made the garrison, with occasional detachments from other commands, and in the summer of 1814 there were more than a thousand officers and men at the post. The only blood shed, however, was that of deserters shot on the parade with

Ceded to the United States 1800

all the dishonors of war,—soldiers drawn up in a hollow square with one side open; the victim kneeling on his coffin, the death warrant read, the fatal shot discharged, and the band playing softly the customary dirge, old "Roslyn Castle."

But with the coming-in of the present century the Island ceases to be a subject for a chronicle. Its modern history begins, and a capital testimony it is to the old saw, "Happy is the island that has no history." Nothing exciting has happened upon it, and yet it is said to be the favorite post of the United States Army!

In 1800 it was ceded by the State of New York to the United States, and in 1821 Federal military headquarters were transferred to it from the city. In 1832, while the works were being thoroughly repaired, the Island had an unwelcome guest—the cholera. In 1836 its garrison made a trip to Florida. But its soldiers came back to it in the next year; and it served as an artillery post for fifteen years more, until 1852, when it was made the principal depot of the general recruiting service. The thunders of the Civil War could scarcely shake it from its tranquillity, though then for a second time Fort Columbus "killed its man." When Lafayette was too much crowded with prisoners, Castle William caught the overflow, at one time as many as a thou-

Garrison Life in 1897

sand. Among these prisoners was John Yates Beall. In 1864 he had tried a form of piracy on the Lakes, making an attempt to capture the *Michigan* in Sandusky Bay. He failed, was captive instead of captor, and in 1865 was hanged by Governor Dix's orders on the parade ground at Fort Columbus. When on June 30, 1878, the Island was made the headquarters of the Department of the East, with the "Superb" Hancock as the first general in command, the life of to-day was ushered in.

It is the life of an ordinary garrison, plus the distinctions of department headquarters and the distractions of the metropolis, its neighbor. In the garrison are three companies of infantry, and the Governor's Island band. At six o'clock of a morning the buglers stand on the parade before the fort, and blow the reveille. In military parlance, this fort is "an enclosed pentagonal work, with four bastions of masonry." To the eye it is a beautiful star, near the centre of the Island, outlined in gray on a gentle rise of green lawn. The moat which surrounds it is green. The glacis sloping away on all sides toward the water is green. The trees which line the brick sidewalks are green and shady, though not one nut-tree remains to justify the old name.

The sally-port and the drawbridge, the unfilled moat and the unused cannon, are

Castle, Battery and Arsenal 1897

gentle witnesses to the green old age of this relic of outgrown military science.

Castle William still stands on the northwestern corner of the Island, on a bed of rocks which it rescued from the covering tide. "This," said the Secretary of War when it was first completed in 1811, "is a stone tower, with fifty-two, forty-two, and thirty-two pounders mounted on two tiers under a bomb roof, and the terrace above is intended to mount twenty-six fifty-pound Columbiads." In untechnical description it is one of the beauties of the Bay,—a round tower, stately and imposing, like St. Angelo, but quite harmless and comfortable in these homely, practical days, when men-of-war six miles off can shell the town without coming within sight of these time-honored guns. Green and picturesque, too, is the old South Battery, set to protect Buttermilk Channel on the southeastern point of the Island, completing the fortifications of the army post, Fort Columbus. This post includes the whole of Governor's Island except six acres, and its commanding officer rules the garrison and reports to headquarters with the same authority and through the same channels as if his post were a thousand miles away. The six acres on the northeastern shore of the Island belong to the New York Arsenal, whose commanding officer is a second Federal military power, and

Chapel of St. Cornelius 1847

whose pyramids of cannon-balls and rows of guns threaten ominously. But they, too, mean no harm, the dangerous material being stored out of sight. Still a third quite separate authority on the Island is the Major-General, with his personal staff and his department staff, commanding the Department of the East, of which Fort Columbus is one post. The little chapel of St. Cornelius, maintained by Trinity Church, and the symbol of a still higher power, has stood for fifty years just north of the South Battery. A professor in Columbia College, Dr. McVicar, built it in 1847, and preached in it for years, until an order requiring all post chaplains to live at their posts, obliged him to choose between the Island and the College. As he preferred the latter, the little church was bought from him for the post, and is a part of old Trinity Parish, its vicar serving as Acting Post-Chaplain.

The Hospital, the Military Institute, and the Museum with its Indian curiosities, its colonial relics, and, *facile princeps*, Sheridan's horse, Winchester, all invite us to consider how interesting they too are.

But the bugler whom we left sounding the reveille has passed on to the guard mounting, the drill-call and recall, the parade and the retreat. The sunset gun is fired from the sea-wall below Castle William. The hundred prisoners who have been at work on the roads and lawns are again confined within its walls. The bugler calls to quarters. Night settles down. The lights die out. There is no sound but the wash of the water and the click of the sentry's heel. Fort, battery, castle, arsenal, and magazine are asleep. Governor's Island is as peaceful as when, three hundred years ago, "Pagganck" lay like an emerald gem pendent on the green chain of Long Island,—and the bugler blows "Taps."

"Taps" 1897

HE HALF MOON SERIES OF PAPERS ON HISTORIC NEW YORK

WILL BE ISSUED MONTHLY DURING THE COMING YEAR UNDER THE EDITORSHIP OF ❧ ❧ ❧ ❧ ❧ ❧ ❧ ❧

MAUD WILDER GOODWIN
ALICE CARRINGTON ROYCE
AND RUTH PUTNAM ❧ ❧ ❧

❧

AMONG THE SUBJECTS OF THE PAPERS WILL BE THE FOLLOWING

The Stadt Huys of New Amsterdam
By Alice Morse Earle

The Fourteen Miles Round ❧ ❧ ❧
By Alfred Bishop Mason
and Mary Murdoch Mason

Wall Street
By Oswald Garrison Villard

❧ ❧ ❧

Annetje Jans' Farm
By Ruth Putnam

The Bowery
By Edward Ringwood Hewitt
and Mary Ashley Hewitt

King's College
By John B. Pine

Old Wells and Water-Courses
By George E. Waring, Jr.

Governor's Island
By Blanche Wilder Bellamy

Defences of Old New York
By Frederick D. Grant

Old Greenwich
By Elizabeth Bisland

Tammany Hall
By Talcott Williams

Barnard College

343 MADISON AVENUE

COURSES IN AMERICAN HISTORY

For Undergraduates. General course, reading, recitations and lectures.—Three hours a week: H. A. Cushing, A.M.

For Graduates. Political History of the Colonies and of the American Revolution.—This investigation course, extending through two years, deals in the first year with the settlement of the Colonies and their development in the seventeenth century, and in the second year with the growth of the system of colonial administration, the conflict with the French, and the revolt of the Colonies. The work of the students consists chiefly in the study of topics from the original sources, with a formal account of the results of such study.—Two hours a week for two years: Professor Herbert L. Osgood, Ph.D.

These courses are open not only to candidates for degrees, but to special students who can show ability to read French and German, and can satisfy the Dean and Faculty of their general competence.

Half Moon Series

Published in the Interest of the New York City History Club.

VOLUME I. NUMBER VI.

"THE FOURTEEN MILES ROUND."

BY

ALFRED BISHOP MASON

AND

MARY MURDOCH MASON.

ON December 12, 1789, which was one hundred and three years after the charter of Governor Dongan had declared New York to be "an ancient citie," but was the first year of the United States of America, Franklin Square was quiet and majestic, as befitted the court-end of town. When the first President took a house there, there were complaints that it was too far out of the city; yet thirty-seven years before, William Walton had built there the finest house in the Colonies. There were eight windows across each upper story of its spacious front. Two stately doorways opened upon the Square. The

The Franklin House

grounds behind the house sloped greenly to the East River. The great merchant was known as "Boss" Walton, the first recorded instance in our history of that bad eminence. His entertainments were so magnificent, his wines so rare, his silver so superb, that when the Stamp Tax was opposed in Parliament on the ground of the poverty of the colonists, the feasts at the Walton House were cited as proofs of colonial wealth.

Near it, at the northwest corner of Franklin Square and Cherry Street, whence one of the arches of the Brooklyn Bridge now springs, stood its rival, the Franklin House, which Washington occupied from April 23, 1789, when the first President of the United States arrived in New York. The house, built in 1770, was a mansion of the solid colonial type. In a slight central projection which ran from ground to roof, a wide door opened into a broad hall. Two other doors, also opening upon Cherry Street, were probably added later. The second story was amply lighted by five windows on the Cherry Street front, and as many on Franklin Square, the sashes filled with the small square panes characteristic of that time. The third story repeated the second. Above it was a balustrade, behind which were the five dormer windows of the low attic. Washington walked thither from the foot of Wall Street, between shouting thou-

Washington Irving

sands. There is a pretty story that, on that day, Washington Irving's parents held him above the heads of the crowd, and prayed the President that the boy might bear his name, and were rejoiced by his prompt permission. But the scene of the pretty story is laid on Broadway, which was untouched by the procession; and Irving was born April 3, 1783. Charles Dudley Warner gives a variant of this tale: When the first President was in New York, he says, a Scotch maid-servant of the family one day followed the hero into a shop and presented the lad to him. "Please, your honor," said Lizzie all aglow, "here 's a bairn was named after you." And the grave Virginian placed his hand on the boy's head and gave him his blessing. But did the President go shopping?

A list of the residences of public officials in 1789 begins with "George Washington, Esquire, President of the United States and Commander of the Army and Navy thereof when in actual service: No. 3 Cherry Street." Franklin Square was then St. George's Square, just as Broadway, from Vesey Street, north, was Great George Street. When business pushed northward, the Franklin House became a music-store and a bank in turn. Then it fell to baser uses. It was torn down in 1856. The only bit of it known to exist is the President's chair of the New York Historical So-

The City in 1789

ciety, which is made of wood taken from the old house. The Walton House, built eighteen years before the Franklin House, survived it for twenty-five. It became a tenement, and stood in its shame until 1881. These are but two of the notable houses of Cherry Street. At No. 27 the first American flag of the present style was made, in 1818, "by Mrs. Reid in her drawing-room." In 1823, at No. 7, then the home of Samuel Leggett, president of the New York Gas Light Company, illuminating gas was first used in this country. A few blocks eastward, at the corner of Jefferson Street, stood the stately mansion of Colonel Rutgers, where Lafayette was entertained with splendor in 1824, and where (perhaps) a man who shared Washington's heart with Lafayette, was hung in 1776. Three points in New York compete for the honor of the hanging of Nathan Hale,—the Rutgers Place, the Commons, and Beekman Hill at the foot of East 51st Street. The last fragment of the Rutgers mansion disappeared in 1875.

New York was a dull and dirty little town in 1789. It was a city without a bathroom, without a furnace, with bedrooms which in winter lay within the Arctic Zone, with no ice during the torrid summers, without an omnibus, without a moustache, without a match, without a latch-key. Of every hundred inhabitants, seven were slaves. There were about twenty-three hundred slaves in 1790, two hundred and fifty in 1820, and none when the sun rose on July 4, 1827, the Empire State's "emancipation day." The streets were narrow,—how narrow may be judged from the fact that both Wall and Liberty, from Broadway to Nassau, were widened in 1790 to their present petty dimensions. Pearl was so narrow that sidewalks were forbidden. A State law provided that people going north must always make way for those coming south. In May, 1788, the Grand Jury had reported the streets "to be dirty and many of them impassable." Pigs were the only scavengers. They ran at large in the streets of New York until within the memory of many men now living. Most of the garbage was thrown into the streets. A little of it went to the river at night in tubs on the heads of slaves. On December 19, 1789, the *Daily Advertiser* appealed to the High Constable, who was supposed to do thoroughly what the pigs did in part, in this moving fashion: "AWAKE, THOU SLEEPER, let us have clean streets in this our peaceful seat of the happiest empire in the universe. That so our national rulers and their supporters may with convenience and decency celebrate a merry Christmas and happy New Year." All wood delivered at store or house (there was no coal) was sawed and split on the street, after delivery. Street-lamps had

Highway Robbery

been introduced in 1762; but they were few and poor, apt to go out, often left unlighted. In 1789, a citizen asked for relief, because, as not a lamp was burning, he had walked into a pump on Nassau Street, near the Mayor's house; and on December 31, 1778, the firemen formally complained that they had been greatly hindered at a recent fire because most of the lamps had gone out.

There were too many trees for health, The penalty for planting a tree south of Catherine Street, except in front of churches or public buildings, was a fine of £5. The city waterworks consisted chiefly of the Tea-Water Pump on Chatham Street (now Park Row) near Queen (now Pearl). Water drawn from it was said to make better tea than that from any of the minor pumps or private wells. The water came from the Collect, where the public washed its dirty linen. Highway robbery was common. The newspapers claimed that all the footpads came from Philadelphia. This was a spiteful saying by the little town against the big. In this year of 1789, Tammany Hall was founded by William Mooney, an upholsterer. Its objects were announced to be "the smile of charity, the chain of friendship, the flame of liberty, and in general, whatever may tend to perpetuate the love of freedom and the political advantage of the country." Its officers were to be native-born Americans, but natu-

Postal Service 1897

ralized citizens could become members. It was then, and for many years afterwards, a thoroughly respectable society. George William Curtis, in one of his earlier novels, speaks of a man's being a sachem of Tammany as a proof of his high standing. It was both non-partisan and non-predatory. The city post-office had just been moved from 8 Wall Street, near the ferry, to 62 Broadway, at the corner of Liberty, and there was public complaint that the postmaster had not chosen "some more central place." The post-office receipts for the three months ending January 5, 1790, were $1,067.08 : for the three months ending January 1, 1897, they were $2,112,675.07. On January 1, 1790, the service to Philadelphia was increased to five mails per week : January 1, 1897, the Philadelphia mails were ninety-six per week. There were then only seventy-five post-offices in the whole country: now there are seventy thousand, five hundred and sixty-two. The southernmost was Savannah. The postage there from New York was thirty-three cents.

There was but one theatre in the city until 1798. It stood on John Street, near Broadway. Founded in 1767, it was closed in 1774 at the suggestion of the Continental Congress, and stayed shut until the British occupation, when it was re-opened as the Theatre Royal. In 1785, against much violent opposition, its

The Theatre

players presented "moral lectures," which were really more or less moral plays. This thin disguise was soon dropped. In 1789, tickets were sold at the box-office and at Gaines's bookstore in Hanover Square, the Sign of the Bible. The season extended this year from April 14th to December 15th. There was a "Last Night" December 9th, a "Positively Last Night" on the 11th, and really a last night on the 15th. During the season, sixty-one performances were announced, among them those of the *School for Scandal, She Stoops to Conquer, Richard III, Merry Wives of Windsor*, and *The Tempest.* Washington attended on May 11th, June 5th, November 24th, and November 30th. On November 24th he noted in his diary that he had invited "Mrs. Adams, lady of the Vice-President, General Schuyler and lady," etc. On this occasion the play was *The Clandestine Marriage.* It is reported by an awe-struck reporter that the President actually laughed. His contemporaries, in trying to make him more than human, made an imaginary prig out of a very real man. Whenever he entered his box, the orchestra played the President's March, composed by its leader, Pfyles, first performed at Trenton on the triumphal journey from Mount Vernon to New York, and known to every American since Judge Hopkinson wrote his verses to this air,

Fashionable Dress

in 1801, as *Hail, Columbia*! The little city contented itself with one public lecture during 1789. It was delivered at Aaron Aorson's tavern, on the Divinity of Jesus Christ, "by a man more than thirty years an Atheist"; and all the aldermen sold tickets for it at twenty-five cents apiece. There were not half a dozen private carriages and not one rubber shoe in town,—facts which explain Washington's diary for November 29, 1789: "Being very snowy, not a single person appeared at the Levee." Clothes were too costly to be lightly risked. Merchants tempted their feminine customers with amens, cordurets, camblets, callimancos, casserillias, durants, duffils, dowlas, fearnaughts, florentines, honey-comb thicksetts, hairbines, lutestrings, moreens, osnaburgs, platillas, rattinetts, romalls, ribdelures, shalloons, taboreens, tammies, ticklenburgs, velverets and weldbores. Tailors offered men, as fashionable colors, bat's wing, mouse's ear, and drake's head. One dame of high degree wore a pierrot of gray Indian taffeta with dark gray stripes; two collars (one white, one yellow), both trimmed with blue silk; a yellow corset (called "shapes") with large blue cross-stripes; and a white satin hat with a large wreath of artificial roses. A well-known man was clad in a scarlet coat, white silk waistcoat embroidered with colored flowers, black satin breeches with paste knee-buckles, white silk

The Drive December 12th

stockings, low shoes with large silver buckles, and "a small cocked hat on the upper part of his powdered hair, leaving the curls at his ears displayed." He carried a gold-headed cane and gold snuff-box, and is rather an agreeable bit of color against the gray background of the New York of 1789.

On this December morning the door of the Franklin House opened, a liveried servant stood on either side, and the President of the United States, with Mrs. Washington and her two grandchildren, entered his coach. It was globular, canary-colored, with cupids and nymphs disporting themselves upon its panels, with six horses drawing it, sometimes with liveried outriders trotting before it, and with a couple of mounted officers following behind it. The family party was a tulip-bed of bright hues, the President not the least gorgeous flower of the four. He had a weakness for velvet, and purple satin was irresistible to him. As the coachman let the impatient horses start, the party passed along that part of Pearl Street, then called Queen Street, which had "grand buildings, four to six stories high," saw Golden Hill on John Street, where the first blood of the Revolution was shed, two months before the Boston Massacre and five years before Lexington, and turned westward on Wall Street. This was the fashionable promenade, "more elegant" than Broadway,

Nassau Street

though that was also much favored of fashion, chiefly for driving, from the Battery even as far north as St. Paul's, where the sidewalk and the name of the street both ended. They passed the residence of General John Lamb, first Collector of the Port, who, to the day of his death, kept open house for every soldier of the Revolution, and never forgave a Tory. Up and down William Street, then called Smith, where it crossed Wall, they looked to right and left upon the dry-goods shops where the feminine half of New York's thirty thousand people bought garments equally strange to their great-grand-daughters in shape and stuff, in color and name. On the corner of Wall and Broad Streets dwelt Alexander Hamilton. A few doors away, on Nassau Street, was his rival and slayer, Aaron Burr, who lived up—and down—to the code of his time. His house was hidden by Federal Hall,—a structure on arches, built in 1699 as a city hall, converted at a cost of $32,000 (raised by private subscription) into a Capitol, and given by the city to the nation when the nation was born. It has left one permanent trace on the map of the city, the jog in the sidewalk at the northwest corner of Wall and Nassau Streets. The building extended from the east line of the present assay office to the west line of Nassau Street. This jog is the place then left for a passage around it. The architect who

Federal Hall 1812

transformed the building was Major Peter Charles L'Enfant, who designed the City of Washington and the medal of the Order of the Cincinnati. The Common Council voted to pay him by giving him ten acres of land where the Third Avenue and Sixty-eighth Street now are; but he declined the trifling gift, probably for the same reason which led the Lutheran Church, years afterwards, to refuse a donation of six acres on Canal Street, near Broadway. The Church records say the land was "not worth fencing." Federal Hall was sold in 1812 (to be torn down) for $425. In 1790 and 1791, the city repaid the private subscriptions and recouped its own expenditures by a special tax of $32,000 and two lotteries which produced as much more. The drawing of the first lottery went on for thirty days, and of the second for twenty-three, so that the ticket-holders had plenty of excitement for their money.

Nassau Street was opened in 1696, when the city granted Teunis de Kay's petition for leave to make a cartway through "the street that runs by the pie-woman's, leading to the commons," and gave him much of the land along it for his labor. Federal Hall looked down Broad Street, past the corner of the present Exchange Place, where the first exchange was established in March, 1670. The merchants met every Friday morning, between

Bowling Green

eleven and twelve, "at the bridge which crossed the ditch at Broad Street"; and Governor Lovelace bade the Mayor see to it that during that hour boys should not coast down the hill from Broadway and make havoc with mercantile legs and feelings. Farther south was the mansion whence Philip Livingston was buried in 1749, when all the houses in the block were thrown open, and when each of the eight bearers was given gloves, scarf, handkerchief, a mourning ring, and a monkey-spoon. Still farther south was and is the old home of Etienne de Lancey, then and now Fraunces Tavern, then kept by "Black Sam" Fraunce or Fraunces (authorities differ, and Black Sam himself probably did not know), where Washington had his headquarters in 1776, and where, in 1783, his famous farewell to his generals etched itself into history.

As the carriage turned from Wall Street into Broadway, the children on the front seat may have caught a glimpse of the Bowling Green, the heart of old New York, the centre of popular sports and popular riots since New Amsterdam was born. The iron railings now about it surrounded it then. They were imported from England in 1771, and they protected a noble lead statue of King George III. on his horse. Said a stout-hearted merchant in 1776, "The British shall have melted majesty fired at them," whereupon a respect-

Trinity Church

able mob tore down the statue, which was melted into bullets, and duly fired at the King's soldiers. The rails are said to have had above them the heads of other members of the royal family, which were knocked off when Georgius Rex was knocked down; and it is further said that "evidences of the fracture are yet visible." Seekers after these evidences should carry to Bowling Green sharp eyes, plenty of faith, and a fund of historic imagination. The mob of 1776, like Tam O'Shanter's witch, tore out the horse's tail. It is now one of the treasures in the almost unknown collection of the Historical Society.

The ruins of Trinity frowned upon the Presidential party; but masons and carpenters were hard at work there upon the new building, the immediate predecessor of the present one. It was consecrated in 1790, and provided the President with a canopied pew, which he occupied from February, 1791, when he left Franklin Square for the McComb mansion at 39 Broadway, and St. Paul's for Trinity. The McComb mansion, some sixty feet broad and four stories high, with grounds running back to the North River (the shore-line was where Greenwich Street now crouches under the elevated railroad) was rented to him for $2,500. One of the forgotten graves in Trinity churchyard is that of Mrs. Clarke, wife of Lieutenant-Governor George Clarke. She died

The City Tavern 1775

in 1740, an embodiment of Ruskin's phrase: "Lady means 'bread-giver' or 'loaf-giver.'" Her gracious memory is embalmed in the records of the corporation, which voted, that, as it was "a pleasure to her in life to feed the hungry, a loaf of bread should be given to every poor person who would receive it,"—a bit of heartfelt simplicity which sounds better than the preamble of a bumptious little law passed by the same body in 1732, creating the first free school: "Whereas, the youth of this colony are found by manifold experience to be not inferior in their natural geniuses to the youth of any other country in the world, therefore," etc.

Just beyond Trinity, where the Boreel Building (115 Broadway) now stands, was the famous City Tavern, once the James de Lancey residence, with its shady grounds sloping to the Hudson, and its broad piazzas crowded with people to see the President pass by. Here the merchants of New York met, October 31, 1775, and put two hundred bold signatures at the foot of a non-importation agreement,—New York's ringing reply to the Stamp Act. Here was the favorite lounging place of the British officers during the Revolution, partly because good liquor was to be had, and partly because pretty women were to be seen on "the Mall," the sidewalk in front of Trinity. It must have been a small

Broadway

society which strutted its brief day then and there; for even in 1789, when the town, after being half ruined by the Revolution, had doubled its population and its house-rents, only three hundred persons were "in society." It took a hundred years to add a hundred men and women to the list. In the City Hotel, built on this site in 1793, Washington Irving was welcomed back to America at a great dinner in 1832.

The President drove by the Market-house in Broadway, opposite Liberty Street, the uptown market, forty-two by twenty-five feet, where the aristocrats, living on the west side of Broadway, went every morning and filled the baskets carried by their black slaves. Dr. John Bard, the leading physician of the time, in a paper extolling the healthfulness of the city, wrote of the people "on the west side of the Broadway" as enjoying "fragrant odours from the apple-orchards and buckwheat fields in bloom on the pleasant banks of the Jersey shore in view of their delightful dwellings." Dr. Bard's son, meanwhile, had had Washington as a much-suffering patient for several weeks that summer. He seems to have been generally repaired at the same time; for John Greenwood, dentist, of 56 William Street, made him a full set of "sea-horse teeth," and told somebody, who told everybody else, that the great man had but a single

Summer Beverages

tooth of his own. It was a hard summer. In one week there had been twenty deaths from heat (equal to eleven hundred deaths for the present population). A newspaper sagaciously said, "Raw rum has been found exceedingly pernicious in this extreme heat." There was certainly plenty of choice in the way of drink. The President's table was supplied (through his steward, Sam Fraunces) with madeira, claret, champagne, sherry, arrack, spirits, brandy, cordials, porter, beer, and cider. There seems to have been little indecorous intoxication. Haswell, in his *Reminiscences of an Octogenarian,* says that as late as 1816 "American whiskey was not known as a general drink, and mint-juleps were only heard of as a mixture said to be taken by people in the Southern States as a preventive against malaria." But Dayton, in his delightful *Last Days of Knickerbocker Life in New York,* describes the "substantial citizens" of 1830 as sitting on the flat roof of Rabineau's swimming-bath, by the Battery, every afternoon, enjoying their mint-juleps and sherry-cobblers. Haswell returns to the charge, and says that in 1823 "American whiskey was wholly unknown north of Baltimore."

At the calaboose on the common, the city maintained an official who whipped a servant, whether free or slave, for his master, and charged one shilling for a thorough job. It

Sorry Sights

was a cruel age,—as cruel to petty criminals as we have been to our pauper insane, up to two years ago. Master Custis and Miss Custis may have peeped out of the front seat of their grandfather's carriage at sundry persons branded T on the left cheek near the nose, in token of conviction for petty thievery. Only a few years before, Mrs. Johanna Young "and another lady," convicted of grand larceny, were paraded around town in a cart, then stripped to the waist and given thirty-nine lashes apiece in public, then banished,—whereupon they went to Philadelphia.

Above St. Paul's, Broadway was no place for pleasure-driving in 1789. So the Washington carriage turned down Park Row, then Chatham Row, with the green fields of "the Commons" on their left, disfigured by neither the Mullett nightmare of to-day's post-office, nor the Tweed memory of to-day's courthouse. Instead, there were the jail; the calaboose or bridewell; the gallows, covered by a Chinese kiosk, in order that the hangings might not pain the passers-by (there were eleven capital crimes then), the pillory, stocks, and whipping-post in a little group of trees; and the new almshouse. The first poor-house was built on the Commons in 1734, at which time also the minutes of the Council show that "a convenient place, or whipping-post," was provided for incorrigible

The Debtors' Prison

persons. In 1678, the year of the famous Bolting Act, under which the city throve mightily at the expense of the province, it is recorded that "ministers were scarce and religions many, but there were no beggars in New York and all the poor were cared for." In 1795, the poor-house had six hundred and seventy-two inmates, not counting the yellow-fever cases. The jail on the Commons, built about 1760, was the finest public edifice of its day. It was a torture-chamber for patriot prisoners during the Revolution. Thereafter, as a debtor's prison, it became the most popular public edifice of its day; for from January 2d to December 3d of 1788, eleven hundred and sixty-two persons, one out of every twenty-five citizens, were jailed there for debt. Even in our day, when it is used as the Hall of Records, is neglected and dingy, and is said to have recorded within it all the smells of the Island from the Dutch days down, it is still beautiful. It has a right to be, for it is a reproduction in miniature of the great fane of Diana of Ephesus. On November 26th the President had given fifty guineas to the Society for the Relief of Distressed Debtors. The prisoners published a card of thanks. The Society thereupon announced that this was all wrong, because it had agreed not to tell who gave the money. Such secrets are better kept in New York to-day. Any one who has

The Collect

to do with our charities knows how many people here "do good by stealth."

Now the carriage rolls on, past the Collect, or Fresh Water Pond, recommended for a water-supply in 1790, but rejected as being too far from town, where the Indians left shell-mounds after their clam and oyster feasts; where New York used to skate; where Fitz Greene Halleck's father saved the Duke of Clarence, afterwards William IV., from drowning when that gay midshipman was visiting Admiral Digby, quartered in a "rebel mansion" on Hanover Square; where John Fitch exhibited the first practicable steamboat in 1796; where the Tombs now stands. It rolled up the Bowery Lane,—to the right the three Stuyvesant houses and the famous old Governor's pear-orchard, whereof men of to-day have seen the last tree, at the northeast corner of Third Avenue and Thirteenth Street; to the left, in the distance, the gentle slope of Richmond Hill, where Varick Street now crosses Charlton in poverty-stricken flatness and ugliness. The Richmond Hill mansion was a centre of history. It was built by Abraham Mortier, paymaster of his Majesty's forces in America, about 1760. In 1789, Vice-President Adams lived there. His delightful wife wrote of it: "In natural beauty it might vie with the most delicious spot I ever saw. It is a mile and a half distant from the city of New

Richmond Hill

York. . . . Upon my right hand are fields beautifully variegated with grass and grain. . . . Upon my left the city opens to view, intercepted here and there by rising ground and an ancient oak. . . . Venerable oaks and broken ground covered with shrubs surround us, giving a natural beauty to the spot which is truly enchanting. A lovely variety of birds serenade me morning and evening, rejoicing in their liberty and security." Here, in 1776, after the victorious defeat on Long Island, Washington had his peripatetic headquarters for several days. Here, Nathan Hale was sent out on the mission which ended in his trial in the greenhouse of the Beekman mansion at the foot of East 51st Street, in his ignominious death at dawn on the gallows, and in his statue in City Hall Park, looking calmly down upon the roar of Broadway. Here, Aaron Burr, also Vice-President of the United States, lived. From Richmond Hill, in the early morning of July 11, 1804, he started for Weehawken to kill Alexander Hamilton, and here he returned to breakfast, that deed done and himself undone. Hamilton started that morning from his country-seat, "The Grange," still standing near One Hundred and Forty-fifth Street, opposite the group of thirteen gum-trees which he planted as a symbol of the thirteen States. When Burr fled from the city, a bankrupt, his cred-

The Potter's Field

itors seized his sixty-two-year leasehold estate in Richmond Hill, and John Jacob Astor paid $25,000 for it. The house stood a hundred feet above the present level, but a tiny bit of its ancient garden still survives. A bit of the house itself survived until 1849.

In this December of 1789, Washington may have pointed out in the distance, to his wife and the children, the meadow which the city had just decided to buy for a potter's field; which became six years afterwards, under the stress of yellow-fever, a burial-place for rich and poor alike and which thereafter became Washington Square. It and Union Square and Madison Square and Bryant Park were all potter's fields in turn, and all thus saved as open spaces to become centres of fashion in turn. South of Union Square, on the old Bowery, now Fourth Avenue, the coach passed the famous estate "Minto," owned by a baron whose many names ended with Poelnitz. Washington had already visited it in May, and had ordered sent to Mount Vernon one of Poelnitz's numerous inventions, a horse-hoe for weeding vegetables. "Minto" was advertised for sale in 1789 as about two miles from the city, with a great variety of the choicest fruit-trees and flowering shrubs and with the richest soil on Manhattan Island. It afterwards became the Randell Farm, and now belongs to the Sailors' Snug Harbor. The rich soil still continues to produce. Ground-rents grow all over it in abundance. The statue of Washington in Union Square stands about where New York, delivered at last from its British garrison, welcomed its deliverer November 25, 1785. He had slept the night before at the Van Cortlandt Manor-house, built in 1748, still standing in strength and beauty at the southern end of Van Cortlandt Park.

Inclenberg 1776

At what is now the northeast corner of Broadway and Twenty-third Street, the old Boston road left the Bloomingdale road, and ran northeast across Madison Square. The carriage turned to the right, and was soon rounding the eastern slopes of Murray Hill. At what is now Thirty-sixth Street and Park Avenue stood "Inclenberg," the country-seat of Robert Murray, the birthplace of his son Lindley Murray, the house where Mrs. Murray's wit and Mr. Murray's wine saved Putnam's army from destruction. It was September 15, 1776. The Americans, retreating from Long Island, were marching northward to Bleecker Street, when the victorious English, marching westward, reached "Inclenberg." They had the ragged Continentals in a trap. But while they tarried at Mrs. Murray's table, Aaron Burr led Putnam's weary troops by leafy lanes, hidden from the ships-of-war on the Hudson and the men of war on Murray Hill, safely to Broad-

The Beekman Mansion

way and Forty-third Street, where Washington met them, galloping down from his headquarters at the Apthorpe house. The Murray house was burned in 1835, sixteen years before the destruction of the then oldest house on the Island,—The Kip mansion, at the corner of Second Avenue and Thirty-fifth Street. It was built in 1655 by Jacob Kip, and torn down in 1851 by some unknown person who should have known better, and, if he had, would have been better known himself. In Washington's time this region was called Kipsborough.

Now, on his peaceful journey, the President passed the Beekman mansion, and must have felt the shadow of Hale's death upon his soul, for Hale was his friend as well as his aide. He was accused of sacrificing André to Hale's memory, but André's gibbet casts no shadow across Washington's fame. André started from the Beekman house on the journey after glory which led him to the gallows. The roof that sheltered him then survived him nearly a century,—until 1874. Another roof-tree of that time still stands near by. At the foot of East 61st Street, in a wilderness of gas-works and stone-yards and tenement-houses and garbage-dumps, is the fine old stone residence of Colonel William S. Smith, who built the house about 1770, who married the only daughter of John

The Kissing Bridge

Adams, and who ruined himself by speculating in East River property a century too soon.

A mile beyond, at Seventy-seventh Street, was the Kissing Bridge, where the President, who was ever a stickler for the rigid observance of laws and customs, must have preserved his reputation by kissing Mrs. Washington and by making Master Custis permit his sister to kiss him. (Janvier declares that the original Kissing Bridge was in Chatham Street, and quotes the Rev. Mr. Burnaby's journal of 1740 as saying that here "it is customary, before passing beyond, to salute the lady who is your companion,"—a custom which was "curious, yet not displeasing.") A few rods farther the carriage turns to the west, plunges down and up some leafy hillsides through McGowan's Pass, and reaches the Bloomingdale road, passing north of the Apthorpe house, which stood until 1892 at (about) Ninety-first Street. Washington dined there September 21, 1776, and supped that night at the deserted house of Colonel Roger Morris, Tory, and husband of Mary Philipse, who listened to Washington's wooing in 1770 at the Philipse manor-house, now the beautiful City Hall of Yonkers, and perhaps said him nay. The Morris house, confiscated after the Revolution, bought by John Jacob Astor, sold by him to Stephen Jumel, whose eccentric widow married Aaron Burr and speedily thrust him out of her

End of The "Round"

home and dropped his name, still stands on Harlem Heights. Lord Howe, on the evening of that September day, fixed his headquarters at the Apthorpe house, and ate the supper cooked for the Rebel general. The last appearance of the Apthorpe mansion in history was on July 12, 1870, when the Orangemen held a picnic there, and afterwards fought the battle of the Boyne over again in the streets of New York.

Southward on Bloomingdale road, through a park-like region studded with villas, the carriage rolled homeward to the vicinity of Twenty-third Street, and so down the Bowery to Franklin Square and Cherry Street, in time for the four o'clock dinner.

That evening the President wrote in his notebook that he "exercised with Mrs. Washington and the children in the coach between breakfast and dinner,—went the fourteen miles round."

Barnard College

343 MADISON AVENUE

COURSES IN AMERICAN HISTORY

For Undergraduates. General course, reading, recitations and lectures.—Three hours a week: H. A. Cushing, A.M.

For Graduates. Political History of the Colonies and of the American Revolution.—This investigation course, extending through two years, deals in the first year with the settlement of the Colonies and their development in the seventeenth century, and in the second year with the growth of the system of colonial administration, the conflict with the French, and the revolt of the Colonies. The work of the students consists chiefly in the study of topics from the original sources, with a formal account of the results of such study.—Two hours a week for two years: Professor Herbert L. Osgood, Ph.D.

These courses are open not only to candidates for degrees, but to special students who can show ability to read French and German, and can satisfy the Dean and Faculty of their general competence.

Half Moon Series

Published in the Interest of the New York City History Club.

VOLUME I. NUMBER VII.

THE CITY CHEST OF NEW AMSTERDAM.

BY EDWARD DANA DURAND.

"AT the meeting of the burgomasters and schepens of this city of New Amsterdam held at the City Hall on the 2d of August, 1653, to which had been called some of the principal citizens and inhabitants, there was read a specified account of the expenditures made so far for the entrenchment of this city and similar works, which amount to about 7000 florins. . . . It is unanimously agreed and voted that nothing more shall be contributed until the Director-General surrenders the whole excise on wines and beer, and if then they are short of money, they will consider measures to raise more for the above said purpose."[1] Dispute over the Excise 1653

In this bold language did the newly established municipal councillors of New Amsterdam address Peter Stuyvesant, the unpopular

Previous Conflicts

representative of the unpopular West India Company. They demanded that one of the chief sources of revenue to the company be given over to the city's chest, as a condition of further contributions to the public defence. Scornfully and instantly was the proposition rejected ; as promptly, on that very day, the burgomasters and schepens declared their persistence in this stand.

Thus began a conflict between city and company that knew scarcely the briefest truce till the end of Dutch rule, a conflict whose record constitutes far the greater part of the history of the finances of New Amsterdam. Throughout, neither party showed a spirit altogether admirable or patriotic. The harshness and arbitrariness of the Director-General possibly repel us less than the tardy, shuffling, and at times almost dishonest behavior of the city fathers.

Ill feeling between the West India Company and the people of New Amsterdam and of New Netherland generally, was indeed no new thing. From the outset, perhaps inevitably, they had clashed. Only two or three years before the establishment of the municipal government, Adriaen Van der Donck had gone to Holland with bitter remonstrances from the citizens of the province, and from the Nine Men upon whom the utterly powerless position of councillors on behalf of the people

Municipal Government Established 1652

had been bestowed. He had labored long and zealously, and all but succeeded in obtaining the removal of the hated Stuyvesant. Though this object failed, it was chiefly through the influence of his embassy that, "to stop the slandering mouth . . . of many who show their malice under this garb" of demands for liberty, the Lords Directors, in 1652, granted the petition for a municipal government for New Amsterdam.[2] With however ill-grace this was done, the Company probably scarcely expected that the new government could be restricted to such a weak and dependent position as that to which Stuyvesant succeeded in reducing it. Instead of allowing the magistrates to be chosen by the people as in the Fatherland, the Director-General insisted upon himself appointing the two burgomasters, the five schepens, and even the city secretary, while none other than the Company's own *Fiskaal*, Cornelis Van Tienhoven, was made *ex-officio* schout or sheriff. Whether, however, the Governor's sense of fair play prevented it, or whether he could find not a single burgher upon his side, the magistrates thus chosen for the first two or three years were quite as far from being mere creatures of Stuyvesant's as were those who were thereafter selected by him from a nomination of double the number made by the burgomasters and schepens themselves. As

City Wall and Debt 1653

a further means of control the Director-General refused to allow a single florin of municipal revenue to be raised without his sanction. The strength of the traditions of free Holland, on the other hand, made him hesitate long before himself levying direct taxes on behalf of the Company, without consent of the people's representatives.

The immediate cause of the rupture of August, 1653, was the question of payment for the city's fortifications, and this same matter remained to the end the chief bone of contention. Scarcely had the burgomasters and schepens taken office in January of that year, when rumors of war led to a consultation between them and the Director-General regarding the strengthening of the fortifications. At the special promise of the municipal authorities "to contribute from 5000 to 6000 florins, to be collected from the interested commonalty," Stuyvesant deferred his plan of improving Fort Amsterdam, in favor of the scheme of constructing a palisade around the entire land side of the city.[3] By means of a loan of 5050 florins, subscribed by about forty of the leading burghers,[4] together with the personal labor of the people, the wall was rushed to completion. Stuyvesant now, with characteristic impatience, demanded immediate steps to raise money to pay off the debt according to promise. After some parleying and evasion the city fathers presented their ultimatum—the surrender to them of the tavern keepers' excise on wine and beer as a condition of any subsidies on their part.

Excise Surrendered to City 1653

The deadlock following Stuyvesant's rejection of these terms could not long continue. In November, a conference was held between the Director and his Council and the city magistrates, leading burghers were called in, and at last the Company's representatives, grumbling enough, agreed to permit the city to collect the excise, "provided that the burgomasters and schepens, as they promised, provide subsidies, by which the public works may be repaired, and their ecclesiastic and political ministers may be sustained."[5] The excise, as was and long continued to be the prevailing custom regarding all indirect taxes, was to be farmed out to the highest bidder.

The additional burden of the support of the church and of the city officials, which was thus made a condition of the grant of the excise, pleased the burgomasters and schepens very little indeed ; and hard would have fared Dominies Megapolensis and Drisius if no other salaries had come to them than were drawn from the city chest. The magistrates, in fact, were quite unwilling to make themselves unpopular by levying the direct taxes which Stuyvesant expected them to raise for paying off the debts. They appear, accordingly, to

Le Bleue's Mission to Holland

have used a considerable proportion of the first year's excise revenue in defraying the expense of a mission of remonstrance to the Lords Patroons in Holland, by which it was hoped to obtain more liberal financial grants. In their petition the worthy burgomasters and schepens asserted, somewhat mendaciously, it must be feared, that the excise would cover barely a third of the ecclesiastical and civil salaries, and accordingly begged to receive it without the requirement of paying these. They further besought the right to farm the ferry to Brooklyn, the revenue from which now belonged to the Company, and the right to collect fees for sealing deeds and other conveyances. They asked that the schout might be appointed by themselves, and made various other requests not connected with financial matters.[6] The emissary who was sent to push these demands, François le Bleue, bore also the remonstrances of a convention of representatives from the various communities of the colony concerning the management of affairs in general—remonstrances which the fiery Director-General had hurled back with reproaches and threats.

Pending action in Holland on their petition, the city fathers undertook to obtain further privileges from the Director-General and Council at home. As continued to be their practice, they sought the concession of indirect im-

Further Revenues Secured 1654

posts, and especially of such as would fall on the whole province. In February, 1654, they petitioned for a "small or burghers' excise" on liquors, for a duty on exports and imports, and for a duty on wine and beer sent out into the province from the city. These latter two somewhat unreasonable demands were refused, "as relating to the general and not the private consumption of a particular city"; but the burghers' excise was established. This appears to have been a tax on liquors bought directly from the maker or wholesale dealer for private use, as distinguished from the tax on liquors handled by tapsters. The rate was twenty stivers per tun of strong beer, six stivers per tun of small beer, thirty stivers per anker of wine or distilled liquor.[7]

It was about this same time that the burgomasters and schepens obtained consent to receive a salary from the city treasury, the former three hundred and fifty and the latter two hundred and fifty florins per year.[8] The salary of the secretary at this time was two hundred florins, with extra allowances for making up the city accounts.[9]

Early in the summer of 1654, new quarrels began between the Director-General and the municipal authorities. Danger of war was again impending; the fortifications needed repair. But it seemed out of place to incur new expense while not a stiver had yet been

Severity of Lords Patroons

paid toward the old debts. Stuyvesant reproached the city magistrates for not living up to their fair promises in this regard ; he reminded them, moreover, that none of the six months pay due the ministers had been received by those reverend gentlemen. After some negotiations in which the burgomasters and schepens showed considerable meanness of spirit, the Governor was forced to put up with allowing a further loan to repair the fortifications, the city fathers agreeing as usual that they would seek some means of revenue.

In the midst of these dissensions came the reply from the Lords Patroons in Holland to the petition sent by the city the preceding winter. This was forwarded through Stuyvesant himself, who accordingly summoned the burgomasters and schepens and, in the presence of the injured dominies, joined his severer reproaches to the rebuke contained in the letter from the Company. This document declared that such remonstrances as had been sent by "disaffected persons" were "highly inexpedient" under the present circumstances, and urged the people to "demean themselves quietly and peaceably, submitting to the government," on which condition restoration of cordial relations was promised. Withal, however, a few of the demands which had been made were granted, but none of financial

Excise Revenue Lost 1654

importance, save an indefinite permission to levy some small new excise or tax.[10]

The energetic Director-General waited but a few days to see if his verbal exhortations at this meeting would stir the sluggish burgomasters and schepens to action ; then he sent a written demand for subsidies, and an order that an account of the receipts and expenditures of the excise moneys be rendered forthwith. The worthy magistrates complied with the latter behest. To the former they replied that according to their calculations the amount now due for the defences of the city was about 16,000 florins; that this ought to be raised proportionably by the various villages in the province ; and that the city was willing to pay its share, which they supposed would amount to perhaps 3000 florins, if permission were given to levy a tax on all real estate within the walls.[11]

To this niggardly proposal the choleric Director gave not the slightest attention. Regarding the accounts, however, he had many faults to find ; especially did he condemn the expenditure of "a certain sum of money paid to François le Bleue." Without more ado, accordingly, Stuyvesant ordered the tavern-keepers' excise to be again turned into the Company's treasury, and therefrom he undertook to pay the long-suffering ministers. Even further, he resolved now to take matters

Stuyvesant's Mighty Letter 1654

quite into his own hand, and gave public notice that he would levy a tax on farming land and cattle, (*morgen talen* and *hoorn geld*) and another of one per cent. on city real estate.[12] This proposition was scarcely to the taste of the burgomasters and schepens. They hastened to write again, promising to support one of the ministers, one chorister, one "dog-whipper" or beadle, the schout, the secretary and the court messenger, as well as to pay their own salaries and contribute toward the debt, if only the excise be restored and the city permitted to levy the proposed tax of the hundredth penny. The long-pent rage of the old Governor now burst forth in a mighty letter, which must have been punctuated with many a fierce stamp of his wooden leg. He rehearsed all the promises of the magistrates, all their failures to perform. Five or six thousand florins they had agreed at the very outset to raise for the fortifications; now they offer a paltry three thousand as their share forsooth of the debt of five times that amount—verily, the single year's farming of the excise had amounted to more than this. To be sure, however, he conceded, it was a matter of indifference whether the Company or the city collected the hundredth penny tax.[13]

Throughout the days of Dutch rule, and indeed for long thereafter, it was the custom to require citizens individually to perform various

The Schoeyinge 1654

duties which, while largely for their personal benefit, also affected the public welfare—duties now left exclusively to municipal authorities. One of the most important early instances of this practice was in the construction of the *Schoeyinge,* or sheet piling along the water front and the *Heere Gracht* or grand canal. This appears to have been previously built, in whole or in part, at the voluntary initiative of burghers owning adjoining lots, but first in November, 1654, was it provided by city ordinance that such citizens must construct and keep up the *Schoeyinge.* In default, the city was to do the work and collect the cost from the owners. The expense of maintaining this protection along the canal, however, was apparently borne by the general treasury until 1660, when, as we shall see, a new plan was tried.

Stuyvesant did not at once levy the *morgen* and *hoorn talen,* which he had proposed in August; he hesitated to depart from the traditional principle of no taxation without representation, and awaited further orders from the Lords Patroons, of whom he especially asked advice as to the tax on city lands and houses. The burgomasters and schepens, on their own behalf, likewise addressed their High Mightinesses in Holland. The latter replied to Stuyvesant, under date of April 26, 1655, reiterating their reproaches against the

Stuyvesant Plans Direct Taxes 1655

delinquent commonalty of New Amsterdam, and declaring that in levying taxes he should "have nothing to care about their consent." It appears, however, that the Director yielded to the arguments of his own councillors, who pointed out the growing distress of the province, and refrained from levying the tax he had threatened.[14] Possibly he felt somewhat more lenient than usual in view of the fact that just about this time (October, 1655) the burgomasters, with his consent, at last undertook to levy a tax or contribution, not, to be sure, for paying off the old debts but for strengthening the city wall by running up a shield of planks.

This, the first direct burden ever laid upon the inhabitants of this now much-taxed city, was peculiar in that an attempt was made to give it somewhat the color of a voluntary contribution. Each burgher was asked to give "according to his state, condition and good-will," but force might be employed in case of "disaffected or malevolent persons." No formal assessment of the value of any man's property was made, but to each the burgomasters and schepens assigned roughly the amount they thought he should pay. Of the two hundred and twenty-eight names on the list, fortunately preserved, less than half are indicated as subscribing voluntarily ; quite a few offered sums which the city fathers deemed insuffi-

First City Tax or "Contribution" 1655

cient and which were increased accordingly; all the rest had to be taxed compulsorily, since they "always resorted to one excuse or another." Governor Stuyvesant himself, by no means lacking in public spirit, "presented" one hundred and fifty florins; only three absent skippers of vessels were taxed at that high figure. A dozen or more burghers gave or were taxed one hundred florins. The least money payment was four florins. Two citizens contributed a beaver each; two others, carpenters, made their gifts in days' labor. The total sum, as listed, was 6305 florins; of this, after even more difficulty than the tax-gatherer experiences among us to-day—for the collection dragged on into 1657, when 1408 florins were still unpaid—nearly six thousand florins were ultimately realized.[18]

Another curious action of the same city magistrates who had undertaken this assessment, must likewise have tended to placate the old Director-General. Their economical worships proposed nothing less than that, in view of the chronically low condition of the chest, they should forego the cash payment of their own salaries, but instead "open an account with the city." It would be only just, they continued, that their predecessors in office should be required to refund the moneys paid them and likewise wait a more pros-

Additional Minor Revenues 1656

perous state of the finances. *Fiat ut petitur,* wrote the laconic Stuyvesant; let us hope the deed was accomplished as easily as the authority was secured.[16]

Substantial evidence soon was given of the somewhat more friendly relations between the Director-General and the burgomasters and schepens. Four new sources of revenue, of minor importance, indeed, were granted to the city chest early in 1656. In the first place, a general ordinance imposed throughout the province a duty on slaughtering animals, the proceeds of which were conceded to the various local bodies. The right to collect certain dues from grocers was also conferred on New Amsterdam, but of this we learn nothing further. Moreover, the city was allowed to receive fees of from three to twenty stivers each for branding the size of measures, barrels, etc. Finally—a step of considerable importance in furthering the growth of the municipality, but of little financial consequence—a resurvey and subdivision of vacant lands within the wall was made, the city being granted the proceeds of the sale of new lots upon reimbursing the claims of the former owners.[17]

The truce between city and Company, if such it could fairly be considered, lasted barely a year. In September, 1656, at the suggestion of the Lords Patroons, the Governor once

Burgherrecht Established 1657

more reverted to the still unpaid debts for the fortifications. Evasive promises to "levy some duties," rehearsals of the hardness of the times, and petitions for aid from the Company's treasury, constituted the characteristic response of the burgomasters and schepens.[18] Stuyvesant's answer took the accustomed angry tone; he demanded definite action. At last, partly as a financial measure but more largely to protect the trade of their city, the magistrates sought leave to establish the system of close citizenship, after the fashion of the Fatherland. They complained bitterly of the unfair competition of the Scotch merchants, who gave to New Amsterdam no benefit whatever by the trade they carried on up the river. This important petition was granted; unfortunately, the undemocratic distinction between the *groot* and *klein Burgherrecht,* which had but recently been invented in Holland, was introduced. Aside from those possessed of various qualifications of birth, residence, or station, any person could acquire the greater citizenship by a payment of fifty guilders, or the lesser by a payment of twenty guilders; this was the revenue side of the measure. Only citizens could carry on any trade or business in the city or traffic upon the Hudson.[19]

It was shortly after this time that, on the petition of the burgomasters and schepens that

Unsatisfactory Accounts 1657

they be allowed to establish the office of city treasurer independently of that of clerk, the Director ordered this position thereafter to be filled by the outgoing burgomaster, for the year following his retirement. Oloff Stevensen Van Cortland was the first city treasurer.[20] About this time, too, some difficulty arose over the accounts of the expenditure of the money raised by the tax of 1655–6, the sharp-eyed Stuyvesant as usual discovering items wherein he sniffed corruption. The burgomasters, however, explained that the thirty-six florins for a tun of beer for the carpenters had been paid in pursuance of a contract made in the presence of Councillors Van Tienhoven and La Montagne themselves; that, moreover, doughty Captain de Coninck and his crew by their labors on the fortifications had far more than earned the various gratuities that had been paid them. We know not whether the Governor was satisfied with these explanations.[21] It was in 1657, likewise, that the city obtained a loan of a thousand florins from the Company's treasury to pay for work on the *Schoeyinge* along the canal.[22]

Several very important events, in their bearing both on the finances and on municipal activity generally, occurred during the latter part of 1657 and the year 1658.

In the first place, a more efficient fire pro-

Fire Apparatus Purchased 1657

tection was undertaken. Unpaid fire wardens had long existed, whose duty it was to inspect fireplaces and chimneys. It was now determined to purchase fire ladders, hooks, and buckets. For defraying the original cost of these a tax of one beaver or eight florins was levied. The city was also authorized to collect annually, for maintaining the apparatus, one florin for each chimney ; in 1661, however, the honest city fathers called Stuyvesant's attention to the inequality of this tax, since the rich often had several fireplaces connected with one chimney, and the amount was accordingly ordered to be levied upon each fireplace. It was also provided that tenants of houses might deduct half of this tax from the rent paid to the owner.[23]

Much more important, especially because of the financial method employed, was the laying of what was probably the first regular pavement in New Amsterdam. This was in Brewer Street, which soon after came to be called Stone Street. The noteworthy feature of the event was the introduction in very nearly its modern form of the system of local assessment for special benefits derived from public improvements. The matter of this much-needed work had been debated by the burgomasters and schepens early in 1658, the alternative lying between the plan of requiring each lot-owner himself to perform

Brewer Street Paved 1658

the work, as had been done in the case of part of the *Schoeyinge,* and that of making the cost a general city burden. It was a petition of the citizens themselves along the street which proposed the intermediate and far preferable course of having the work done by the city and the cost assessed on the abutting property; such assessments they declared themselves willing to pay. This plan was adopted by the city council, January 21, 1658. Two burghers were appointed to manage the work, and they were authorized "to assess proportionably for the expense incurred each house standing in the aforesaid street." A few of the citizens were afterward somewhat unwilling to pay, yet there was no such difficulty as occurred a year or two later when the assessment system was tried without petition of the interested owners.[24]

While all this was going on, new negotiations and conflicts arose between the ever hostile city and provincial authorities. For the avowed purpose of preventing the holding of large blocks of real estate for speculation, the Director, anticipating the single-tax principle, had levied a tax of the fifteenth penny on vacant lots in New Amsterdam. The proceeds were to go to the city chest, owners being given the alternative of surrendering their lots to the burgomasters and schepens at an appraised value.[25] Perchance

Salaries of Magistrates 1658

the worthies who then graced the magistracy felt that this new grant of revenue would be of little gain to their own administration, now soon to close. At any rate, but four days after the ordinance bestowing it, in marked contrast to the behavior of their predecessors two years before, they barefacedly begged Stuyvesant to inform them "from what source they may expect to obtain" the salaries he had long since promised them; in order that they "might be prompted to acquit themselves of their duty with alacrity and vigor." The abrupt reply was a reference to the ordinance by which the salaries had been granted. This had, of course, provided for their payment out of the city treasury; but the fawning burgomasters and schepens refused to observe the plain implication, and besought the Governor for "further explanation." A brief but severe lecture was the only response; they were reminded in the customary strain of the unfulfilled promises of subsidies for paying the debts and for maintaining the fortifications.[26]

Along with this ignoble petition of the city fathers had gone yet another—for more revenue. Let the income from the weighing house, they besought, "agreeably to the laudable customs of the Fatherland," be conferred upon the municipality. Stuyvesant replied that such a right or regalia properly be-

First City Wharf 1658

longed to the general government, since all imports and exports from New Netherland were weighed here; the citizens directly benefited by public works ought to raise means to pay for them. He then proceeded to enumerate accurately all the ten sources of revenue, either temporary or permanent, so far granted to the city chest. The yearly receipts from the burghers' excise, he declared, were 4200 florins, those from the duty on slaughtered animals 1457 florins; presumably these were the largest forms of income or he would have specified the amount from other sources, which he must have known approximately. Notwithstanding these objections, he promised to grant the fourth part of the receipts of the scales, if the Lords Patroons should approve; it was not till two years later, however, that any income from this grant was actually obtained by the city.[27]

The present great financial importance of New York's system of municipal docks and wharves makes especially noteworthy the beginning of this form of city property, in the fall of 1658. Hitherto, vessels had been unloaded either directly upon the shore of the Great Canal, or upon the bridge which crossed it at the site of the present Bridge Street. This being unsatisfactory the worshipful burgomasters and schepens petitioned for leave

Night Watch Established 1658

to construct a suitable wharf (*hoofd*, wrongly described by some writers as a "hoist"), apparently in close connection with the bridge. An extension of this dock, four rods long, was built in 1660 at a cost of two hundred and twenty-five florins. For the use of the wharf the city was allowed to charge eight stivers for each *last* (about two tons) loaded or unloaded, and for smaller weights in proportion. This wharfage was reduced to five stivers a few years later; certain coasting vessels, moreover, were allowed to commute by bringing stone for the city fortifications. In 1662, likewise, the shipping interests were further encouraged by the construction of a small breakwater, and charges were levied on vessels for its support.[28]

The last important event in this year of busy municipal activity was the establishment of a city night-watch. During the times of danger in 1653, bands of citizens had been called on to patrol the streets. Rumors of war were now again stirring. Not merely were the good burghers summoned once more to form train bands and prepare for emergencies; a "rattle watch" of paid guards, eight in number, was also employed, it being understood that four should be on duty each alternate night. Each of the watchmen received twenty-four stivers for every night of service, and they were promised

Stuyvesant Relents 1660

"one or two beavers besides for candles, and two hundred or three hundred sticks of firewood." The expense of this new enterprise was met by a tax of fifteen stivers monthly on each family, and not a little trouble had the bold police captain in collecting this charge. It seems that the rattle watch was discontinued temporarily a year or two after its establishment, but we find it renewed in 1661.[29]

Nothing of consequence affecting the city chest occurred in 1659, but early in the following year the Director-General took a step which we should little have anticipated from his previous harsh attitude on the same subject. The city magistrates, despite the various revenues they had succeeded in worrying out of Stuyvesant, found the treasury still chronically bankrupt. The original debt of six thousand guilders for the fortifications, despite so many negotiations, had remained, these seven years, unredeemed, though the West India Company itself appears to have paid off some of the later obligations which it had hoped to lay upon the city. The burgomasters and schepens now besought aid in satisfying these old creditors, by whom they were "troubled day after day," and promised thereupon to seek some measures to meet the other debts of the municipality. "After many discussions *pro* and *con*, and the examination

Repairing Heere Gracht 1660

of the city accounts," the Director and Council agreed to assume certain enumerated claims, amounting altogether to 3849 florins, provided the city fathers keep their fair promises. Presumably they did not.[30]

The *Schoeyinge* along the *Heere Gracht* now needed repairing once again, and it was resolved to make a more thorough job than ever before. Hitherto, apparently, this work (so far as the canal was concerned) had been partly, if not wholly, done at the expense of the general treasury. Now, it was resolved to make use of the system of special assessment for benefit, which had been so successful in paving Brewer Street. When the work had been completed by the city itself and the cost had been reckoned up, it was found that it could be defrayed if " on both sides of the canal each resident or occupant of a lot shall pay . . . on so much as he possesses the sum of forty guilders in seawant per rod." We have preserved for us the measurements of the various lots and the amount assessed against each. Hans Dreper on a frontage of 1 rod 10 feet, was to pay seventy-three florins (the Dutch rod being 12½ feet) ; Hendrick (Willemsen) the baker, on 5 rods 4½ feet, 214 florins 17 stivers, etc. The total assessment was 2792 florins.

Never in nineteenth century days did a greater wail over the burden of special assess-

Special Assessment Difficulties

ments arise than forthwith greeted the burgomasters and schepens of 1660. Not only had no petition of the interested owners been made for this work, but apparently they had not even been warned that they would be forced to bear this expense. One and all they complained, refused, stormed ; but to little avail. Poor baker Hendrick maintained that so far from receiving any benefit from the work, he had actually been much damaged by the loss of a lot of stone which had been undermined. He would not contribute, and he and another neighbor were accordingly "led to the prison chamber"; chiefly to scare them, presumably, for they were soon brought back and the suggestion was made to them that they pay in four instalments. The baker consented to this, but his obstinate companion swore he could and would not, do what they might with him. What they did is not recorded. So many were the remonstrances that finally the privilege of paying in four annual instalments was extended to all those most heavily assessed, while the others were allowed to pay in three instalments.[31]

Perhaps because of these difficulties with the *Heere Gracht,* the older plan of ordering work to be done by each abutting owner at his own expense and by his own methods, was reverted to in the case of the pavement of the paths running along both sides of the *Prince*

Last Fortification Loan 1664

Gracht (now Beaver Street) in the fall of 1660.[32] This probably continued to be the ordinary manner of paving streets in New Amsterdam and New York throughout most of the seventeenth century.

Little more of importance is recorded concerning the management of the city finances till the very close of Dutch rule, now drawing near. To be sure, the burgomasters and schepens could not refrain from occasionally petitioning for new sources of revenue, but they were not successful. Doubtless the chest remained habitually vacant ; doubtless creditors went, as usual, unpaid. The last financial event which preceded the capture of the city by Colonel Nicolls had to do, like that with which the history of the finances opened, with the fortification of the city. In the spring of 1664, danger of British attack loomed up far more real than ever before. However averse the burghers afterward showed themselves to resistance when they saw it was too late, they were not wanting in spirit now. Stronger fortifications were imperative. When it was proposed to borrow money, nearly a hundred citizens stood ready to offer no less than 27,500 florins—at a good ten per cent., it is true, Curiously, the city magistrates officially subscribed for 6300 florins ; the church organization likewise offered 2000. Before actually

Spirit of the Finances

incurring this heavy new debt the burgomasters and schepens felt that larger revenues must be guaranteed them. On their petition Stuyvesant reluctantly surrendered once more the tavern-keepers' excise of wine and beer, although this revenue, he declared, which had amounted to 8035 florins the preceding year, was all that kept the "sinking ship" of the Company's own finances above water. The city in turn pledged every stiver of its income, save moneys for a few small necessary salaries, toward redeeming the debt.[33]

How far this loan was actually secured and how far its proceeds were spent, the records do not show. It was but a few months after this that the English ships arrived in the harbor, and the futility of all these efforts became apparent.

Without referring to the unimportant events of the short period of Dutch restoration in 1673-4, we may briefly call attention to the chief characteristics of financial policy shown in the history we have traced.

That policy was in general such as was to be expected in a city where semi-mediæval methods and traditions of municipal government prevailed, but it was naturally modified not a little by the small size and the newness of the community, and especially by its dependence upon a private company, bent on

Indirect Taxation

deriving as much gain as possible from the people. The practice of calling upon the citizens personally, without pay, for public duty, that of making the municipality a close corporation and of confining trade to its members, and, finally, that of relying for revenue chiefly upon fees and indirect taxes, all these were quite in the spirit of European towns of that day. On the other hand, the extreme difficulty with which these sources of revenue were won from the Director-General shows how far short stood the new city of the large autonomy which then usually belonged to old-world municipalities. Direct taxation was highly unpopular; indeed the city never resorted to it in quite unalloyed form. The tax of 1655–6 had been treated so far as possible as a voluntary contribution, and, at any rate, was not based on a formal assessment of the value of property. The fire and police taxes were put on the basis of immediate payments for services, and were levied accordingly not on property but on the fireplace or the house. The custom of relying mainly on indirect revenues continued till toward the close of the eighteenth century.

Of perhaps the greatest interest is the early application of the principle of special assessments for local improvements, so clearly employed in the case of Brewer Street. This practice is almost unknown in Europe to-day

Special Assessments

and is often pointed out as a great forward step of our own continent in local finance. It was once supposed to have originated with a New York provincial law of 1691, but a prototype of this was found in England in 1667 in connection with the rebuilding of London after the great fire. Whether the honor of establishing the system in 1658 must be again conceded to New York, or whether she but copied Dutch methods, is as yet uncertain, as is also the question whether direct connection can be traced between the early practice and the law of 1691. The subject of the origin of the system is of no little interest, for the use of special assessments is of even greater relative financial importance to-day than it was so long ago in aiding the City Chest of New Amsterdam.

REFERENCES.

1. *Records of the Burgomasters and Schepens of New Amsterdam* (translation as published by the city, 1897), i., p. 92.
2. Letter, April 2, 1652, N. Y. Col. Mss., *New Netherland Records* (Van der Camp's translation), iv., p. 68.
3. *New Netherland Records*, vi., p. 61.
4. O'CALLAGHAN, *History of the New Netherlands*, ii, p. 215.
5. *New Netherland Records*, ix., p. 8.
6. *Records of New Amsterdam* (printed translation), i., pp. 144–5.
7. Ordinance, May 4, 1654. *Ibid*, p. 193.
8. *Ibid*, p. 157.
9. *Ibid*, p. 150.
10. *New Netherland Records*, iv., pp. 136–43; ix., pp. 175, 212.
11. *Ibid*, pp. 182, 211.
12. *Ibid*, pp. 189, 205.
13. *Ibid*, pp. 212, 216–26.
14. *Ibid*, iv., p. 175; xiii., pp. 150 *ff*.
15. *Ibid*, xiii., p. 107; xi., p. 211; xiv., p. 56; *Records of New Amsterdam* (printed translation), i., p. 366; (manuscript translation), iii., p. 257.
16. *New Netherland Records*, xi., p. 185.
17. *Ibid*, xi. pp. 165, 171, 260; xiv., p. 56.
18. *Ibid*, xvii., pp. 188–90.
19. *Ibid*, xv., pp. 39, 54 *ff*.
20. *Ibid*, xv., p. 30.
21. *Ibid*, xiv., pp. 44, 122.
22. *Records of New Amsterdam*, June 26, 1657.
23. *Laws and Ordinances of New Netherland*, p. 322; *New Netherland Records*, xix., p. 204.
24. *Records of New Amsterdam*, iii., pp. 5, 34, 113.

25. *New Netherland Records*, xiv., p. 24.
26. *Ibid*, pp. 30, 71.
27. *Ibid*, pp. 55-58; *Records of New Amsterdam*, iii., p. 387.
28. *New Netherland Records*, xiv., p. 414; xxiv., p. 17. *Records of New Amsterdam*, iii., p. 435.
29. *Records of New Amsterdam*, iii., pp. 314 *ff.*, 438–40.
30. *New Netherland Records*, xxiv., p. 28.
31. *Records of New Amsterdam*, iii., pp. 413–25.
32. *Ibid*, p. 429.
33. *New Netherland Records*, xxii., p. 78 *ff.*

The Southern Workman and Hampton School Record ⚜ ⚜ ⚜ ⚜ ⚜

is a twenty-page monthly published by the Hampton Institute in Virginia in the interest of the two races it represents—the Negro and the Indian.

It is a record of the practical working out of the race problems, not only at Hampton but at Tuskegee and other schools, and contains much interesting matter from graduates in the field and from prominent students and writers representing the best thought of the country.

A few pages are devoted each month to the local affairs of the School, to letters from Negroes and Indians in the South and West, to folk-lore, and to reviews of books bearing upon race problems.

Subscription, $1.00 a year. This may be sent to

REV. H. B. FRISSELL,
HAMPTON, VA.

Half Moon Series

Published in the Interest of the New York City History Club.

VOLUME I. NUMBER VIII.

FORT AMSTERDAM IN THE DAYS OF THE DUTCH.

By MAUD WILDER GOODWIN.

IN the autumn of 1626, the good ship *Arms of Amsterdam* sailed away to Holland bearing tidings of the tiny Dutch colony at the "Manhattes," which it left in a thriving condition. The report, forwarded to the West India Company, pictured the settlers as already making comfortable dwellings for themselves. Thirty log-houses, with roofs made from the bark of trees, huddled close together at the end of the island. The counting-house boasted walls of stone and a thatched roof, and François Molemaecker was building a mill with two stories, of which the upper one was to form a spacious room large enough to serve as a meeting-place for almost the entire colony, and the mill was to be still further

Condition of Colony 1626

Planning of Fort 1626

adorned by a tower wherein should be hung bells brought hither from Porto Rico.

In those days no settlement was complete without a fortification, and the first care of the colonists was to build a fort which should prove both a protection and a refuge from their enemies. As they had paid the natives for their land, it was not so much the Indians whom they feared, as other Europeans, covetous, like themselves, of possessions in the New World.

After much discussion as to the position of this fort, the settlers finally decided to place it boldly at the very point of the island where their flag of orange and blue might wave defiance to any alien vessel seeking to penetrate Hudson's River, or any adventurer aiming to appropriate the territory of the Dutch West India Company.

The green-turfed land which forms the end of Manhattan Island to-day was then under water at high tide, and the Capske, a sharp ledge of rock dividing the North and East rivers, terminated a little south of State Street. On the slope of land to the north of this, the site of the fort was laid on the ground now marked by a row of steamship offices at the foot of Bowling Green.

The engineer who superintended the building of this early fortification was named Kryn Fredericksen. He found material scarce, and

Blockhouse Built 1626

labor in such demand for house-building, that he could plan only for a blockhouse, encircled by palisadoes built of red cedar, and sodded earthworks.

While this rude structure was in process of erection, an episode having serious consequences occurred. A friendly Indian of the Weckquaeskeeck tribe, who inhabited what is now Westchester County, came with his nephew to trade at the Dutch village. Three servants belonging to Peter Minuit, then Director of the colony, fell upon the Indian, robbed him of his wares and finally murdered him. The nephew escaped, and returned to his tribe vowing vengeance, which he wreaked to his full satisfaction nearly twenty years later.

Except for this ominous episode, the upbuilding of the little town went forward prosperously. The new fortification was completed and christened Fort Amsterdam and the hamlet nestling under its protection was declared the capital of New Netherland.

The relations between the Dutch settlers and their colonial neighbors were now, as always, uncertain, and ready at any time on slight provocation to break out into open warfare. In 1627, there was some threat of difficulty with the English concerning the right of trading with the Indians ; but it ended amicably. Governor Bradford of Massachusetts received from Director Minuit of New Nether-

Threat of War with the English 1627

land "a rundlet of sugar and two Holland cheese," and the nations whom the governors represented continued at peace. This experience, however, impressed upon the settlers at New Amsterdam the necessity of strengthening the very primitive defences which were their only reliance in case of war, and, accordingly, in the year 1633, Wouter van Twiller, who had succeeded Minuit as Director, ordered the construction of a fort more nearly adequate to the needs of the settlers.

So substantial was this fort that two years passed before its completion. Its shape was a quadrangle with a bastion at each corner. The northwest bastion was faced with "good quarry stone," and the earthworks were thoroughly repaired by negroes in the employ of the Dutch West India Company, under the superintendence of Jacob Stoffelsen.

Within the enclosure stood three windmills, a guardhouse and barracks, besides the "big house" built by Van Twiller for his own occupancy. The fort itself was not very extensive according to modern ideas. It measured only some three hundred feet in length by two hundred and fifty in breadth, yet the cost of completing it (including probably the buildings within) was 4172 guilders, or between sixteen and seventeen hundred dollars. One of the buildings in the enclosure soon came to an untimely end. A man named

Arrival of Kieft 1638

Van Vorst undertook to fire a salute in honor of the Director-General from a stone gun which stood near the house. A spark from the wadding lodged on the roof, which, being covered with reed, caught fire at once, and the whole building was destroyed in less than half an hour.

The old fort witnessed scenes of jollity in those early days. On one occasion, the first gunner held a festivity at one of the angles of the fort, where a tent had been erected and tables set out. In the midst of the feasting, a trumpeter blew a sudden blast upon his trumpet, much to the alarm of the revellers. The Coopman of Cargoes and the Coopman of Stores[1] were so wrathful, that, they called the trumpeter hard names, and he in return administered to each a sound thrashing, which put an end to the merry evening.

Van Twiller's control over the colony lasted only a short time after the completion of the fort. In March, 1638, Kieft arrived to take the reins of government from his hand. Kieft found the defences in a ruinous state. The fort, finished only three years before, was in a shameful condition of disrepair; the guns dismounted, the public buildings within the walls in ruins. Of the three windmills only one was in operation, and the walls of

[1] "Coopman of Cargoes" *i.e.*, supercargo of a ship, and "Coopman of Stores" store-keeper.

Troubles with Indians 1641

the fort were so beaten down that any might come in or go out at their will "save at the stone point."

This state of things was the more unfortunate inasmuch as Director Kieft's injudicious belligerency soon plunged the colony into a series of quarrels with the natives. Under orders from Holland, as he declared, Kieft undertook to lay a tax upon the Indians, who expressed their wrath in vehement protest against "the Sakema of the Fort." He was but a mean fellow, they declared. He had not invited them to come and live here that he should now lay claim to the corn which they had planted.

So violent did this feeling become that Kieft found it necessary to order every inhabitant to provide himself with a gun, and warned the settlers that, in case of a night attack, at a preconcerted signal of three cannon shots they were to appear armed at the fort in military order.

The position of the settlers on outlying "*bouweries*" grew more and more perilous. Massacres were reported from Staten Island, massacres often too cruelly avenged by the Dutch, who grew more and more blood-thirsty and greedy for plunder. One day in the summer of 1641, word was brought to the fort of the murder of Claes, "the Raadmaker" (in English, wheelwright) living on the west shore of the river. The old man, so the story

Murder of the Raadmaker 1641

ran, had received a visit from a young Indian, who had been in the habit of working for the son of Claes and who came to the house professedly to purchase cloth. Claes hospitably set food before him and then went to a chest, wherein the cloth was kept. As the Raadmaker stooped, the savage struck him dead with an axe.

This story naturally filled the settlers with horror, nor was their rage diminished by learning that the murderer was no other than the nephew of the Weckquaeskeeck Indian, who had met with foul play at the hands of Director Minuit's servants twenty years before. On receiving the news of the Raadmaker's murder, Kieft sent at once to the Chief of the Weckquaeskeeck tribe demanding the surrender of the murderer; but the Sachem haughtily replied that he wished the young warrior had slain twenty Christians instead of one and that he had justly carried out the traditions of his race in avenging the murder of his relative. This answer roused the Director to a state of frenzy. He determined to call a council of war to authorize him in proceeding against the contumacious Indians. On the 28th day of August, 1641, accordingly, all the masters and heads of families dwelling in or near New Amsterdam assembled in the fort to consider the question of the punishment of the Weckquaeskeecks.

First Attempt at Popular Government 1641

This gathering was noteworthy as the first effort at popular government in the colony and the burghers shrewdly made the most of it by appointing a committee of the Twelve Men to co-operate with the Director. Kieft himself began to realize that he had raised spirits which he could not lay, and bitterly resented the restrictions which the Twelve Men sought to lay upon his impetuosity. He desired to attack the Indians at once ; but the Twelve counselled delay and the popular will so enforced their authority, that Kieft was compelled to yield to their judgment and to postpone action.

It would have seemed natural, that this period of delay should be spent in preparation for the strife to come, in strengthening the defences and arming the outposts ; but, instead, Kieft began the erection of a series of elaborate, expensive and comparatively unneccessary buildings inside the fortification, and spent upon them the money which should have been laid out upon stout masonry and iron guns. Besides the fine, stone tavern erected among the thatched-roofed, wooden-chimneyed cottages huddling about Fort Amsterdam, within the walls of the fort rose still more substantial buildings. The most imposing of these was the new church, which owed its origin, it is to be feared, less to piety than to vanity, since, until the taunts of De

Contract for Building a Church in the Fort 1642

Vries called attention to "the mean barn" which was all that the dwellers in New Amsterdam had to show in contrast with the well-ordered meeting-houses of New England, the old chapel in the village had been deemed sufficient by the worshippers of the little colony. Now, however, it was determined to erect a fine church, which should be a credit to the whole province of New Netherland, the expense of the building to be borne partly by the West India Company and partly by private subscriptions.

A contract, "done at Fort Amsterdam," and dated May, 1642, sets forth the agreement between William Kieft, church-warden and John and Richard Ogden, by which the Ogdens bind themselves to build a church seventy-two feet long, fifty-two broad and sixteen feet high above the soil, for the sum of 2500 guilders equal to about $1000, the price to be paid in beaver, or other merchandise. It is stipulated that the contractors shall procure the stone and bring it ashore near the fort, for which purpose they shall be allowed the use of the Company's boat for a month or six weeks. The church-wardens agree to convey the stone from the shore to the fort, and to furnish the lime with which to lay it. If the work is done "in a workmanlike manner" and to the satisfaction of the employers, the contractors are to receive a bonus of an additional hundred guilders.

Church Completed 1642

There were not wanting carping critics who spoke of the *kerck* as "the fifth wheel to a coache," objected to such a use of money, and even doubted the wisdom of building a new church at all, especially in the fort where, as they pointed out, it occupied a quarter of all available space and, moreover, by its location would necessarily shut off the southeast wind from the gristmill on which the settlers depended for grinding their corn.

Director Kieft and Dominie Bogardus proved too strong for the objectors, however, and the church finally raised its steep double-pointed roof above the walls of the fort. That the building might preserve his own memory, as well as testify to the glory of God, the Director caused to be inserted in the front a tablet bearing the inscription:

> "*An. Dom—MDCXLII*
> "*Willem Kieft, Directeur Generael*
> "*Heeft De Gemeente Desen Tempel Doen Bouwen.*"[1]

A century later the church was burned and the slab buried in dirt, whence it was dug up when the fort itself was demolished in 1789. The slab was removed for safe-keeping to the Dutch church in Garden Street; but on the de-

[1] "An Dom—1642
[When] Willem Kieft was Director-General
The Congregation built this temple."

Other Buildings in the Fort 1642

struction of that building by fire, the slab commemorating Kieft and his greatness disappeared forever.

Besides the ground given up to the new church the space in the fort was further encroached upon by other buildings civic and domestic rather than military in character. The quaint windmill, with its long arms and revolving tower, occupied one corner, and near the *Gevangen Huys* or jail, stood the Governor's house, which for that day was an elaborate and elegant mansion, having an "entry" twenty feet wide, and a double-faced chimney to keep it warm. It was surrounded by walks measuring ten feet in width, and altogether must have required much money and labor to equip and maintain. It is not strange that there should have been some murmuring among the thrifty burghers over such expenditures, especially at this crisis when matters were growing daily more threatening, and the settlers dared scarcely stir abroad for fear of savages.

The conduct of the colonists in general and the Director in particular was marked at this time by a mixture of ferocity and cowardice. A large number of Weckquaeskeeck Indians were massacred in cold blood by the Dutch, after they had sued for peace and sought shelter in the fort from their powerful enemy, the Mohawks. Other tribes had been treated

General Indian Warfare 1643

with equally brutal disregard of both principle and policy, till, at last, in 1643, the settlers found themselves by their own folly involved in a general Indian warfare. The only hope of the colony on Manhattan Island now lay in the protection afforded by Fort Amsterdam, and its inadequacy was painfully apparent. A Jesuit priest who travelled through New Netherland at this time, writes thus of its condition :

> "This fort which is at the point of the island, is called Fort Amsterdam. It has four regular bastions mounted with several pieces of artillery. All these bastions and curtains were in 1643 but ramparts of earth most of which had crumbled away so that the fort could be entered on all sides. There were no ditches. There were sixty soldiers to garrison the said fort and another which they had built still farther up against the incursions of the savages, their enemies. They were beginning to face the gates and bastions with stone."

In October, 1643, the Eight Men who had succeeded the Twelve as representatives of the colony, wrote home to the "Honorable, Wise, Prudent Gentlemen of the XIX. of the General Incorporated West India Company, Department of Amsterdam," complaining bitterly of the harrying they were undergoing at the hands of the allied Indians, who having sent their old men, women and children into the interior, were in excellent fighting condition. "The most expert warriors," the complaint says, "hang daily on

Letter of the Eight Men 1643

our necks with fire and sword, and threaten to attack the fort with all their force of about fifteen hundred men. This we hourly expect." The only place of shelter the letter declares to be Fort Amsterdam, and this so poorly supplied with men and ammunition as to be nearly useless. "The fort is defenceless and entirely out of order, and resembles (with submission) rather a molehill than a fort against an enemy."

The colonists must now have bitterly regretted the eight thousand guilders which, as we learn from later records, proved the actual cost of the fine new church, a sum which might well have fitted out a stout defence around the little colony. Feeling had already begun to run high against Kieft and his mismanagement; but for the present no one had any thought except for immediate defence against the enemy. Fearing that their appeal to the West India Company might prove insufficient, the Eight Men ten days later sent a still more pressing letter addressed this time to the "Noble, High and Mighty Lords, the Noble Lords, the States-General of the United Netherlands Provinces." This appeal sets forth that

"we poor inhabitants of New Netherland were here in the spring pursued by these wild Heathen and barbarous Savages with fire and sword. Daily in our houses and fields have they cruelly murdered men and women, and with hatchets

Desperate Condition of Colonists 1643

and tomahawks struck little children dead in their parents' arms, or before their doors, or carried them away into bondage. The houses and grain barracks are burnt with the produce; cattle of all description are slain and destroyed, and such as remain must perish this approaching winter for the want of fodder. Almost every place is abandoned. We, wretched people, must skulk with wives and little ones that still survive in poverty together in and around the fort at the Manahates where we are not safe even for an hour; whilst the Indians daily threaten to overwhelm us with it. Very little can be planted this autumn and much less in the spring; so that it will come to pass that all of us who will yet save our lives must of necessity perish next year of hunger and sorrow with our wives and children unless our God have pity on us.

"We are all here, from the smallest to the greatest, devoid of counsel and means, wholly powerless. The enemy meets with scarce any resistance. The garrison consists of but fifty to sixty soldiers unprovided with ammunition. Fort Amsterdam, utterly defenceless, stands open to the enemy day and night.

"The Company have few or no effects here (as the Director has informed us). Were it not for this, there would have been still time to receive assistance from the English at the East ere all had gone to ruin; and we wretched settlers, whilst we must abandon all our substance are exceedingly poor.

"These heathens are strong in might. They have formed an alliance with seven other Nations, are well provided with guns, powder and lead, which they purchased for beaver from the private traders who have had for a long time free range here; the rest they take from our fellow-countrymen, whom they murder. In fine, we experience the greatest misery, which must astonish a Christian heart to see or to hear."

The case of the settlers under the shadow

Peace Declared 1645

of the fort, and of the fugitives who crouched within its feeble shelter, was pitiable indeed. The wonder is that the fort and its garrison survived at all ; but the colonists struggled on under difficulties and discouragements, as their countrymen have had a way of doing the world over ; and, at last, in the summer of 1645, a general peace was declared between the colonists and the natives. After four years of warfare, the settlers breathed again. Men went out into the fields by day in quiet and slept at night without dream of war-whoops or fire-brands. The coming of peace, however, did not diminish the importance of the fort. It still continued the *cor cordium* of New Netherland. The weightiest communications addressed to Their High Mightinesses, the States-General, were dated from the fort and here counsel was taken on things spiritual and temporal, peaceful and warlike. Here, too, punishments were meted out, and the punishments of our ancestors were formidable matters.

The Dutch archives contain accounts of the discipline of a female, who was found guilty of slandering the Reverend Everardus Bogardus, Pastor of the church within the fort. It was decreed that the "said female" should be obliged to appear at the sound of the bell before the Governor and Council in the fort, and there solemnly to declare that

Kieft's Discipline 1638-46

she knew the dominie to be honest and pious, and that she had "lied falsely." Sterner punishments awaited evil doers of the male sex. Jan Hobbes, for theft, was put to the torture and two soldiers found guilty of blasphemy were condemned to ride the wooden horse, an animal more awful than that within the Trojan walls. It stood under the shadow of the fort, and on its razor-back the criminal was seated, with iron stirrups and leaden weights attached to his unlucky legs.

Kieft, who in spite of his shortcomings was a rigid disciplinarian, achieved order, where anarchy had formerly reigned among the garrison at the fort. He laid down a strict code of laws and penalties, applying especially to those on guard. This code reads :

"Section I : Whosoever abuses the name of God when on guard shall pay a fine for the first offence of ten stivers ; for the second, twenty stivers ; for the third, thirty stivers.

"Section II : He, who speaks scandal of a comrade during the time he is on guard, shall pay thirty stivers.

"Section III : He, who arrives tipsy or intoxicated for duty, shall pay twenty stivers.

"Section IV : He, who neglects to be present without sufficient cause, fifty stivers.

"Lastly, He who, when the duty on guard is well performed, and the sun is risen and reveillé beat, fires a musket without his corporal's orders, shall pay one guilder."

This code of military law was read aloud by a corporal every time the soldiers went on guard, that none might plead ignorance as an

Letter from West India Company 1645

excuse for failure in obedience. Besides this reading of the code, the corporal's daily task was the superintendence of the cleaning and charging of muskets, the examination of cartridge-boxes, and, most difficult of all, the prevention of the smuggling of liquor into the fort. The many records of drunken frays among the soldiers bear witness that this part of the corporal's duty was sometimes slighted, or else that the soldiers had opportunities of securing liquor when they were off duty.

"William the Testy," with his sharp gray eyes and his round, red face was always on the watch for offenders, and woe to the laggard coming sleepily to his post after reveillé had called to duty at daybreak, or to him who loitered with his sweetheart by the shore when tattoo had sounded at nine o'clock in the evening!

About the time of the closing of the Indian war, the colonists received a document from the Assembly of the XIX. or Governing Board of the West India Company containing valuable advice, which like much good advice came rather late. The letter recommended that colonists should be compelled to settle near each other in towns and villages in order to be able to give mutual assistance in time of danger; and it further advised the repairing of Fort Amsterdam, which was now in such a state of utter ruin and collapse, that men went

Repairs to Fort Ordered 1645

in and out over the wall instead of through the gate. This repairing was ordered to be done with stone, and the expense was estimated at a sum between twenty and twenty-five thousand guilders. In addition to the masonry, the earthworks were to be restored with "good clay and firm sods" and the soldiers were to be employed as laborers to reduce the cost.

A list of the officers, employees and garrison to be engaged, together with their salaries is annexed, and includes,

1	Director,	3000 fl
1	Clergyman,	1440 "
1	Constable, (gunner)	240 "
1	Schoolmaster and Sexton,	360 "
1	Provost,	180 "
1	Corporal to act as Gunsmith,	180 "
1	Commander,	720 "
1	Ensign,	540 "
2	Sergeants,	600 "
2	Corporals,	432 "
1	Drummer,	156 "
4	Cadets,	720 "
40	Soldiers,	6240 "
1	Surgeon,	300 "
1	Skipper,	300 "
4	Sailors,	624 "
1	Boy,	108 "

A florin was equivalent to about forty cents. This number of florins therefore represented

Kieft Superseded 1647

less than half the same number of dollars, so that the pay of a common soldier in the Fort Amsterdam garrison was about fifty dollars yearly, while the Director himself received between twelve and fifteen hundred. Even at these moderate wages, the West India Company was losing money on its venture, and its books show that the colony of New Netherland had cost the Company more than half a million guilders, over and above returns, during the years from 1626 to 1644 inclusive. As Kieft and his mismanagement were responsible for much of the loss it is not surprising that his recall was agreed upon by the Assembly in old Amsterdam, greatly to the delight of the settlers in New Amsterdam, by whom he was thoroughly detested.

The newly appointed Director, Petrus Stuyvesant, came over heralded by the fame of his statesmanship and military powers. He had been Governor of Curaçao, and the loss of his leg at the siege of St. Martins (then occupied by the Portuguese) had established his claim to doughty soldiership. Now, surely, the seaport fortress of New Netherland might look for better days. This old soldier would see to it at once that its defences were put in order and its guns made ready to belch defiance at the foe.

No wonder that there was much rejoicing throughout the little Dutch town on the point

Stuyvesant's Arrival 1647

of Manhattan Island, on that May morning in 1647, when the news spread abroad that the fleet bearing the new governor, Director Stuyvesant, his lady and their suite, had cast anchor in the bay. The inhabitants in their best attire thronged to the shore below the fort, and the fort itself brave in banners opened salute from all its great guns at once. The four ships in the harbor responded with similar salutes, and afterward Stuyvesant came ashore amid much waving of flags and a tumultuous greeting from the people.

This was a gala day long remembered, but by no means the only one in the history of the fort, which was the scene of most of the merrymaking as well as most of the solemn ceremonials of the colony. On *Nieuw Jaar* and *Kerstydt* (Christmas) the Governor's house was ablaze with candles and the young men and maidens danced in the "entry." On *Paas* (Easter), the villagers collected in the stone church at the summons of those Porto Rico bells, whose chimes were rung by a "klink" or bell-ringer, who lodged under the belfry in the fort, and over the door of whose chamber was carved a quaint inscription dedicating "the holy cell" to the Son of Peace.

Of all the festivals which were held in the old fort none was gayer or more memorable than that celebrated one day in February,

New Amsterdam Becomes a City 1653

1653, when the village of New Amsterdam became the *City* of New Amsterdam. On this day, the city fathers marched to the *kerck* in the fort in solemn procession, preceded by the bell-ringer bearing cushions of state for the pews of the dignitaries. At their head strode Peter Stuyvesant the stout-hearted hero described by Irving, with his regimental coat decorated with brass buttons from chin to waistband, the skirts turned up at the corners, and separating at the back to display the seat of a sumptuous pair of brimstone-color breeches ; his hair standing out on each side stiff with pomatum, his wooden leg set boldly in advance, one hand firmly grasping his gold-headed cane, the other holding the hilt of his doughty sword.

All these festivals and merrymakings were very pleasant, no doubt, and perhaps served their purpose in easing the strained relations between the citizens of New Amsterdam and the West India Company, with which they were continually at odds ; but they did little toward solving the problems of defence from hostile attack which perpetually stared the settlers in the face. The relations with the neighboring settlers, the Swedes on one side and the English on the other, were so uncertain that in a petition to the States-General, the first application for a municipal charter, the burghers humbly beseech Their High Mightinesses

Character of Stuyvesant

"to be pleased to determine and so to establish and order the Boundaries of this Province, that all causes of difference, disunion, and trouble may be cut off and prevented; that Their High Mightinesses' subjects may live and dwell in peace and quietness, and enjoy their liberty as well in trade and commerce as in intercourse and settled limits. (2d.) That Their High Mightinesses would be pleased to preserve us in peace with the neighboring Republics, Colonies, and others, Their High Mightinesses' allies."

This mild request to be kept in prosperity and at peace with all the world in these troublous times was far from being fulfilled. Not only did the neighbors continue to snarl at each others heels over questions of boundary, etc., but the Governor himself, to whose coming the New Netherlanders had looked forward with such delight, had grown wellnigh as unpopular as his predecessor in the eyes of the colonists. He early displayed the arbitrariness of his disposition, when in one of the first contests with the burghers over some injustice of Kieft's he exclaimed, "These boorish brutes would hereafter endeavor to knock me over also; but I shall now manage it so that they will have their bellies full in all time to come."

On another occasion when Cornelis Melyn pleaded for grace till the result of his appeal to the court over-seas could be heard, the Director sternly replied, "Had I known, Melyn, that you would have divulged our

Stuyvesant's Threats

sentence, or brought it before Their High Mightinesses, I should have had you hanged forthwith on the highest tree in New Netherland."

The irascible old Governor afterward made his censure still more general, and announced that as it had come to his knowledge that some people were thinking of appealing from his judgments, he wished it understood that should any one attempt such a piece of insubordination, "I would have him made a foot shorter, pack the pieces off to Holland and let him appeal in that way."

Director Stuyvesant did not know the men with whom he had to deal, if he thought to frighten them into subserviency. Adriaen van der Donck and his fellows fought stubbornly for their rights and privileges and especially against unjust taxation. They declared they would not be unequally taxed for the support of the government and the strengthening of defences, and refused the amounts demanded, unless the Governor would supply a fair amount from the revenues derived from excise, etc.

The result of all these petty bickerings was of course most disastrously felt in the condition of the fort. Times continued hard, the Company niggardly, the Governor tyrannical, and the burghers recalcitrant. In March, 1653, the Director sent the following appealing letter

Stuyvesant's Letter to Burgomaster and Schepens 1653

to the burgomasters and schepens of the little town:

"Honorable, Dear and Distinguished [Friends]:

"We see with great grief the damages done to the walls of the fort by hogs, especially now again in the spring, when the grass comes out. We made an order concerning it last year at the request of the Select Men, who promised properly to fence in the fort and to keep the hogs meanwhile from the walls. But seeing, after the lapse of a year, that nothing or at least only little has been done and that what has been done at the fort has again been destroyed by the pigs, as may daily be learned, we are compelled to enter a protest about the non-fulfilment of the promise, being told that the failure of it, the destruction of the walls and all our works, is caused by the Select Men having been superseded and their authority and duties transferred to Burgomasters and Schepens, who had accepted to do the work. How this is, we do not know, but we see, to our trouble and shame, the pigs daily on the walls, busy with their destruction. Therefore we request Burgomasters and Schepens to give an order in accordance with the beforementioned promise and prevent the pigs. Else we shall be compelled to carry out our former order. Relying thereon we remain, Honorable, Dear, Distinguished [Friends],

"Your well-meaning friend,

"P. STUYVESANT."

"The Burgomasters and Schepens decided, upon the letter of the Director-General, provisionally to engage a herdsman and in the meantime to make the fence as quickly as possible, the Director-General having promised to furnish the posts. Done, etc., this 31st of March, 1653.

(Signed) "ARENT VAN HATTEM,
WILH. BEECKMAN,
ALLARD ANTONY."

Hogs Damage the Fort 1653

It would appear that the herdsman did not understand his business very well, or else that there were more hogs than people in New Amsterdam, for the records five months later harp on the same old complaint from the Governor:

"Respected and Very Dear:

"We cannot, consistently with duty, omit calling your Worships' attention to the injurious and intolerable destruction, which we, to our great dissatisfaction, daily behold the hogs committing on the newly finished works of the fort, whence the ruin thereof will certainly ensue.

"And whereas Burgomasters and Schepens, in violation of their solemn promises made both in writing and orally, will not lend a hand to repairing and strengthening the same, we can certainly expect they will adopt measures and take care, that what we with great pains and labor have brought so far will not again be destroyed by hogs, and thus all our labor be rendered useless, it being certainly the practice in no place to permit cattle to run at large to the injury and damage both of individuals and the public. Without more remonstrance then, in case this matter is not speedily and promptly attended to by your Worships, we hereby protest, that necessity compels us to provide therein by the following Ordinance and Placard, whereof we by these presents, do first notify the Burgomasters and Schepens, and clear ourselves of all damage and injury that may follow therefrom. Done at Fort Amsterdam in New Netherland the 12th August, 1653.

(Signed) "P. STUYVESANT."

"City Hall, Tuesday, the 12 August, 1653, 4 o'clock in the afternoon. Present.—Arent Van Hattem, Marten Krigier, Poulus Leendersen, and M. Van Gheel.

Meeting of Schepens 1653

"Having taken into consideration the foregoing Remonstrance of the Honble General, the same is postponed until the arrival of the other Schepens, who are absent.

"Wednesday afternoon Burgomasters and Schepens again met except Pieter Couwenhoven. Adjourned to 8 o'clock to-morrow.

"Burgomasters and Schepens of this City New Amsterdam assembled together.

"Having seen the Remonstrance of the Honble General and his complaint concerning the damage the hogs are daily doing to the fort and the newly erected works, the Burgomasters and Schepens do therefore order their Court messenger to notify the Burghers that every one of them shall take care of his hogs or keep them in the sty until the fort and recently constructed works have been fenced in with palisades to preserve said works from damage, or in default thereof, such persons shall be held responsible for the damage and injury. Thus done and enacted this 14 August A^o. 1653, New Amsterdam. (Signed) Arent Van Hattem, 1653, Martin Krigier, Pouls L. Van die Grift, Wilh: Beeckman, Pieter Wolfersen, Maximilianus Van Gheel."

The flurry of the threatened English invasion in 1653 brought about some improvement in the condition of the fort, as well as in the defences to the northward along the Singel : but the zeal for fortifying died out with the alarm and was finally buried when on July 18, 1654, amid much bell-ringing and public rejoicing, a proclamation was affixed to the wall of the *Stadt-Huys* announcing that a compact of "Peace, Union, and Confederation" had been made and concluded at Westminster between the commissioners of the Lord Protector and the ambassadors of the Lords States-General.

Rumors of War 1664

For ten years longer the old fort mouldered peacefully away, as tranquil in its decay as though it had received a certified discharge from active duty. But at length, in the early summer of 1664, startling rumors began to fly about of a threatened invasion, which might drive the hogs off the earthworks once more and set the rusty guns to a trial of their strength. Stuyvesant's troublous rule, after a duration of seventeen years, was about to be brought to a violent, if not untimely end at last. Shortly after the Restoration of Charles II., that monarch by a royal charter ("the most despotic instrument recorded in the colonial archives of England") conveyed to his brother, the Duke of York, a vast tract of American land, including on the east the country between the Saint Croix and the Pemaquid, and on the west the tract between the Connecticut and the Delaware rivers with all adjacent islands, thus completely obliterating the Dutch ownership of New Netherland.

Without warning to the Dutch of approaching hostilities the Duke despatched four vessels, the *Guinea*, the *Elias*, the *Martin*, and the *William and Nicholas*. These ships bore five hundred soldiers and had also on board Richard Nicolls, who was to be Deputy-Governor of the conquered province, Sir George Cartwright, Robert Carr and Samuel

English Fleet Sent to New Netherland 1664

Maverick. These commissioners were ordered to take possession of New Netherland and establish an English settlement to be known as New York. Rumors of the proposed onslaught reached New Netherland from Boston, where the English squadron had put in for further reinforcement; but the suddenness of the attack gave little time for preparation of defence, and the Governor himself came flying back post haste from Fort Orange,[1] whither he had been called by some disturbance among the Indians.

On the 28th of August, 1664, the English fleet came to an anchor in Gravesend Bay, and the garrison at Fort Amsterdam knew that the struggle was at hand and that sure defeat awaited them. Stuyvesant's position was a most difficult one. The inhabitants of the town had no spirit for resistance, the fort was in no state of readiness for a siege, the hostile vessels were already preparing to open fire; but still he strove to parley. On September 3d, a deputation was sent to Nicolls, the English commander, but he refused discussion.

"When may we visit you again?" the deputation asked.

"On Thursday," answered Nicolls, "for to-morrow I will speak with you at Manhattan."

[1] Albany.

Negotiations with Nicolls 1664

"Friends are welcome there," answered the Dutchman diplomatically.

"Raise the white flag of peace," answered Nicolls, "for I shall come with ships of war and soldiers."

While these negotiations were proceeding the burghers of New Amsterdam were constantly sending remonstrances to Stuyvesant and his advisers demanding a surrender. These remonstrances set forth the weakness of their situation :

"We shall now examine," they said, "your Honors' fortress. You know in your own consciences that it is incapable of making head against so powerful an enemy. Granting even that it could hold out against its assailant, one, two, three, five, or six months (which to our sorrow it cannot) it is still undeniable that it cannot save the smallest portion of our entire city, our property, and, what is dearer to us, our wives and children from total ruin ; for after considerable bloodshed even the fort itself could not be preserved. Wherefore, to prevent and arrest all the aforesaid misfortune, we humbly and in bitterness of heart, implore your Honors not to reject the conditions of so generous a foe, but to be pleased to meet him in the speediest, best, and most reputable manner."

Stuyvesant himself, in the letter which he afterwards sent home to the West India Company excusing his surrender, enlarged still further upon the hopelessness of defence.

"The fort," he wrote, "is situated in an untenable place where it was located on the first discovery of New Netherland for the purpose of resisting any attack of barbarians rather than an assault of European arms. Having within

Condition of the Fort 1664

pistol-shot on north and northeasterly sides higher ground than that on which it stands, so that, notwithstanding the walls and works are raised the highest on that side, people standing and walking on that high ground can see the soles of the feet of those on the esplanade and bastions of the fort, where the view is not obstructed by the houses and church in it, and by the gabions on the wall.

"Secondly, the fort was and is encompassed only by a slight wall, two or three feet thick backed by coarse gravel, not above eight, nine, or ten feet high in some places, in others higher according to the fall of the ground.

"Thirdly, it is for the most part crowded all round-about with buildings better adapted for a cidatel than for defence against an open enemy. The houses are in many places higher than the wall and bastions, and render these wholly exposed. Most of the houses also have cellars not eight rods distant from the walls of the fort ; in some places, not two or three, and at one point scarce a rod from the wall, so that whoever is master of the city can readily approach with scaling ladders from the aforesaid houses the walls of the fort, which is unprovided with either wet or dry ditch ; and also if need be run a mine from the so close adjoining cellars and blow the place up. Besides this, the fort was and is without either well or cistern."

The struggle was clearly hopeless and at last the old hero consented to the surrender. By the articles of capitulation Stuyvesant and his comrades were permitted to march out carrying arms, with drums beating, colors flying and matches lighted. On the *vlag-spil* in the corner of the fort, the English banner was raised, the name of the fort changed to Fort James and the bloodless victory accomplished.

Treaty of Breda 1667

The treaty of Breda, signed in July, 1667, confirmed England's possession of New Amsterdam. For nine years English rule prevailed in the colony, and English officers sunned their red coats on the bastions of the fort; but, before yielding the supremacy, the Dutch made one more gallant struggle crowned by temporary success. In the spring of 1673, Holland and England being then again at war, the States-General despatched a fleet of five vessels under command of Commodores Cornelis Evertsen, Jr. and Jacob Benckes, Captains Antonio Colvé, Nicholaes Boes and Abram Van Zyll. At the end of July, this fleet appeared in the bay, and their commander sent an abrupt summons to Deputy-Governor Manning, then in control of the fort, calling for immediate surrender. Manning, who was in control in the absence of Governor Lovelace, the successor of Nicolls, strove to delay the issue by parley, but the Dutch would not be put off, and really in the condition of the fort, which was as usual in a chronic state of disrepair, platforms and gun-carriages out of order, only four gun-sponges and but seventy or eighty gunners with neither spade nor handspike nor other implement of defence, it is hard to see what course but surrender was open to him, unless he was willing to see all the thatched roofs of the town go up in flame as soon as the enemy opened fire. The

Attack of the Dutch 1673

surrender, however, was bitterly resented by the authorities in England, and a series of charges was brought against "John Manning, Commander-in-Chiefe of James Forte." These charges set forth that on or about the 28th day of July, 1673, "he having notice of an enemy's fleet coming into the bay," did not endeavor as he might to put the garrison into a state of defence. That on the 30th of July "he suffered the said enemyes with their Fleet to come and moare their ships under the fort." That he permitted boats to come ashore "loaden with men," and, worst of all, "that Hee strooke his Majestie's Flag before the ennemy that had landed, were in sight of the fort." There was so much swearing and counter-swearing in the course of this trial that it is difficult now, after the lapse of more than two centuries, to form any judgment of the rights of the controversy ; but it is evident that poor Manning made a convenient scapegoat and, though he prayed on "the bended knees of his harte" that his excuses might be "pondred," he was found guilty of cowardice, and his sword broken over his head in symbol of his disqualification for office.

But the punishment of Manning did not help the British to recover New Amsterdam. The fort was taken, and though Manning strove to make terms stipulating that "all officers and

Dutch Triumphant 1673

souldiers of ffort James should march out with armes, Drumes beating, cullers flying, Bagg and Baggage without Hindrance or Molesta-c̃on," yet the agreement was not kept; for Manning declared bitterly afterward that Col. Calvert "ingaged, his hand on his Brest," that upon "ye word and Honor of a Gentleman, they should be Puncktually P'formed; but p'fidiously breaking his faith and his word."

The Dutch were triumphant. On the surrender of Manning, the commander of the Dutch fleet took possession of the town and the fort. Down came the English flag once more, and up went the ensign of Holland. The name of New York was changed to New Orange, and Fort James became Fort "Willem Henrik." Antony Colvé, one of the commanders of the fleet, was made Governor of the colony and commander-in-chief at the fort.

During his rule the town was practically under martial law. At sunset each night, the guard at the fort, called the *hoofd wagt*, delivered over the keys of the city to the Mayor, who proceeded to lock the gates and place the *burger wagt*, or citizen guard, on night watch. In the morning at sunrise this guard was relieved, and the Mayor again made the rounds of the city, unlocking gates.[1] Mrs. Sigourney,

[1] Instructions to Jacobus Van Der Water, as Mayor of New Orange, done at Fort Willem Henrik 12 January, 1674. "The

Fort James 1674

in a poem commemorating this time and custom, writes:

> "Hail mighty city!—high must be his fame
> Who round thy bounds at sunrise now should walk.
> Still art thou lovely what so e'er thy name,
> New Amsterdam, New Orange or New York."

The condition of the fort at the end of the second Dutch occupation was described by a traveller who visited it soon after it had passed into English hands. He says:

"It is not large. It has four points or batteries. It has no moat outside, but is enclosed with a double row of palisades. It is built on the foundation with quarry stone. The parapet is of earth. It is well provided with cannon for the most part of iron, though there were some small brass pieces all bearing the mark or arms of the Netherlanders. The garrison is small. There is a well of fine water dug in the fort by the English, contrary to the opinion of the Dutch, who supposed the fort was built upon rock, and had therefore never attempted any such thing. There is indeed some indication of stone there, for along the edge of the water below the fort there is a very large rock extending apparently under the fort. It has only one gate, and

---

Mayor shall take good care that in the morning the gates are opened at sunrise and locked again in the evening with sunset, for which purpose he shall go to the principal guard and there address himself to the commanding officer and demand to conduct him thither at least a sergeant with six soldiers all armed with guns. With these he shall proceed to the fort to fetch the keys and return these again there as soon as the gates are opened or shut."

that is on the land side, opening upon a broad plane or street called the Broadway or Beaverway. Over this gate are the arms of the Duke of York. During the time of the Dutch there were two gates, another on the water side; but the English have closed it and made a battery there."

New Orange again becomes New York 1674

In 1674, New Orange was returned by treaty to the British and resumed permanently its title of New York. The fort also resumed its name of Fort James, but only for a short time; since on the accession of William and Mary it was rechristened in honor of the king, and finally, when Anne, who married Prince George of Denmark, ascended the throne, it received the name of Fort George, and under that title it continued until its final demolition at the close of the Revolutionary War.

From beginning to end of its long life, this strange fortress continued a picturesque cumberer of the ground, useless in war, worse than useless in peace; and when at last it succumbed before the march of commerce there were few to regret its fall.

The authorities for this paper are drawn chiefly from the Documents Relating to the Colonial History of the State of New York, the Documentary History of New York, O'Callaghan's History of New Netherland, the accounts of their travels, written by Captain

De Vries, Father Jogues and others, and the early City Records, now in process of translation from the Dutch, which by the courtesy of the translator, Mr. Berthold Fernow, I have been enabled to see in proof.

Barnard College

343 MADISON AVENUE

COURSES IN AMERICAN HISTORY

For Undergraduates. General course, reading, recitations and lectures.—Three hours a week: H. A. Cushing, A.M.

For Graduates. Political History of the Colonies and of the American Revolution.—This investigation course, extending through two years, deals in the first year with the settlement of the Colonies and their development in the seventeenth century, and in the second year with the growth of the system of colonial administration, the conflict with the French, and the revolt of the Colonies. The work of the students consists chiefly in the study of topics from the original sources, with a formal account of the results of such study.—Two hours a week for two years: Professor Herbert L. Osgood, Ph.D.

These courses are open not only to candidates for degrees, but to special students who can show ability to read French and German, and can satisfy the Dean and Faculty of their general competence.

The Southern Workman and Hampton School Record ⚜ ⚜ ⚜ ⚜ ⚜

is a twenty-page monthly published by the Hampton Institute in Virginia in the interest of the two races it represents—the Negro and the Indian.

It is a record of the practical working out of the race problems, not only at Hampton but at Tuskegee and other schools, and contains much interesting matter from graduates in the field and from prominent students and writers representing the best thought of the country.

A few pages are devoted each month to the local affairs of the School, to letters from Negroes and Indians in the South and West, to folk-lore, and to reviews of books bearing upon race problems.

Subscription, $1.00 a year. This may be sent to

REV. H. B. FRISSELL,
HAMPTON, VA.

Half Moon Series

Published in the Interest of the New York City History Club.

VOLUME I. NUMBER IX.

OLD GREENWICH.

BY ELIZABETH BISLAND.

Antiquity of Greenwich Village

NO part of the City of New York has so good a claim to antiquity as Greenwich Village. Before Hendrik Hudson steered his *Half Moon* through the Narrowe, before New Amsterdam was dreamed of, this spot was occupied by an Indian village, whose exact locality corresponds very nearly to that of the present Gansevoort Market.

There is some reason to suppose that those Indians who came out in their canoes to Hudson's ship, who brought him vegetables and fruits, and who, in the enthusiasm of their first intoxication upon European strong waters, caused him so much trouble, were from this village, which was called by the early settlers —with their almost hysterical uncertainty as to Indian orthography and pronunciation—in-

Early Names of Greenwich

differently Sappokanican, Shawbackanica, and Tapokanico.

As soon as Governor Kieft had purchased the Island of Manhattan he undertook to set aside certain portions for the special use of the Dutch West India Company, the title of which should be vested in perpetuity. Of these four farms or bouweries thus reserved Sappokanican was number three, and was set down in the deeds as the Bossen Bouwerie—or the "Farm in the Woods." It was known sometimes by the one name and sometimes by the other until, under English rule, its title was finally changed, about 1721, to Greenwich, and this still clings to it despite its having been swallowed up in the general mass of Greater New York, as sections of London are still known as Chelsea, Kensington, or Knightsbridge, although only antiquarians can distinguish the boundaries of the original villages.

There appears to have been the best of reasons for the favor in which this section was held by the intelligent savage and his discriminating successor. It was markedly healthful, owing to a substratum of fifty feet of clear sand underlying the fertile topsoil. It was well wooded, and gave, on the river side, upon a charming beach washed by waters teeming with fish. The Zandtberg hills that crossed the tract were in some places fully a hundred feet above the tide level; to the south was a

Bestavaar's Kill

marsh much affected by wild-fowl, and the bright, quick brook that emptied into the river afforded numerous trout.

This brook—called by the Dutch, Bestavaar's Kill, and by the English, Manetta Water—marked the boundaries of the bouwerie. Although no longer visible it flows in diminished volume in its old channel. Its east branch rises east of Fifth Avenue between Twentieth and Twenty-first Streets, whence it flows in nearly a straight line to the southwest corner of Union Square ; thence in a slightly curving line to the junction with the west branch (which rises east of Sixth Avenue between Fifteenth and Sixteenth Streets), near the middle of the block bounded by Eleventh and Twelfth Streets and Fifth and Sixth Avenues ; from this junction it flows to Fifth Avenue and Clinton Place ; thence across Washington Square through Minetta Street to the North River, between Charleton and Houston Streets.

There is no record of the passing away of the Indian village, but probably Dutch rum and frequent hostilities with the new settlers succeeded in depopulating it of savages early in the Colonial period. When Wouter Van Twiller without undue ostentation transferred the title of the Bossen Bouwerie from the West India Company to himself and immediately set about turning it into a tobacco farm,

Van Twiller's Tobacco Farm 1633

there were apparently no Indians in occupation to object to his agriculture or to discommode him in his questionable occupation of the place. His farm buildings—as far as is known—were the first houses built north of the fort (the date was 1633) and the little cluster of cabins that gradually gathered about them formed the nucleus of the future Greenwich Village. This annexation of the West India Company's property and the building of the farm-houses took place some dozen years or so after the formal colonization of the New Netherlands, and makes the village the respectable age of rather more than two hundred and sixty years.

Whatever may be thought of Van Twiller's honesty, his judgment as an agriculturist was unimpeachable. The tobacco grown on the new farm was the best in the colony, and made a name for itself abroad. In 1638, two inspectors were appointed to regulate the cultivation of what was then the staple export of the colony, in order that it might maintain the high character it had achieved in foreign countries. Later, the Governor found it necessary to remonstrate with the farmers for planting tobacco to the exclusion of food crops, a practice which brought about a scarcity in the new colony, and obliged him to put an embargo upon the exportation of all bread-stuffs.

Visit of the Labadists 1679

It is not quite clear whether or not the Bossen Bouwerie reverted to the ownership of the West India Company after Van Twiller was recalled in disgrace. Governor Stuyvesant refers casually in a State paper to the "little village of Sapokanigan," but no clue as to its title can be inferred from what he says.

The transference of the colony to English rule left no mark upon the hamlet at the forest's edge, which lay a little to the north of the present Cunard steamship piers. The next definite mention of it is in the Journal of the Labadists in 1679. Their minute and painstaking record of all they saw in the colony to which they had been sent to find a home for the sect founded by Jean de Labadie, gives the best picture obtainable of life and conditions in the town of New York and in the surrounding villages. Referring to their visit to "Sapokanikee"—still another version of that flexible name—which they passed through on foot while exploring Manhattan Island, they speak approvingly of the fertility of the soil, of the excellent beer they drank there, and of the sweet odors in the air, which were so delicious as to cause them to pause many times and endeavor, fruitlessly, to discover their origin—"we stood still because we did not know what it was we were meeting," they say. Hendrik Hudson remarked upon

Nature's Bounty

the pleasing perfumes he smelled upon his first visit here, and it has been customary to attribute these to the blossoming of grape flowers, but as he and the Labadists were both here in the autumn, this explanation will not serve, though Callaghan in a later description of the neighborhood says: "The entire land, both forest and bottom land, was moreover covered with vines, climbing up the loftiest trees, or creeping along the lowly valleys, and bearing loads of grapes, some white, some blue, some large, some small, some very juicy, and all promising, if properly cultivated, an ample return to the vine dresser."

Van der Donck says, that in the river from the Sappokanican beach, lobsters, four and six feet long, were frequently captured, but were thought coarse and not such good eating as those of a lesser size. The oysters were enormous, and could be bought at from eight to ten stivers the hundred. The waters were full of shrimp and tortoise, and he remarks that "some persons prepare delicious dishes from water terrapin, which is luscious food." Wild turkeys, weighing from twenty to thirty pounds, were numerous in the woods surrounding the village, and so were deer and elk, the former being so fat in the early autumn as to spoil their meat. The edges of the swamp were full of wild raspberries, cran-

The Village in 1727

berries, and blackberries, while in the fields wild strawberries were so abundant that "people lay down and ate them to satiety."

In spite of its exposed condition, far from the protecting fort, so inviting a spot could not long want settlers. Several times the townspeople fled from epidemics to the salubrious little village, and by 1727 it was a flourishing settlement, connected with the city by an excellent road which followed very nearly the course of the present Greenwich Street. The inhabitants were mostly farmers and such few mechanics and artisans as served for the village needs, and the title of the place was fluctuating uncertainly between its two original names of Sappokanican and Bossen Bouwerie, and a new English one of Greenwich, when the fortunes of the place received a sudden uplift in the coming of Sir Peter Warren, "Knight of the Bath, Vice Admiral of the Red Squadron of the British Fleet, and Member of Parliament for the City and Liberty of Westminster"—as his monument in Westminster Abbey pompously sets forth. He—according to the same authority, and he had the honor to have his epitaph written by Dr. Samuel Johnson—"Derived his Descent from an Antient Family of Ireland," and the virtues attributed to him by the monument he must certainly have possessed in some measure, since he was in command of H. M. S. *Grafton*,

Sir Peter Warren's Mansion

and gazetted to a Post Captaincy at the early age of twenty-four years.

It was in 1744 that Sir Chaloner Ogle left him in command of a squadron of sixteen sail on the Leeward Islands station, where in less than four months he captured twenty-four prizes, one of them a plate-ship with a cargo valued at £250,000. These prizes were sent to New York to be condemned, and, as appears from an advertisement in the *Weekly Post Boy* of June 30, 1744, Messieurs Stephen De Lancey & Co. were Captain Warren's agents for the sale of his French and Spanish loot. Captain Warren married Miss Susannah De Lancey, the daughter of his agent, and chose Greenwich as his home, purchasing some three hundred acres near the river. The estate was afterwards enlarged by a gift from the city, which gift was an acknowledgement of Sir Peter's services at Louisburg. The house stood some three hundred yards back from the river on an eminence that fell away in a gentle slope toward the water side. The main entrance was from the east ; and at the rear—on a level with the drawing-room, a dozen feet or so above the sloping hillside—was a broad veranda commanding the view westward to the Jersey Highlands, and southward down the bay, clear to the Staten Island hills. The grounds were laid out like an English park, planted with clumps of Lombardy

Division of the Warren Estate

poplars and a fine avenue of locust trees. Immediately about the house was a hedge of box, which afterward grew to noble proportions.

Here were born three daughters, Charlotte, Anne, and Susannah, and not until after the election of Sir Peter to Parliament did Lady Warren abandon her beautiful residence by the river side, and permanently remove to London. The three daughters grew up in course of time to be beauties and heiresses, and made brilliant marriages. Charlotte, the eldest, became Countess of Abingdon ; Anne, the second daughter, married Charles Fitzroy, Baron Southampton, and the youngest, Susannah, became the wife of a certain Colonel Skinner. On the death of Lady Warren the whole estate was broken up into three lots numbered A, B, and C, and for these the trustees threw dice in order to decide which daughter should have the right to a first choice. The lot containing the house fell to Lady Abingdon, and was sold by her to Abijah Hammond, who in turn sold it to Abraham Van Nest. It remained intact until 1865, when it was swept away by the rising tide of brick and mortar, and the beautiful avenues of locust trees and great box hedges were destroyed.

The rest of the estate was divided up into small holdings of ten or fifteen acres, and the

Colonial Assembly Meets at Greenwich

roads cut through them bore the names of Sir Peter's daughters—Skinner Road, is now part of Christopher Street ; Fitzroy Road lay very near to what is now Eighth Avenue from Fourteenth to Forty-second Streets, and Abingdon Road (later Love Lane) was on the line of Twenty-first Street. The only survival of this early nomenclature is to be found in Abingdon Square, but it was along the lines of this first parcelling out of the land that Greenwich developed, until the rectangular City Plan of 1811 rigidified its easy going methods of growth. Some traces of the old carelessness of method still are visible in such anomalies as that Fourth Street crosses Tenth, Eleventh, and Twelfth Streets nearly at right angles.

When the epidemic of small-pox attacked New York, Sir Peter, who was almost as important a personage in the colony as Governor Clinton, invited the Colonial Assembly to meet at his house, and the members were so pleased with the beauty and healthfulness of the site that it at once became the fashion for New Yorkers to seek health and recreation in the pretty rural village. Lady Warren's brother, Oliver De Lancey, built a country house there, which was confiscated later by the Revolutionists, because of his loyalty to the crown. Other rich men followed suit, among them William Bayard, the sugar refiner, James

The Fashionable Drive

Jauncy, and Abraham Mortier, Commissary to His Majesty's Forces, who, in 1760, purchased Richmond Hill, the southwestern outjut of the Zandtberg, and built there "a wooden building of massive architecture, with a lofty portico, supported by Ionic columns, the front walls decorated with pilasters of the same order, and its whole appearance distinguished by a Palladian ornament of rich though sober character." It was at Richmond Hill that Sir Jeffrey, afterward Lord, Amherst was entertained when he had ended those successful campaigns that broke the power of France in America.

The road to Greenwich was the fashionable drive of the period, lying—until 1767—along the water side through the present Greenwich Street, crossing Lispenard's Meadows and Manetta Water upon a raised causeway. This was apt to be wet after a rain, and for that reason the route was changed to the Post Road—the present Bowery—whence it turned along Greenwich Lane to the Obelisk erected as a monument to the memory of General Wolfe (which caused this to be also called Monument or Obelisk Lane), then by the Great Kiln or Southampton Road (the present Gansevoort Street) to the river, and so homeward again along the riverside. Parties of pleasure to the country houses were frequent, and because of the perennial thirst of

Removal of the Potter's Field 1797

that generation whenever diverting itself, many small taverns sprang up beside the way. A lady from Boston, visiting New York in the winter of 1768, mentions in her letters home the excellent sleighing to be had on this road, and the many drinkables offered her. She says:

"We met fifty or sixty slays that day; they fly with great swiftness, and some are so furious they 'le turn out of their way for none but a loaden cart."

A pauper cemetery lay along the route of this fashionable drive, near the present Madison Square, but to give space for an arsenal, in 1797 it was moved to what is now Washington Square, still on the line of the drive and still causing great disatisfaction to the gay world, who found the squalid pauper funerals a melancholy *memento mori* as they interrupted their summer afternoon drive, or slackened the passage of the furious "slays."—When the Square was laid out in 1823, the Potter's Field, which had long been disused, was swept away, but the excavations for the foundation of the Washington Arch, in 1890, brought to light some few remaining relics of the past in the shape of broken tombstones. There is a tradition that, in 1823, when the remains were removed the coffin of a child fell open and displayed one of those abnormal posthumous growths of hair, the remains of

Richmond Hill

the nameless little pauper being entirely shrouded in a mass of blonde curls.

A small triangular space at the corner of Eleventh Street and Sixth Avenue, is all that remains of the Jewish Cemetery of New York. The first Beth Haim or Place of Rest was just south of Chatham Square; this was closed early in the present century and the Beth Haim in Greenwich was purchased by the congregation of Sharith Israel, and in its turn was obliterated by the opening of Eleventh Street, in 1830.

The Revolution brought no great changes to Greenwich. General, and afterwards Senator, Richard Henry Lee, of Virginia, made the village his home during the Session of Congress in 1789. Richmond Hill was used for a time by General Washington, as his headquarters, and then passed into the hands of Vice-President Adams, when Washington went to live in Franklin Square. Mrs. Adams was much pleased with it and wrote to her sister of the surrounding park "that nature has so lavishly displayed her beauties she has scarcely left anything for her handmaid, art, to perform." Gulian Verplanck, writing in *The Talisman* in 1829, gives a description of a Vice-Presidential dinner-party:

"There in the centre of the table sat Vice-President Adams in full dress, with his bag and *solitaire*, his hair

Richmond Hill Acquired by Aaron Burr

frizzled out on each side of his face. On his right sat Baron Steuben, our royalist republican disciplinarian general. On his left was Mr. Jefferson, who had just returned from France, conspicuous in his red waistcoat and breeches, the fashion of Versailles. Opposite sat Mrs. Adams with her cheerful, intelligent face. She was placed between the Count de Moustiers, the French Ambassador, in his red-heeled shoes and earrings, and the grave polite Mr. Van Birket the learned and able envoy of Holland. There, too, was Chancellor Livingstone, then still in the prime of life, so deaf as to make conversation with him difficult, yet so overflowing with eloquence and information that while listening to him the difficulty was forgotten."

When Aaron Burr became the owner of the place in 1797, he undertook, despite Mrs. Adams' judgment, to improve the grounds. He put a handsome gateway at the entrance —which is now the terminal of Macdougal Street—made many plantings, and arranged the ornamental water known as Burr's Pond, later a favorite place for skating. He lived here in considerable splendor for ten years, his beautiful daughter, Theodosia, who afterwards fell a victim to the Barataria pirates, being at the head of his house, and aiding him in entertaining the distinguished visitors whom he attracted about him—such. men as Volney, Talleyrand, Louis Philippe, and even Brant the Indian Chief. As Senator and Vice-President and one of the most brilliant figures of the New Republic he naturally took first place in the village as long as he lived there. It

Last Days of Richmond Hill

was from Richmond Hill that he went, on a morning in July, 1804, to fight his duel on the Weehawken Heights with Alexander Hamilton, and thus to end his own political career, as well as the life of his adversary.

Twenty-nine years later Philip Hone makes this record in his diary :

> "Wed : July 3, 1833.—The celebrated Col. Burr was married on Monday evening to the equally celebrated Mrs. Jumel, widow of Stephen Jumel. It is benevolent in her to keep the old man in his latter days. One good turn deserves another."

His marriage was a last desperate expedient, no more successful than those which had preceded it, and ended in Burr's seeking seclusion on Staten Island.

Verplanck says that Counsellor Benzon was the last person of importance to occupy Richmond Hill. It was, later, transformed into a theatre, sank to being the home of a circus and menagerie : the City Plan brought about the levelling of the height on which it stood, and the house, by ingenious methods being lowered with it, was turned into a road tavern and finally destroyed.

The coming of all this fashionable society greatly stimulated the growth of the little village, which threw out two humble offshoots, known as Lower Greenwich, which lay at what is now the foot of Spring Street, and Upper Greenwich, whose site was at the

The State Prison 1796

foot of the present Christopher Street. Some traces of the latter remain in the shape of a row of low wooden houses on West Street, between Tenth and Christopher Streets.

The next important event was the building of the State Prison, in 1796—Governor Jay's proclamation declaring that "It shall be considered the Prison for the whole State." It stood at the foot of Tenth Street, and portions of the old wall may still be seen, incorporated with those of the brewery that now occupies its site. The prison was about two hundred feet long and the twenty-two-foot stone wall surrounding it enclosed four acres of ground. A pier was built into the river to facilitate the landing of prisoners, as well as to accommodate De Klynn's ferry from New Jersey. The prison was opened on November 28, 1797, and seventy prisoners were transferred to it. It continued in use thirty years, until Sing Sing superseded it.

Among the convicts sent to this new penitentiary, was a man named Noah Gardner, who had been, through the efforts of the Society of Friends, reprieved at the gallows' foot. His crime was forgery, the penalty for which was death. Grant Thorburn referring to this case, says: "One day I went up to the Park to see a man hung. After gazing two hours at the gallows the Sheriff announced a reprieve. I must own I was disappointed."

Prison Labor

Gardner was anxious for occupation, and was allowed the tools of his trade, and began to manufacture boots. He undertook to teach his trade to his fellow-prisoners, and soon had organized a body of three hundred skilled shoemakers, and thus began the system of State Prison Manufactures. His services proved so valuable that after seven years of his life term had been served, a general petition secured his pardon, and, aided by loans and patronage, he became a successful shoe merchant. It is said that on one occasion he was bitterly reviling a workman for failure to deliver promised work, who humbly urged excuses of a sick wife and children. Failing to placate him, the workman cried out: "Yes, I know it 's a terrible thing to be disappointed. I remember I went to see you hanged and was so disappointed when the Sheriff read the reprieve."

After many years of respectability, Gardner gathered up all the money he could lay hands on, eloped with a young and pretty Quakeress, and was never heard of again.

The discipline appears to have been somewhat ineffective in this institution. It was in the work-rooms that frequent conspiracies were hatched, this assembling of the convicts being a new condition with which the authorities had not yet learned to cope. The first revolt was in 1799, and was only quelled by

Revolt of the Prisoners

firing upon the prisoners who had seized and made prisoners of their guards. In 1803, the prison was set on fire by the convicts, and they were only reduced to submission by the shooting of the ring-leaders. A year later the guards were again overpowered, shut into the wing of the prison, which was fired: many prisoners escaped, but the guards were rescued before the wing was consumed. Nevertheless, the people of Greenwich were disposed to consider the prison an attractive feature of the village.

An advertisement of the Greenwich Hotel, in *The Columbian*, of September 18, 1811, says:

"A few gentlemen may be accommodated with board and lodgings at this pleasant and healthy situation, a few doors from the State Prison. The Greenwich stage passes from this to the Federal Hall and returns five times a day."

These frequent trips of the stage showed how active was the intercourse between the village and the town. Previous to this time the stage had made but one trip daily, starting from the foot of John Street and charging a fare of two shillings either way. This was much too expensive a vehicle for the school children, who walked all the way to and from the Dutch Reformed School in Nassau Street, making their way across Manetta Brook, and

The Old Stage Lines

by Burr's Pond. The school-house stood upon the site of the present Mutual Life Insurance Building. This country road, which the school children followed, was the present Greenwich Street, south of Leroy. They could see across the open fields to Washington Square, where in that day a gallows used to be erected when criminals were to be executed.

Asa Hall's line of stages was established in 1816, leaving Greenwich on the even hours, and New York on the uneven ones, starting from the corner of Pine Street and Broadway, but taking a most devious course by reason of calling for all passengers who had sent in the morning and booked a seat. The fare was reduced to a shilling, and the arrival and departure of the coaches was announced by the blowing of a horn. Kipp's stages, of a later day, started from the corner of Pine and Nassau Streets, passed up Broadway to Canal, and made their way past farms and gardens to Greenwich. Sol. Kipp, of the firm of Kipp & Brown, was a famous character in the village, and unable to reconcile himself to the loss of his right-of-way by the introduction of the horse cars, he battled for years in the courts against the starting of the Eighth Avenue Line, but succumbed before the power of George Law and his millions.

Tom Paine took up his residence in Green-

Randall's Memories of Paine

wich in the early part of the century, and died there on the eighth of June, 1809. His home was a small house in Herring Street, (now 293 Bleecker), where he had lodgings along with Madame Bonneville, and her two sons.

Mr. John Randall, Jr., engineer to the Commissioners who were laying out the City Plan, thus records his memories of the great infidel. He says :

"I boarded in the city and in going to the office, (the Commissioners had their office in Greenwich) I almost daily passed the house in Herring Street where Thomas Paine resided, and frequently in fair weather saw him sitting at the south window of the first story room of that house. The sash was raised, and a small table or stand was placed before him with an open book placed upon it which he appeared to be reading. He had his spectacles on, his left elbow rested on the table, and his chin rested between the thumb and fingers of his hand ; his right hand lay upon his book, and a decanter containing liquor, of the color of rum or brandy, was standing next his book or beyond it. I never saw Thomas Paine at any other place or in any other position.

The commissoners out of compliment to the author of the *Age of Reason* named a small street in their new plan, running parallel with Grove, and between Herring and Asylum Streets, Reason Street ; a name corrupted by common parlance into Raisin, and finally altered to Barrow Street.

It was in the summer of 1801 that Robert Richard Randall died, and left by will twenty-one acres of land in Greenwich Village to found an asylum for superannuated sailors. This land was north of Greenwich Lane, extending from the Bowery to about the eastern line of the present Fifth Avenue, and was originally known as the Eliot estate before it passed into the hands of Captain Randall, who bought it, in 1790, for £5000. There already existed a Marine Society, of which Randall had been one of the founders, whose object was the increase of maritime knowledge, and the aid of indigent masters and their families. The fund of this society was limited to $15,000, to which each member contributed $2.00 yearly. Captain Randall had himself been a ship master and merchant, and was deeply interested in the success of the Marine Society, to which he left a small sum of money as well as the aforementioned land, appointing the Chancellor of the City of New York, the Mayor and Recorder, and the senior clergymen of the Episcopal and Presbyterian churches of the city, "To receive rents, issues, and profits thereof," and to build and organize a Sailor's Snug Harbor. A charter was secured in 1806, but, owing to a long contest in the courts with relatives who endeavored to have the devisor's benevolent intentions set aside, nothing in aid of the sailors was done until 1831, when a farm on Staten Island was purchased, as already it was evident that bet-

Founder of the Sailor's Snug Harbor

Greenwich Market 1800

ter use could be made of the twenty-one acres than to devote them to a site for the required buildings. Captain Randall's original plan was that the Snug Harbor should be built upon this land which he bequeathed, and that if properly farmed it would supply all the grain and vegetables required by the inmates. Very wisely, however, he left the trustees free to use their own judgment. The cost of the litigation had been so heavy that despite the great increase in the value of the land it was not until more than thirty years after the testator's death that his charity began to have practical results. To-day the income from the Randall bequest, which at the time of the issuance of the charter was only $4,243, reaches the sum of nearly half a million yearly, and serves to support some five hundred old seamen and their families.

In the year 1800, the first Greenwich market was established in Brannon Street, at the request of many local petitioners, of whom one was Aaron Burr. In 1804, two butchers put up a shed near the State Prison, and in spite of protests from the holders of stalls in the Greenwich, or Spring Street Market, as it was afterwards called, continued to sell meat there, and finally established a general market, known as the State Prison Market, and from this the prison itself derived its necessary supplies. How low was the cost of living at that

Stringent Market Regulations

time may be inferred from a table of the prices of daily food in the prison, where the three meals for two hundred and thirty-five persons cost but $10.11.

It appears that the Corporation was so particular in granting licenses to the holders of stalls in the market, that young butchers were not only required to serve a regular apprenticeship, but their conduct and morals were also particularly considered, and if they were very young someone had to go their surety for good behavior. Trinity Church had contributed to the erection of Greenwich Market, and when Jefferson Market superseded it there was some fear that the Church would resume the gift, which had been made with the understanding that the land should be used only for market purposes; so the Common Council ordered the place "paved and appropriated for market purposes," though no market stood there.

When the old Spring Street Market was swept away, the butchers who owned stalls were required to buy others in the New Clinton Market, and were allowed no preference over outsiders. Henry Cornell, who was unable to pay the purchase-price demanded for the stalls established himself in a "meat-shop," which was then a complete innovation. The market butchers made loud outcries against this infringement of the law and their rights,

A Refuge from Epidemics

and Cornell, often convicted and fined, but always sustained and assisted by his patrons, finally carried his point and was relieved from persecution by the bill which was passed in 1843, making it legal to sell meat outside of the markets.

Because of its superior healthfulness, Greenwich always profited by the epidemics which visited the lower city. In 1742, and 1743, Mayor John Cruger reported the death of one hundred and sixty-five persons from "an epidemical distemper or plague," which was probably yellow fever. The population of the city was then about 10,000, and many went to Greenwich to escape infection, remaining as long as the plague lasted. Small-pox sent them there again in the following year, and once more in the year 1739, as appears from a letter from Lieutenant-Governor Clarke to the Duke of Newcastle, dated April 18th, of that year, which begs leave "to inform Your Grace that the Small-pox being in town and one-third part of the Assembly not having had it I gave them leave to sit at Greenwich." But although even a flight to Greenwich was not always a certain escape from small-pox, yellow fever seems never to have crossed the swamp and the meadows between the town and the village. In 1798, the scourge appeared with great suddeness and fury and again there was an exodus to Greenwich, where many re-

The Epidemic of 1822

mained after all danger of infection in the city had passed. The farmers brought their produce here instead of to the town, where it was almost impossible to obtain fresh food in the markets. The fever reappeared four times within the following six years, and on every occasion Greenwich added to its permanent inhabitants.

It was the epidemic of 1822, that gave the most sudden and vigorous impetus to the growth of Greenwich. Mr. John Lambert describing the hegira caused by the pestilence, says :

> "As soon as this dreadful scourge makes its appearance in New York the inhabitants shut up their shops and fly from their houses into the country. Those who cannot go far, on account of business, remove to Greenwich, a small village, situate on the border of the Hudson River, about two or three miles from town. Here the merchants and others have their offices and carry on their concerns with little danger from the fever, which does not seem to be contagious beyond a certain distance. The banks and other public offices also remove their business to this place ; and markets are regularly established for the supply of the inhabitants. Very few are left in the confined parts of the town except the poorer classes and the negroes. The latter, not being affected by the fever are of great service in this dreadful crisis ; and are the only persons who can be found to discharge the hazardous duties of attending the sick and burying the dead."

In one season of epidemic, he says, upwards of 20,000 people fled from the city.

The Epidemic of 1822

Hardie gives a vivid picture of the exodus in 1822 :

"Saturday, the 24th of August, our city presented the appearance of a town besieged. From daybreak till night one line of carts containing boxes, merchandise and effects were seen moving toward Greenwich Village and the upper parts of the city. Carriages and hacks, wagons, and horsemen, were scouring the streets and filling the roads ; persons with anxiety strongly marked on their countenances, and with hurried gait, were hustling through the streets. Temporary stores and offices were erecting, and even on the ensuing day (Sunday) carts were in motion and the saw and hammer busily at work. Within a few days thereafter the Custom-house, the Post-office, the banks, the insurance offices and the printers of newspapers located themselves in the village, and these places almost instantaneously became the seat of the immense business usually carried on in the metropolis."

Devoe in his *Market Book* says :

"The fever of 1822 built up many streets with numerous wooden buildings for the uses of the merchants, banks, (from which Bank Street took its name), offices, etc., and the celerity of putting up these buildings is better told by the Reverend Mr. Marcellus, who informed me that he saw corn growing on the present corner of Hammond and Fourth Streets on a *Saturday* morning and on the following *Monday* 'Sykes & Niblo' had a house erected capable of accommodating *three hundred* boarders. Even the Brooklyn ferry-boats ran up there daily."

This influx of business completely changed the character of Greenwich, from a quiet, dreamy village where the magnates of the city

The University of the City of New York 1830

loved to come for rural retirement and repose, to a bustling part of the metropolis.

Such an expansion was too sudden to be entirely permanent ; but the tide, when it ebbed at last, left so much behind it that Greenwich ceased forever to be a detached village and became a well-defined suburb of the town. The most interesting development of its new life as part of New York, was the founding of the University of the City of New York, in 1830. It grew from a general desire that the city should be supplied with a system of education more complete than the schools, or even Columbia College, could afford, and that independent research should be pursued under the patronage of this new institution, which was to be founded on the broadest lines of encouragement to intellectual endeavor.

How great and immediate were the fruits of this wise decision is shown by the fact that Samuel Morse perfected the electro-magnetic telegraph in one of the rooms of the new University Building whose foundations were laid on the east side of Washington Square in 1833, and from the roof of that Gothic structure of white freestone, which has now vanished, Professor John W. Draper took the first daguerreotype ever made of a human face.

The story of Greenwich from that day is merged in the history of the City of New York as a whole.

Barnard College

343 MADISON AVENUE

COURSES IN AMERICAN HISTORY

For Undergraduates. General course, reading, recitations and lectures.—Three hours a week: H. A. Cushing, A.M.

For Graduates. Political History of the Colonies and of the American Revolution.—This investigation course, extending through two years, deals in the first year with the settlement of the Colonies and their development in the seventeenth century, and in the second year with the growth of the system of colonial administration, the conflict with the French, and the revolt of the Colonies. The work of the students consists chiefly in the study of topics from the original sources, with a formal account of the results of such study.—Two hours a week for two years: Professor Herbert L. Osgood, Ph.D.

These courses are open not only to candidates for degrees, but to special students who can show ability to read French and German, and can satisfy the Dean and Faculty of their general competence.

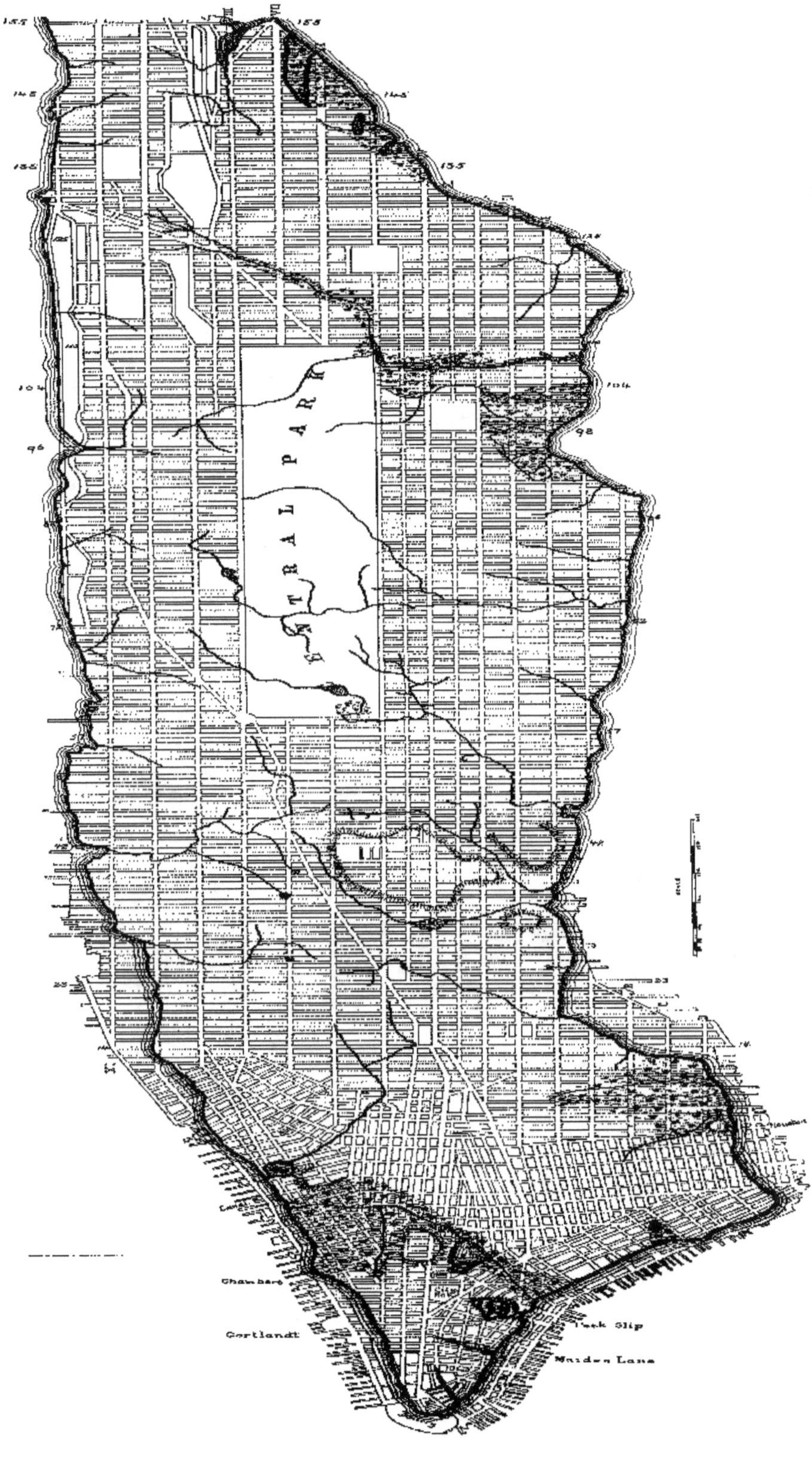
CENTRAL PARK
155
145
135
104
96
98
42
23
14
Chambers
Cortlandt
Peck Slip
Maiden Lane

Half Moon Series

Published in the Interest of the New York City History Club.

VOLUME I. NUMBER X.

OLD WELLS AND WATER-COURSES OF THE ISLAND OF MANHATTAN.

BY GEO. EVERETT HILL AND GEO. E. WARING, JR.

PART I.

THE Reverend James Wolley, Chaplain of the British soldiery in New York under Sir Edmund Andros,—but much better known to us in his sporting capacity, as hero of the famous bear hunt in John Robinson's orchard on Maiden Lane,—published, when he returned to England in 1681, *A Two Years' Journal of New York,* in which he set forth, in quaintly pedantic phrase, the charms of the Island of Manhattan. In the estimation of this clerical Nimrod, not the least of the blessings enjoyed by the desirable region was the goodly provision under which "Nature kindly drains and purgeth it by Fontanels and Issues of run-

General Original Topography

ning waters in its irriguous Valleys." We read with approval; for the springs and streams of the land of the Manhatoes were remarkable for their number, their diverse characteristics and—considering the limited drainage area of each—for their size.

But we open our eyes in mild astonishment when the worthy clergyman describes this paradise as "free from those Annoyances which are commonly ascribed by naturalists for the Insalubriety of any Country, viz. South or Southeast Winds, stagnant Waters, lowness of Shoars and"—but enough! Surely the reverend gentleman had land to sell, probably in Beekman's Swamp! For, apart from the remarkable constancy which he ascribes to the fickle breezes (which alone are responsible for the behavior of the notoriously fickle weathercock), we know that there was but little elevated ground to be found in the ordinary peregrinations of the citizen of that day, and that the shores were deeply indented with frequent marshy inlets and salt meadows; while a continuous swamp extended from river to river, separating the lower part of the island from the higher land above, and spreading out on its western edge into an extensive morass, long famous for its malaria and mosquitoes.

Above this swamp an irregular range of sand hills marked the beginning of better

Choice of Location for Settlement

ground, well elevated, well drained and, for the most part, of fairly uniform grade. Save for an extensive marsh on the east side, these conditions prevailed to the upper border of the lower third of the island. Then the formation gradually became rugged and irregular, the sandy and gravelly soil disappearing, and rock predominating more and more as the elevation increased. Several streams of considerable size traversed this district, running through stony valleys flanked by high rocky hills. On the western side, this bold formation continued to the northerly boundary; but toward the east, at a point distant from the end by about one fifth of the total length of the island, the rugged, rocky character terminated abruptly, and the fertile plains and meadows of Harlem began.

Such, in brief, was the general topographical condition of the island when the early Dutch colonists founded New Amsterdam.

The site for the town was not determined without discussion. Some of the party urged that the settlement be made on the main land, just above the Spuyten Duyvil Creek, ostensibly because it was a secluded place, which would be likely to escape observation and attack; but it is safe to say that they were attracted, to a greater or less degree, by the low fertile plains, intersected with streams and tidal inlets, which resembled their native land

De Heere Gracht

and which invited the construction of canals. For a Dutchman without a canal was like gingerbread without ginger,—a possibility, it is true, but an anomaly ; a fit object for pity or contempt, according to circumstances.

Fortunately for their successors, an inlet of the bay, which could be made to do duty as a canal, extended inland for about a quarter of a mile on the line of the present Broad Street. This ditch was the natural outlet for a marshy section of considerable size lying above what soon came to be known as The Beaver Path, now Beaver Street. A brook trickled through this marsh, from the common lying north of it, called the *Shaape Waytie,* or Sheep Pasture, and received the flow of a small stream which ran through the Company's Valley, as that portion of The Beaver Path was named which lay between Heere Straat (Broadway) and the junction of these two rivulets. From the latter point, the Heere Gracht—or Heere Graft as it was soon called, stretched its odorous length to the bay.

Around this ditch gathered much of the social and business life of the new community. The first church, commenced in 1633, was erected within a stone's throw of its banks, and occupied as a place of worship until Dominie Bogardus, and the after-dinner subscriptions of the guests at his stepdaughter's wedding, built the new church within the fort.

The New Church and the Brewery

Just beside the church was the Company's bakery; and just behind the church, on Brugh Straat, was the Company's brewery; while half-way between the church and the brewery was the house of the preacher himself. Alas! if reports be true, the Dominie's tastes and habits coincided exactly with his geographical position.

Several foot-bridges were built across De Heere Graft, and a wider bridge, "for cattell and waggons," spanned it at Hoogh Straat. Its banks became the public market of the town. Several times was it deepened and otherwise improved. In 1657, it was determined to line the banks of the ditch with plank, and to assess the cost upon the owners of the abutting property. This called forth a storm of indignation from the luckless proprietors, who, with the same breath, declared that the proposed change was useless, extravagant, and undesirable, and that it would be of great benefit to the public at large and therefore should be made at the expense of the town. Governor Stuyvesant, regardless of their threats and petitions, ordered the execution of the project. The work proceeded and was finished in 1659, at a cost of about one thousand dollars. The width of the amended canal was sixteen feet, and the roadway on each side of it was twenty-eight feet wide, making the total width seventy-two

Broad Street and the Canal

feet, the present average of the street. Some of the property-owners refused to pay their assessments, but the testy old Governor, who more than made up in determination what he lacked in legs, ordered the delinquents to be locked up until they should come to his way of thinking. Before nightfall, all had experienced a change of heart and avowed their willingness to pay.

A similar improvement was made to the ditch above The Beaver Path, which afterwards became known as the Prince Graft, the centre of the tanning and shoemaking business. In 1676, however, this industry removed to Maiden Lane, and, a little later, to Beekman's Swamp.

De Heere Graft had now become a desirable residential quarter, and many of the better class of citizens had made their homes upon its well-paved banks. For some time, the merchants of the town had met at the Hoogh Straat bridge for the transaction of business, and in March, 1670, the first New York Exchange was established, which held weekly meetings on Fridays, between eleven and twelve o'clock. In the winter, the boys of the town improved so well the coasting facilities afforded by the hill from Broadway to the bridge, that the merchants were obliged to ask for protection, and Governor Lovelace ordered the Mayor to see that the annoyance was stopped.

New Canal Suppressed

In 1671, further repairs to the big ditch were made, mainly upon the lines adopted in 1657; but in 1676, *horribile dictu,* the edict went forth that the precious canal must be made way with, and the inhabitants were ordered to cover it and fill it up level with the street. One naturally expects the records to tell of violent protest against this assault upon ancient traditions; but the Dutch spirit had declined and we hear not a murmur of remonstrance. Indeed, so complete from the first was the submission to the English rule, that within three months after the capitulation of Governor Stuyvesant, the Dutch magistrates of the town, in a petition addressed to the Duke of York, expressed great satisfaction with "the Hon'ble Col. Richard Nichols," and stated that they were "confident and assured that, under the wings of this valiant gentleman, we shall bloom and grow like the cedar on Lebanon."

So De Heere Graft was buried and its place became Broad Street. At this time the Wet Docks were built, at the foot of the street,—two great basins, sufficiently large to accommodate a whole fleet of the ships of that day, and intended to afford facilities for the rapid loading and unloading of cargoes. This improvement stimulated markedly the price of real estate in that vicinity, and brought to Broad Street even more trade than it formerly enjoyed.

The Broad Street Sewer

Under the street, the canal, turned into a sewer, still serves as outlet for the drainage of about thirty-eight acres of closely built territory; and the extensive systems of piling, needed to support heavy buildings on the site of the old swamp, still call to mind the original condition of the ground.

Prior to 1677, the only public source of water supply was a well and pump close to the gate of the fort. In that year, however, Stephen Van Cortlandt was appointed Mayor, under Governor Andros, and, by his direction, the first public wells of the city were dug. There were six of these, and each was located in the middle of a street. Between this date and 1700, four other public wells were dug, similarly situated, making ten in all. Of these wells, seven are known by name, and the sites of the other three have been established beyond doubt. They were located thus :— "De Riemer's Well," in Whitehall Street, near Bridge; "Well of William Cox," near the Stadt Huys, at the head of Coenties Slip; "Ten Eyck and Vincent's Well," in Broad Street, between Stone and South William; "Tunis De Kay's Well," in Broad Street, a little above Beaver; "Frederick Wessel's Well," in Wall Street, west of William; "Mr. Rombout's Well," in Broadway, near Exchange Place; and the "Well of Suert Ol-

Maagde Poetje Laundry

pherts," in the same neighborhood. Of the three which are not known by name, two were in Broad Street, near Exchange Place, and the third was in Wall Street, between Broad and New Streets. The water from these wells was brackish and the supply was not plentiful; but they were regarded as an important addition to the resources of the fire department, and valued for this, if for nothing more.

Many other wells were dug in the lower part of the city in after years, but the records concerning them are often vague and confusing. We know of one at Church and Cedar Streets, and of another at Dey and Greenwich Streets; also of one seventy-two feet deep in Washington Market, which yielded very poor water.

In a depression which followed the line of the present Maiden Lane from Nassau Street to the East River, a little stream of sparkling spring water rippled and danced over a pebbly bottom. The southerly bank was steep, but not abrupt, while, on the north, a gentle grassy slope extended from the water to a sharper rise just beyond. This spot presented such facilities for the washing and bleaching of linen that it became a resort for laundry women, and because of this it was first called *Maagde Paetje,* or Virgins' Path.

The V'lei

At the foot of this valley, the Brooklyn ferry-boats discharged their passengers and cargoes ; and an enterprising blacksmith, named Cornelius Clopper, established himself on the corner of Pearl Street and Maiden Lane, where he speedily built up a considerable business with the Long Island farmers and traders. Before long his sterner industry completely overshadowed the gentler domestic toil of the washing women, and the Maidens' Lane became the Smith's Valley, or Smit's V'lei. This was afterwards shortened into The V'lei, and then corrupted to Fly ; so that when the first public market-sheds were erected, on land reclaimed from a little tract of salt marsh at the mouth of this stream, they were popularly called the Fly Market.

Close by the ferry stairs lived Philip Livingston, dealer in rum and grindstones, glass and furs, hardware and marble,—an active politician and a signer of the Declaration of Independence.

To this valley the tan-yards removed, when they were banished from the Prince Graft, and from here they went to Beekman's Swamp, or to the Fresh Water Pond. Gradually the hills were levelled and the brook was filled. Although the surface still exhibits a marked depression, there is little to indicate the conditions from which Maiden Lane received its name.

Kripple-bush

Peck Slip marks the entrance to what was another marshy district, extending in the shape of an irregular lozenge from the shore (then at Water Street) to what is now the corner of Frankfort and North William Streets; and with its minor axis running from the present intersection of Beekman and Gold Streets to Brooklyn Bridge at Vandewater Street. The centre of this district, bounded now by Cliff, Frankfort, and Gold Streets, and a southeasterly projection of Spruce Street, was so low as to be in a state of almost continual submersion; while the slightly higher marshy shores were covered with a thick growth of brambles, which gained for the locality the name of Kripple-bush, or tangled briers. The earliest buildings in the vicinity were the storehouses of Isaac Allerton, merchant, which, in 1661, stood on the shore close by, when there were but twelve buildings in all outside of the stockade on Wall Street.

This land was part of a farm owned by Thomas Hall, who, in 1670, sold it to William Beekman, The new owner planted an orchard upon the hill-side running down to the marshy valley, and in time the latter became known as Beekman's Swamp. In 1677, the slaughter-houses, banished from the city by order of Governor Andros, settled here ; and here, a little later, came the tanners from Maiden Lane. Their successors remain to

The Swamp

this day, and the "Swamp" is still the centre for the wholesale leather trade of the city. These industries, naturally, did not tend to make the spot attractive, and, although six ship-yards flourished near Peck Slip in 1728, the entire marsh was sold in 1735 for one hundred pounds. Slowly the tide of life crept up the eastern shore, and, by 1767, the population of the district had so increased that a Lutheran church was built at the head of the marsh, on the corner of Frankfort and King George (now North William) Streets. This low stone edifice was always known as the "Swamp Church." Within its walls minister and people read the words of the "voice crying in the wilderness": "Every valley shall be exalted and every mountain and hill shall be made low." And, close on the heels of prophecy, came a literal local fulfilment; for pick and shovel were soon assaulting nature's surrounding earthworks, and the spoils of their warfare were poured into the ooze of the morass below. The actual site of Mr. Beekman's orchard is many feet in the air above the Beekman Street of to-day, and the "tangled briers" of Kripple-bush lie deep beneath the stones of Ferry Street.

To anyone but a Dutchman—who always preferred a ditch to a lake—there was no more beautiful spot on the lower island than the

The Collect

site of The Collect, or Fresh Water Pond, the largest body of water south of the Harlem River. It covered the territory now bounded by Baxter, White, Elm, Duane, and Park Streets. This clear and sparkling pond was fed by large springs of great reputed purity. Its depth is uncertain, the records ranging from forty to seventy feet, but it was undoubtedly very deep, and was currently reported to be bottomless. Other stranger rumors were rife concerning it. It was said to be the abode of hideous and terrible sea-monsters, which were seen, at intervals, by solitary individuals, and which, on one occasion, during the Revolution, seized a Hessian trooper and carried him off to their subaqueous lair. Tradition's younger and more matter-of-fact sister, history, remarks that "from time to time persons who had drunk too deeply fell from its banks and some of them were drowned." Viewed in this side light, it seems highly probable that the tremendous monsters were of the delirium tremendous variety.

The Indians appreciated the natural advantages of the situation, and their wigwams dotted the groves upon the shores of this lake for many years before Peter Minuit arrived in 1626 and purchased the entire island at the rate of ten acres for a cent. They were a peaceful agricultural people, these Manhatoes,

The Manhatoes

extensive cultivators of peas and beans, corn and pumpkins. To them we owe the knowledge and name of *sickquatash*, or succotash; and such ample provision did they make for the preparation of this dainty that Hudson, on his first visit to these shores, saw, at one of their villages, a quantity of corn and beans "sufficient to fill three ships." They knew also the value of the oyster. Often their canoes, laden with this spoil of the bay, returned to the lake through the stream connecting it with the North River, and were beached upon its western shore. Large quantities of these oysters were preserved, as stores for the winter, by the women, who opened the shells and strung the juicy morsels on long withes, to be dried in the sun. So great was this industry that the western shore became covered with empty shells, which led the Dutch—whose geographical appellations were usually descriptive, rather than commemorative—to call the place *Kalch Hoek*, or Shell Point. The name of Collect, later applied to the pond itself, is probably a corruption of this word.

Near its shores, late in the autumn of 1626, three negro servants of the Governor murdered and robbed a Weekquaesgeek Indian, who had come from Westchester to sell beaver skins to the Dutch. The deed was witnessed by an Indian boy, a nephew of the murdered man, and long years after, when the youth

Cattle, Fish, and Game

had grown to manhood, he fulfilled his vow of vengeance and satisfied his ideas of justice by murdering an inoffensive trader not far from the scene of the former tragedy.

In 1661, the meadows near the Fresh Water, which had previously been used as a common for the pasturing of all sorts and conditions of cattle, were fenced in and reserved for the use of the bovine aristocracy of the city. Gabriel Carpesy was employed as herdsman, and for many years he drove his charges back and forth between the fields and the city. Like his celestial namesake, he carried a trumpet, which he blew "in the morning" at the gates of his clients, who were expected to have their cows in readiness to join the herd; and in the evening, as the procession returned from the green pastures and still waters, a blast of the familiar horn announced to each owner that his particular Grietje or Katrina was at the gate, awaiting admittance.

The pond was known as a famous fishing-ground from the first, and the drain upon its piscatory resources became so great that, in 1734, a law was passed prohibiting the use of a net in its waters, and imposing a fine upon any person catching fish "by any other manner than that of angling." The marshes on the east were the home of the snipe, and we are told that sportsmen visiting this locality generally returned with "a large quantity of fly-abouts."

The Little Collect

On the hill, which rose to the west, was the negro burying-ground, and at its foot, close to the water, criminals were publicly executed. Here, in 1741, were hung twenty of the actual or suspected participants in the plotted uprising of the slaves and massacre of the whites. The sloping hillside formed a natural amphitheatre, where great crowds were wont to gather from time to time, now to witness a hanging, and again to watch the skating. For in winter the Collect made a fine skating-park, and the ice was thronged with the young people of the town. Here William IV., the "Sailor King," amused himself by throwing coins for the skaters to chase; and so great was his admiration of the speed and dexterity exhibited, that he forthwith put on skates himself, and, after many a royal tumble, mastered the gentle art.

South of the Fresh Water Pond, and separated from it by a strip of ground high enough to be dry, lay a small marshy lake known as the Little Collect. Just east of this, at the present intersection of Pearl and Park Streets, was a large tan-yard, and another was located on the shore of the greater pond, where Worth and Elm Streets now cross. Upon the strip of ground between the two ponds stood the City Magazine, or Powder House. The road which led to it from Broadway was called Magazine Street; and on the western side of

John Fitch's Steam-boat

Broadway, directly opposite the head of this street, the city hospital was built on a five-acre lot, occupying the very summit of the hill, and purchased from the Rutgers estate.

In the summer of 1796, seven years before Fulton's first experiments, and eleven years before the success of the *Clermont*, John Fitch sailed a steamboat upon the Collect. The vessel was a ship's yawl, eighteen feet long and six feet beam, with square stern and round bows, experimentally fitted with a screw propeller. A ten- or twelve-gallon iron pot served for a boiler. The little craft made the circuit of the pond several times, at the rate of about six miles an hour. Many spectators were present. Among them were Nicholas Roosevelt, Chancellor Livingston, John Stevens, and others who were deeply interested in the possibilities of the steam-engine. A model of Fitch's boat is owned by the New York Historical Society, but the original, with a part of its machinery, was abandoned and left upon the shore of the pond. Piece by piece the woodwork was carried off for fuel.

Between 1786 and 1796, the population of the city nearly doubled. Streets were laid out to Canal Street, and builders were busy even farther north. Early in this season of prosperity a few shrewd individuals foresaw that the growth of the city would soon enfold the Collect and its surroundings. Efforts were

Schemes of Development

made to form a syndicate to buy up the land around it, improve the lake, lay out a park upon its shores, and thus enhance the value of the remaining property, which was to be sold for building-lots. But capitalists did not take kindly to the proposition, considering that the locality was much too remote to make the enterprise promising. The owners of the land also looked upon the scheme as visionary, and gave no support to the movement, which was finally abandoned. To-day, there are few areas in all Christendom more densely populated than this "remote" region.

In 1790, the city authorities took up the matter, and we find in the records of the Common Council the following entry :

> "Ordered. A Committee to cause a survey to be made of the ancient bounds of the Fresh Water Pond and report the same to the Board."

And, later :

> "The Committee appointed delivered a survey for the several streets in the vicinity of Fresh Water, which was ordered to be filed."

The following year the corporation purchased the interests of the heirs of Anthony Rutgers, for one hundred and fifty pounds sterling.

In 1793, the Council ordered another survey of "the land and meadows at and about the

The Filling in of the Collect

Fresh Water Pond, with the streets which may be necessary marked thereon."

Soon after this, another plan for the preservation of the Collect and the improvement of the surrounding territory was proposed. This project provided for the construction of a navigable canal from the East River to the Hudson, passing directly through the pond and converting it into an inland harbor or basin. The idea met with considerable favor, but before the money needed for the work had been raised, the dumping of rubbish and offal into the Collect had begun. The trees which were once its glory were cut down for firewood; the beautiful shores were disfigured with piles of refuse, often of the most objectionable character; and its clear waters became turbid and offensive. So serious a nuisance was created, that, in 1805, the Council declared the condition of the pond to be "dangerous to the public health," and ordered that it be drained and filled in with clean earth. The filling of the Little Collect was completed soon, and Magazine Street was extended to meet Pearl Street, at first as a muddy lane. But before long the road became so firm and dry that houses were erected on either side, and, in 1807, the Scotch Presbyterians built their church upon it.

In 1808, before the filling in of the large pond was completed, an attempt was made to excavate the accumulation of decomposed vege-

The Old Wreck Brook

table matter, resembling peat, which lay in a thick bed over the entire bottom. This material formed an indifferent fuel when dry, and it was hoped that its recovery would prove remunerative ; but after a short trial the project was abandoned and the work of filling in was resumed. Gradually, in ever narrowing circles, structures of brick and mortar appeared—unfit monuments, on the graves of the pleasant places below ; and in 1838, over the spot where the fish leaped and the waters laughed beneath the bows of the Indian's canoe, there arose, in gloomy pile, the Halls of Justice—The Tombs, wherein Freedom and Joy, sacrificed to Crime, are daily buried.

But the obliteration of the Collect is not to be regretted. In such a location, the pond, had it been preserved, would inevitably have become a receptacle for filth, a cause of much desultory disease, and a possible source of devastating pestilence,—a greater menace to the community than the powder magazine which formerly stood on the little tongue of land jutting into its waters.

The eastern outlet of the Collect Pond was through a small stream called the Old Kill or, later, the Old Wreck Brook, which made its way to the East River, practically on the line of the present Roosevelt Street, through a

The Tea Water Pump

swampy valley known as Wolfert's Marsh. At its mouth there stood, in 1664, a mill which was already called "old," and here in that year, at eight o'clock on Monday morning, September 8th, the gracious conqueror, Nicolls, returned to the sore-hearted Stuyvesant the duly ratified copy of the articles of capitulation, which turned New Amsterdam into New York without changing the municipal machinery or infringing the rights of the humblest citizen.

To the south of the valley, the ground rose so abruptly that the Boston High Road, which followed the line of Chatham Street (now Park Row), curved to the east as far as William Street and back again, to avoid the steep descent.

Close by the brook, on the highway (near the intersection of the present Park Row and Pearl Street), was the great spring called the Tea Water Pump. It was undoubtedly supplied from the same sources that fed the Collect Pond, and, until 1840, its water was considered the best on the island. In fact no other good water could be had, save from the well at the fort; for the supply from the public wells was so brackish that the horses of strangers visiting the city refused to drink of it. As a consequence, the Tea Water was in universal demand, and a large number of carts were regularly employed in distributing

The Kissing Bridge

it, in casks, throughout the city. So great was this industry that, in 1796, complaints were made that the water carts, awaiting opportunity to fill their barrels at the pump, obstructed Chatham Street ; and, to remedy this evil, the spout of the pump was raised some two feet and extended, so as to discharge the water at the outer edge of the walk and allow pedestrians to pass under it without inconvenience. We are told that, in 1798,

> "the average quantity drawn daily from this remarkable well, about 20 feet deep and 4 feet in diameter, is 110 hogsheads of 130 gallons each. In some hot summer days, 216 hogsheads have been drawn from it, and, what is very singular, there are never more or less than 3 feet of water in the well."

In an old advertisement, offering for lease a house on Reade Street, the proximity of the Tea Water Pump is emphasized as one of the special advantages of the premises.

Passing this much valued spring, the High Road crossed the Old Kill by the famous Kissing Bridge, an institution so appreciated by the young men—and possibly by the young women—of the earlier times, that at several other bridges on the island, formerly free, it became customary to collect toll in like manner. But this was the first of its kind. Of it the Reverend Mr. Burnaby, an English clergyman travelling in this country a century and a

Wolfert's Valley

half ago, wrote in his diary: "Just before you enter the town there is a little bridge, commonly called the Kissing Bridge, where it is customary, before passing beyond, to salute the lady who is your companion." Probably the worthy priest, thirsting for knowledge,—or something else,—forced himself to conform to the custom, for he naïvely remarks that he found it "curious, yet not displeasing." We shall hear more of these amatory adjuncts of the civilization of the day as we pursue our journey up the island.

This bridge marked the end of the town from 1755 until the close of the Revolution, and some of the municipal ordinances refer to it as a boundary.

Just north of the bridge the road ascended another hill, so steep that a circuitous route was necessary, and the loop formed in the effort to secure a better grade still exists as Chatham Square. On the hillside, close to the road, stood Wolfert Webber's tavern, for a long time the farthest outlying dwelling on the eastern side. To its right lay the sparkling waters of the Collect, and at its foot the Old Kill danced its way under the Kissing Bridge and through the meadows of the valley which long bore the name of the enterprising and hospitable Wolfert. Beyond it stood the windmill, built by one Hartogvelt, in 1662, for Jan DeWitt, the miller; and behind the

Western Outlet of the Collect

mill arose the hills which shut out the view of the Kripple-bush. It was a fair prospect, but it had its disadvantages; for we find that, when Anthony Rutgers owned the property, he petitioned the King for a better title, so that he might be able to sell the land to some one who would drain it, "because the inhabitants lost one third of their time by sickness."

Behind Wolfert's tavern, on the west side of Bowery Lane near the present Pell Street, there stood, in 1767, the small, two-story frame building where Charlotte Temple met her tragic fate.

The valley was filled early in the present century.

The western outlet of the Collect was a small stream which left the pond at its northern end and flowed, nearly on the line of the present Canal Street, to the Hudson. East of the Church Street of to-day, its course lay through a low, but rather narrow marshy valley, between rolling land, topped here and there with conical sand-hills, on the north, and the *Kalch Hoek*, which arose to a considerable elevation on the south. Beyond this hill, and following the curve of its base, there spread the broad pasture land, swamps, and salt marshes of the Lispenard Meadows, which extended to the shore line (just beyond Greenwich Street) and from Duane Street on

The Lispenard Meadows

the south to Spring Street on the north. Through these meadows the stream from the Collect flowed sluggishly, spreading out over the low land, but maintaining enough of a channel to permit the passage of small boats from the river to the pond. A little brook, draining another swampy valley which lay at the foot of the western slope of *Kalch Hoek*, followed, substantially, the line of West Broadway from Reade Street, and entered the larger stream nearly at a right angle. On the northern side a tiny rivulet trickled down from a fine spring which gave the name of Spring Street to the road which passed it, leading to Broadway.

In seasons of heavy rains almost the whole district was flooded, and in the winter acres of its surface were traversed by skaters, who resorted thither by hundreds when the Collect had been made unfit for this use. During the dry season, however, this region furnished much valuable pasture land. The boys of the period fished in the creeks, or, regardless of brambles, waded through the swamps in search of bull-frogs and water-snakes—joint tenants with the snipe and woodcock, whose cousins inhabited the Jersey shore ; while venturesome girls occasionally risked torn frocks and wet feet in gathering berries or cattails.

In its primitive condition, however, the val-

Anthony Rutgers's Petition

ley was never particularly attractive. The greater part of it was included in the original grant to Roelof Janssen, which, after the marriage of his widow, Annetje Jans, to the Reverend Everardus Bogardus, was known as the Dominie's Bouwerie. Later, the property was swallowed up in the Duke's Farm, which became successively the King's Farm, the Queen's Farm, and, finally, by the grant of Queen Anne, the Church Farm. At no time during all this period was the land a profitable property. It was leased often for merely nominal rentals, but one tenant after another abandoned it. In its pestilential quagmires cattle were lost so often that the Council caused it to be fenced off; and we are told that, where Grand and Greene Streets now intersect, a man, who had mistaken his way in the dark, walked into deep water and was drowned. The Lutheran Church was offered, at one time, a tract of six acres near the present corner of Broadway and Canal Street, which the Trustees deemed "inexpedient to accept as a gift, since the land was not worth fencing in."

The first noteworthy attempt to improve the meadows was made soon after 1730, when Anthony Rutgers, wishing to benefit the public in general and himself in particular, offered to clear and drain the swamps on condition that the land be given to him. His petition to the King and Council contains the following description of prevailing conditions :

"The said swamp is constantly filled with standing water, for which there is no natural vent, and being covered with bushes and small trees is by the stagnation and rottenness of it become exceedingly dangerous and of fatal consequence to all the inhabitants of the north part of the city bordering near the same, they being subject to very many diseases and distempers, which by all physicians and by long experience are imputed to the unwholesome vapours arising thereby ; and as the said swamp is upon a level with the waters of Hudson and the South [East] rivers, no person has ever yet attempted to clear the same, nor ever can under a grant thereof which is to expire with the next new Governor ; for the expense of clearing the same will be so great, and the length of time in doing the same such that it never will be attempted, but by a grantee of the fee simple thereof ; and as the same can be of no benefit until it is cleared, so no person has hitherto accepted a grant of the said land, but the same hath lain and still remains unimproved and uncultivated, to the great prejudice and annoyance of the adjacent farms, particularly to a farm of your petitioner's adjoining thereto, which your petitioner, after having been at a great charge and expense in settling, cannot prevail on any tenant to take the same, or get any servants to continue there for any time while the said swamp remains in its present state."

Accompanying the petition, were opinions from several physicians, stating, in substance, that the marshes were the cause of much sickness, and that their drainage would result in great sanitary benefit to the community. The Council granted his request and gave him a

Improvement of the Canal

title to the swamp, covering about seventy acres, for "a moderate quit-rent," on condition that he should "clear and drain it within a year."

At this time Leonard Lispenard was the lessee, from Trinity Parish, of that portion of the Church Farm which lay between the river and the wet valley now covered by West Broadway, and extended from the neighborhood of Reade Street to the wide swamp through which the stream from the Collect lazily flowed. We can make up our minds, each to his own liking, as to whether or not Mr. Lispenard foresaw a way in which he could secure permanent possession of this property without the annoyance of paying for it. But this much is certain : that, just about the time when a considerable part of the land had been cleared, drained, and converted into good pasture, he made himself very agreeable to neighbor Rutgers and to his pretty daughter, and finally married the latter. About 1750, the enterprising and industrious Anthony died, and the Meadows became the property of Mr. and Mrs. Lispenard, and were known thereafter as the Lispenard Meadows.

Although Rutgers's labors had reclaimed a large part of the wet territory, the low land lying on each side of the stream from the Collect remained unimproved until 1796, when, in furtherance of the long discussed project

St. John's Chapel

for constructing a navigable canal from the Hudson to the East River, a committee, appointed by the Council, secured from the owners of the land the right to cut a channel forty feet wide, and to lay out a street thirty feet wide on each side of it. Nothing further was done at this time. In the city records of 1798 appears the following entry:

"A letter from the Health Commissioners read, representing that the swamp or meadow between the Fresh Water Pond and Hudson River is overflowed with standing water, and requires immediate measures for draining it. Ordered that it be attended to."

When the Collect became a dumping-ground, the projected canal was abandoned; and about the beginning of the present century the brook was straightened, deepened and planked, making a channel about ten feet wide in a street one hundred feet in width. About the same time a stone bridge, with a single central arch, was built across the stream at Broadway. This bridge was ten feet seven inches above the surface of the meadow, and was approached by a narrow embankment from either side. In 1808, it marked the city boundary, and a milestone which stood at its southern end bore the legend, "2 Miles from the Battery." Near Church Street, a single plank, laid across the canal, connected the two ends of a well-beaten foot-path, which

St. John's Park

was used as a short cut by the inhabitants of Greenwich in going to and from the city. At a later date bridges were built at Church Street and at other points.

In 1807, the Vestry of Trinity Church began the erection of St. John's Chapel, on Varick Street, between Beach and Laight. A less attractive location could hardly have been found. It was at the junction of the West Broadway and the Canal Street swamps, and the outlook was over a dreary waste of rushes and brambles, unshaded by a single large tree. The building itself was of stone, a really elegant structure, which cost about two hundred thousand dollars. Having completed the chapel, the Vestry of Trinity turned their attention to the improvement of the neighborhood, and laid out as a park the whole block bounded by Varick, Beach, Hudson, and Laight Streets, which was called Hudson Square or St. John's Park. It was carefully graded, planted, and fenced in; and "old Cisco," a former slave, who was made its keeper, cared for it with such fidelity that the locality soon became one of the most attractive parts of the city. Substantial brick houses arose around it, the homes of many of the best citizens, and the value of property in the vicinity rapidly increased. Wells were dug and pumps erected at the corners. At Laight and Varick Streets, the Presbyterians built a little

Now a Freight Station

church, which appeared so plain and small beside the beautiful stone pile that overshadowed it, that it was dubbed "St. John's Kitchen." Here the Reverend Dr. Samuel H. Coxe, father of the late Bishop Coxe, of Buffalo, thundered his anathemas against slavery, to the discomfort of several of his most influential parishioners. The gates of the Park were kept locked, to prevent the intrusion of strangers, but each resident of the square had his own key, and enjoyed its privileges with certainty that he would meet no objectionable person inside its limits. Facing this park lived the families of Alexander Hamilton, General Schuyler and General Morton, the Aymars, Drakes, Coits, Delafields, and others of equal fame; and here lived many of their descendants until the Hudson River Railroad Company tore down the protecting fence, invaded the sacred precincts with axe and shovel, and blotted St. John's Park out of existence with four acres of freight station. Fashion fled precipitately. Only John Ericsson, the builder of the *Monitor*, remained. He continued in his old home until his death, which occurred not very long ago.

Little by little, the whole wet area of the Lispenard Meadows was drained, filled and built upon.

Many public wells were dug in this vicinity, but it is difficult to locate them. We know

Reclamation of the Swamp

of one on Greenwich Street, between Canal and Watts Streets, and of another at North Moore and Greenwich Streets. A third, at Church and Thomas Streets, on the slope of the *Kalch Hoek,* still exists, and is used for watering horses ; but the original supply from the soil has been shut out and the well converted into a cistern fed with Croton water.

The open channel in Canal Street gave place to a sewer, fourteen feet wide and six feet high, with flat bottom and sides of stone and with arch of brick, which still carries a copious flow of water from the ancient springs that fed the almost forgotten Fresh Water Pond. The work of filling the swamps and raising the grade of this district was tedious and costly, for the mire was so deep and soft that the heavier filling material sank to the bottom as fast as it was poured in. In some places, new ground to the depth of forty feet was made before the surface became dry. In sinking a well at Wooster and Grand Streets, this was found to be the thickness of the filling at that point. But eventually the brooks and meadows, and the hills which bounded them, alike disappeared. Occasional complaints of wet cellars, and a high death rate from pulmonary and diarrheal diseases, alone remain to recall the original conditions.

END OF PART I.

Barnard College

343 MADISON AVENUE

COURSES IN AMERICAN HISTORY

For Undergraduates. General course, reading, recitations and lectures.—Three hours a week: H. A. Cushing, A.M.

For Graduates. Political History of the Colonies and of the American Revolution.—This investigation course, extending through two years, deals in the first year with the settlement of the Colonies and their development in the seventeenth century, and in the second year with the growth of the system of colonial administration, the conflict with the French, and the revolt of the Colonies. The work of the students consists chiefly in the study of topics from the original sources, with a formal account of the results of such study.—Two hours a week for two years: Professor Herbert L. Osgood, Ph.D.

These courses are open not only to candidates for degrees, but to special students who can show ability to read French and German, and can satisfy the Dean and Faculty of their general competence.

Half Moon Series

Published in the Interest of the New York City History Club.

Volume I. Number XI.

OLD WELLS AND WATER-COURSES OF THE ISLAND OF MANHATTAN.

By GEO. EVERETT HILL and GEO. E. WARING, Jr.

PART II.

Minetta Brook

NOT far above the Lispenard Meadows, between Charlton and West Houston Streets, lay a small, swampy tract, through which the "Manetta Water" flowed to its outlet in the Hudson. Until demoralized by this near approach to the slothful stream in the marshy valley below, the brook was a brisk little affair, hurrying along in its well-defined channel, apparently as full of business as it certainly was full of trout. Yes, of trout! They were there in abundance, darting to the higher waters like streaks of smoke and flame, against the foamy rush of a narrow channel, or sulking under the shadow of the bank in the quiet

The Course of Minetta Brook

pool below. Indian, Dutch, and English boys caught them, and so did American boys who had the good—or bad luck to be born in the last century. But, although Minetta Brook still flows in its ancient bed, no finny inhabitants tempt the urchin who would "play truant any day to go fishin'."

Two rivulets united to form the stream. The western one rose near the intersection of Sixth Avenue and Seventeenth Street, and flowed, practically in a straight line, to the middle of the block bounded by Fifth and Sixth Avenues and Eleventh and Twelfth Streets, where it was joined by the eastern branch. The latter had its origin in a spring east of Fifth Avenue and above Twentieth Street, and ran, parallel with the other, to the southwest corner of Union Square ; thence it curved to the west and followed an irregular course to the junction, receiving two tiny tributaries on its way. From this point the brook flowed, in a southerly direction, to Fifth Avenue below Clinton Place. Then curving towards the west, it crossed Washington Square, ran parallel with and just south of Minetta and Downing Streets, across West Houston Street, to the little swamp already mentioned.

Its sources were high, and, save in the vicinity of Washington Square, which was low and flat, the eastern and southern banks of the

Greenwich

stream were hilly. Between West and Amity Streets they were densely wooded, and through the forest which extended toward the south ran the foot-path from the city, which crossed the Canal Street ditch by a single plank and led to Greenwich through the line of the present Bedford Street. On the western side of the stream, broad, fertile fields stretched to the Hudson ; and here, in a little, triangular space between three low hills, lay, in ancient days, the Indian village of Sappokanican. The natural advantages of this plain early attracted the attention of the Dutch settlers, and the first house on the island, outside of the little settlement around the fort, was the farmhouse of Governor Wouter Van Twiller, erected here about 1634. Before long other houses clustered around it, forming a little settlement, which later became the village of Greenwich. At its northern end, on the bank of the river (where Little Twelfth and Washington Streets now cross) stood old Fort Gansevoort ; and close beside the water, on the square now bounded by Washington, West Tenth, West, and Charles Streets, stood the State Prison, which moved to new quarters at Sing Sing in 1828. This district has always been exceptionally healthful, and in 1798, when the city was scourged with yellow fever for the third time, Greenwich became the refuge of many of its citizens. Even the

Richmond Hill

banks of Wall Street closed their doors, and opened temporary offices in what has ever since been called Bank Street.

While the village was still a Dutch settlement, Minetta Brook, or at least its lower portion, was known as *Bestavaar's Killitje,* and as late as 1730, when Governor Montgomery granted a new charter to the city, one of the boundaries specified was "Bestaver's Rivulet."

Near the outlet of the stream, and between it and the Lispenard Meadows, rose a considerable elevation known as Richmond Hill, the southwestern end of a long, irregular chain of sand mounds, called the *Zandt-berg*, which stretched from the present Lafayette Place to the vicinity now marked by the crossing of Hudson and Vandam Streets. Directly over the spot where Charlton and Varick Streets now intersect stood "The Mansion," built about 1760 by Abraham Mortier, Commissary of the British troops. The site was superb. Far off to the south, over the trees and shrubbery which fringed the hill, over the meadows which Rutgers earned and Lispenard won, and over the flank of the *Kalch Hoek,* lay the little city. To the north, beyond the silvery flash of the rippling brook, spread the fertile plains on which nestled the little village of Greenwich; and to the west, the grounds stretched their grassy slopes to the river,

Aaron Burr

which ever rolled by in silent majesty. Within the estate, at the foot of the hill, the waters of Minetta Brook expanded into a beautiful lake, called the Richmond Hill Pond, but better known by its later appellation of Burr's Pond.

Washington occupied the house in 1776; and, after the retreat of the American forces to Harlem, it was tenanted by various British officers. In 1789, which marked the beginning of government under the Constitution, Vice-President Adams and his family lived here, and letters from Mrs. Adams, written during their occupancy, pay glowing tribute to the loveliness of the spot.

But Richmond Hill is best known as the home of Aaron Burr, who, on May 1, 1797, leased the premises for a term of sixty-nine years. Here his lovely daughter, Theodosia, entertained as her father's guests many of the most eminent men and women of the day,—among them Louis Philippe, the "Citizen King," Talleyrand—clubfooted and sarcastic, Comte de Volney, Brant, the Indian chief, statesmen, diplomats, scientific men, and litterateurs. No man was more honored than Aaron Burr until that fatal July morning in 1804, when, under the Heights of Wiehawken, he killed Alexander Hamilton, the beloved of the people. This terminated his own career, and with it ended the fame of Richmond Hill.

Washington Square

No one cared to reside there ; and, when the hill was levelled, the house was lowered to the street grade and moved back to the north of Charlton Street, where it passed through the successive gradations and degradations of boarding-house, theatre, circus and menagerie before its final disappearance.

Washington Square was not always the attractive spot that it is now. When the Minetta Brook traversed its site, the ground was low and wet,—so undesirable, even after it was drained, that it was set apart as the Potter's Field. In it were buried, not only strangers and paupers, but citizens whose families were unable to afford the cost of a lot in the church cemeteries ; and later, when interment in the churchyards of those who had died of yellow fever was forbidden by law, these bodies too were buried here. The total number of burials in this area must have been very great. Certainly the evidence of this use remained for a considerable time; for we are told that, in 1841, long after interments had ceased and the tract had been filled and graded, the water drawn from wells in the vicinity "though very clear and pellucid to the eye, was overcharged with phosphate of lime (bone earth) and an extremely fetid animal matter."

Along the western bank of Minetta Brook, just below the junction of its two branches, there lay, in the early part of the present century, a large Jewish cemetery. So many yellow fever victims were buried here that there was no room for more, and a new tract, on Twenty-first Street, was purchased. Soon afterwards Eleventh Street was opened through the property, and all the bodies were removed to the upper graveyard, except a few which still remain in a small plot protected and hidden by a high brick wall.

Although Minetta Brook has been lost to sight for many years, we have abundant evidence that it still exists. Deep excavations near its course are almost invariably flooded by its waters, and heavy buildings over or beside it require elaborate foundations of piling.

Above Greenwich, the ridge, which formed the water-shed of the island, lay so close to the western shore that the streams emptying into the Hudson were, as a rule, small and insignificant. Furthermore, their memory is almost devoid of historical associations, for the principal growth of the early city was on its eastern side.

One of the more considerable of these streams rose near Eighth Avenue and Thirty-first Street, flowed south to Twenty-sixth Street, west to Ninth Avenue, and then northwest to its outlet at Twenty-ninth Street. It received the waters of several small tributaries

Small Streams above Greenwich

and the overflow from a diminutive pond near Seventh Avenue between Twenty-sixth and Twenty-seventh Streets.

The next stream to the north rose near the southwest corner of Central Park and followed a tortuous course, in a general southwesterly direction, to its outlet, through a marsh at the foot of Forty-second Street. This brook, which ran through the "Glass House Farm," once owned by Sir Peter Warren, collected the flow of a number of minor rivulets. Among them, were the outlets of two small ponds, one at Seventh Avenue and Thirty-fifth Street, and the other east of Seventh Avenue and between Thirty-eighth and Thirty-ninth Streets. A sewer, eight feet and six inches in diameter, discharging at Forty-second Street, still carries a large flow of fresh water from these ancient sources.

Other small and unimportant water-courses, emptying into the Hudson at Fifty-sixth, Sixty-seventh, Sixty-ninth, and Eighty-third Streets, drained the rough country which became the site of the picturesque, though not elegant, "Shantytown."

From One hundred and fourth Street, near Tenth Avenue, another brook made its marshy way to an outlet in Stryker's Bay, at Ninety-sixth Street; and a small branch, from the neighborhood of Tenth Avenue and Ninety-fifth Street, joined it at Eleventh Avenue.

Pond on Corlaer's Hook

The remaining streams on the west side were mere rills, some fed by springs and others carrying surface water only. They emptied into the river at One hundred and fifteenth, One hundred and thirty-eighth, One hundred and forty-second, One hundred and forty-ninth, and One hundred and fifty-seventh Streets, and just south of Fort Washington.

Returning to the eastern side of the island, we stop long enough to note a well at Bleecker Street and Broadway, which was drilled in 1832, through forty-eight feet of earth and four hundred feet into the rock. The water rose to within twenty-nine feet of the surface, and the flow was estimated at forty-four thousand gallons per day.

No streams emptied into the East River between Roosevelt and Houston Streets, and in all this district we know of but one small pond. This was situated on Crown Point, or Corlaer's Hook, south of Henry Street and between Jefferson and Clinton Streets. It was surrounded by large trees, and, although no distinct stream flowed from it, a wet meadow extended to the river and afforded an outlet for its surplus water. This was the region of shipyards, and many a vessel built upon these shores was sent to England for sale.

Beyond the high ground, which extended

The Stuyvesant Meadows

to the north as far as Rivington Street, lay ninety acres of salt marsh, bordered by low sand hills and known as the Stuyvesant Meadows. From Avenue A to the East River and from Houston to Twelfth Streets they stretched their dreary surface, broken only by the lines of the sluggish streams which drained them—or, rather, which failed to drain them. At the southern end of this region of wetness, near the shore, rose a little knoll, covering about an acre, cut off by creeks and marshes from the dry land which bordered the swamp, and completely surrounded by open water during exceptionally high tides. Its site is marked to-day by the narrow thoroughfare, one square long, called Manhattan Street. This inconsiderable eminence has been an occasion of stumbling to many a chronicler; for it alone is entitled to the name "Manhattan Island," which is used so often, instead of "Island of Manhattan," to describe the whole territory covered by that portion of the city lying south and west of the Harlem River.

The exact location of the streams which traversed "The Marsh"—as the Stuyvesant Meadows were frequently called—is not clear; even the number of them is doubtful. We are reasonably sure, however, of the position of two. Of these, the first, called Stuyvesant's Creek, rose in the neighborhood of Rivington

The Stuyvesant Country-Seats

and Suffolk Streets, crossed Stanton Street near Clinton, Houston Street near Sheriff, and Second Street near Houston ; thence it swung around the north side of Manhattan Island, emptying into the river near the foot of Third Street. The second stream, whose course is clearly indicated by existing records, had its origin near First Avenue and Sixth Street, crossed Tompkins Square, and flowed diagonally to its outlet near the foot of Ninth Street. We know that one—and probably two small waterways existed between these well-established streams, but the references to them are too indefinite to permit exact location. These creeks were the home of countless eels, and flounders in abundance could be caught at the bend of the shore near Twelfth Street, called Branda Munah, or Burnt Mill Point. The marsh ended at Twelfth Street, but through the higher ground above it a little stream ran, from near Avenue B and Tenth Street, diagonally towards the northeast, emptying at the foot of Fourteenth Street. In this vicinity was the Stuyvesant Skating Pond, in early years the scene of many a gay skating carnival.

On a hill which rose between the bank of the river and the present Stuyvesant Square, about where First Avenue and Seventeenth Street now cross, stood the country-seat of Petrus Stuyvesant, fourth Governor of New

Proposed Improvement

Amsterdam, whose vigorous policy and incorruptible character left an indelible impress upon the city. Near Twelfth Street and west of Second Avenue, as the streets now run, was the mansion of Gerardus Stuyvesant; and above the trees, on a knoll since furrowed by First and Second Avenues and Eighth Street, and finally levelled, rose the high hip-roof of a house with a lofty portico, the home of Nicholas William Stuyvesant.

Many surveys of the Stuyvesant Meadows were made from time to time, and many plans for their drainage prepared. The most interesting of these is a plan presented to the Council, in 1826, by Edward Doughty, City Surveyor. He proposed to build three canals through the district, running respectively through Sixth, Ninth, and Fourteenth Streets. These canals were each to be twenty feet wide, with plank bottoms and walls of stone, and ornamented with "iron railings and trees on each side, so as to render these streets a pleasant and desirable residence." Sixth Street, from Avenue A to the river, was to be widened by the addition of twenty feet on each side of the existing street, making the total width one hundred feet, and leaving a driveway forty feet wide on each side of the canal. Ninth Street was to be treated in a similar manner. The scheme was approved by Nicholas W. Stuyvesant, Henry Brevoort,

Cedar Creek

Augustus Wynkoop, Nicholas Fish, John Jacob Astor, and many other prominent men, who addressed a communication to "The Honourable, the Corporation," commending the project to favorable consideration. But remonstrances were filed by the score. Many were the objections urged and vigorous were the objectors who urged them. The plan was rejected, and a system of underground drainage and surface-filling was adopted. Its execution was tedious, but, when complete, twenty-one blocks of salt marsh had been reclaimed and made available for building purposes.

Strange as it may seem, the wells in this district yielded excellent water. The flow from one at the corner of Avenue D and Fifth Street, used by many families, was said to be "pure, both good for drinking and washing, and, as we believe, the best and cheapest that can be had . . . on the meadows." Another much-used well, with a good reputation, was located near the corner of Columbia and Rivington Streets.

At Seventeenth Street, just beyond Governor Stuyvesant's country-seat, was the outlet of another stream of considerable size, called Cedar Creek, which was fed by several springs in the district between Fifth and Sixth Avenues and Twenty-first and Twenty-seventh Streets.

The Plan of the Upper City

This stream, in passing through Madison Square, spread out into a pond,—once the duck-pond of Rose Hill Farm, which was bought, in 1747, by John Watts, brother-in-law of Lieutenant Governor De Lancey. Later in the century, during the visitations of yellow fever, Madison Square was used as a public cemetery. In 1806, the city ceded it to the United States Government, as a site for an arsenal, which was erected and occupied until 1823. A district east of the square, betweeen Twenty-third and Twenty-seventh Streets and Second and Fourth Avenues, was once known as Bull's Head Village, and here, for over twenty years, was the great cattle-market of the city.

About 1845, when steps were taken towards the laying out of Madison Square as a public park, and the suppression of the stream was determined upon, it was proposed to construct a diagonal street, over its bed, from Madison Avenue to the foot of Eighteenth Street; but the little brook was finally buried without this honor, and Broadway remained the only line to break the rectangularity of the gridiron on which this portion of the city was toasted.

The commissioners appointed, in 1807, to lay out the upper part of the city were Gouverneur Morris, John Rutherford, and Simeon De Witt. It is said that while examining the ground one fine day, when fleecy

Conflict of Streets and Streams

clouds were flying across the sky, they stopped at noon to discuss the problem near a bank where some workmen had been screening gravel. In illustration of his ideas, one of them—the story does not say which one—began to trace upon the ground with a stick a rough map of the island. Just as he had finished the outline, and was about to sketch in his proposed system of streets, the sun flashed forth from behind a passing cloud and threw across the skeleton map the shadow of the gravel-screen. "There is the plan!" exclaimed another; and forthwith it was adopted. For all time the shadow of that gravel-screen will cover the Island of Manhattan from First Street to Harlem River. Whether or not the plan adopted in 1811 really originated in this manner, it is certain that its absolute disregard of the natural topography of the land, and the blind way in which its provisions have been carried out, have resulted in serious sanitary and financial loss. In opening the streets and avenues, the natural water courses and swamps only received attention in so far as they were impediments to the work of construction. No thought of providing permanent channels, or of the evils which would result from the neglect to do so, received consideration. Streets were built across the beds of streams on solid embankments, like dams. If the

Ash Brook

flow was considerable, a culvert was roughly constructed; but it was usually laid with insufficient foundation and the weight of the superimposed embankment pressed it into the mire until its water way was closed. Stagnant ponds were formed in the hollow squares bounded by the new streets; and these, instead of being drained, were filled in as they lay, and upon them were constructed houses up whose walls the foul dampness continually crept, and whose cellars were veritable lairs of disease and death. In 1871, an extensive system of deep drainage was begun, and this has remedied, at great cost, unsanitary conditions which need never have arisen.

At the foot of East Twenty-fifth Street, lay the estate of John Lawrence. On it was a miniature pond, fed by a spring, and from this ran a tiny rill, which does not appear at all on many of the topographical maps of the island, but which gave its own name to the entire estate, long known as Ash Brook. The little stream was crowded out of existence many years ago, but some of the oaks that once shaded its banks remained to watch over its grave, and are still standing,—or at least were standing, a short time ago.

Above the line of Twenty-seventh Street, the physical structure of the island rapidly

Kip's Bay

changed. The gentle slopes of fertile soil gave place to a rougher and more varied formation; instead of the low, conical, sandy hills, masses of gneiss and granite rose in rugged outline to a considerable elevation; and the water-courses no longer flowed placidly through broad valleys and swampy meadows, but ran in deep channels between high, rocky hills. Some of these streams were fed by perennial springs, and were, therefore, constant in their flow; but many of the smaller ones were mere accumulations of surface water from a limited drainage area, and their beds were often dry in summer.

The eastern shore of the island, between the present lines of Thirty-third and Thirty-seventh Streets, recedes so as to form a considerable indentation, known, from the middle of the seventeenth century to this day, as Kip's Bay. On its shores, in 1653, lay the farm of Jacobus Kip, who was then Secretary of the province. It was a goodly estate, covering about one hundred and fifty acres, and comprising meadow, woodland, and stream. In front, across the river, stretched the fertile fields of *Lange Eylandt*, deeply indented by the estuary later known as Newtown Creek. To the south rose the wooded height, soon to be called Rose Hill; and it was sheltered from the north-west winds of winter by the broad back of the greater eminence to which Robert Murray

Sunfish Pond

afterwards gave his name. In 1655, Mijnheer Kip, having married a wife, and preferring the sweets of rural domesticity to the neighborly interest and surveillance of his fellow-townspeople, built himself a home upon his farm. Of course, a man of his standing and wealth—newly wed at that—must needs do all in befitting style ; so the brick was imported from Holland, and, with it, a stone carved with the ancestral coat of arms, which, in due course, projected over the spacious doorway. The house was a large double structure, so substantially constructed that it remained, in good condition, until 1851, when the fateful shadow of the commissioners' gravel-screen fell upon it, and it was demolished to make room for Second Avenue and Thirty-fifth Street, which cross over its site.

Murray Hill and Kip's Farm were encircled by two water-courses. The more southerly of these rose near Broadway and Forty-fourth Street, and ran, in a rather devious course, but practically parallel with Broadway and about three hundred feet east of its line, as far as Thirty-fourth Street. Thence it curved to the east, flowing between Thirty-first and Thirty-second Streets to the line of Third Avenue, and then swinging towards the north it crossed Second Avenue on the line of Thirty-fourth Street, which it followed to the bay. At Madison Avenue and Thirty-second Street

Stream North of Murray Hill

the stream expanded into a pond, which extended to Fourth Avenue and covered the site of the car-stables located at that point. This little lake, called Sunfish Pond, was famous fishing-ground, although on several occasions, during protracted drought, it nearly disappeared ; for the stream which fed it received very little spring water, and often, in summer, its bed was almost dry. In times of heavy rains, however, it overflowed its banks and spread from Murray Hill to Rose Hill. We are told that the inhabitants of houses along its lower course were compelled, more than once, to resort to boats as the only means of communication with dry ground.

The other stream, which emptied into Kip's Bay at Thirty-sixth Street, collected the flow of several small springs among the rocks in the vicinity of Forty-sixth Street, between Fifth and Sixth Avenues, and flowed, almost due east, to a point near Fourth Avenue, where it curved towards the south and passed, through the valley between Murray and Dutch Hills, to its outlet. On its way it received some little water, mainly surface drainage, gathered by minor tributary channels. The largest of these entered from the north, in the block bounded by Third and Lexington Avenues and Forty-second and Forty-third Streets.

It was at Kip's Bay that the British troops landed when they took possession of the city

Inclenberg

on September 15, 1776. On that memorable day the American forces abandoned their defences without firing a shot, and their compatriots in the city were in imminent danger of being shut in by the exultant Britons, who would speedily have stretched a cordon across the island from river to river, had not Mrs. Murray, the venerable wife of the Friend, Robert Murray, with rare presence of mind, invited the British officers to dine at her home, "Inclenberg," which stood on the Boston High Road near the present intersection of Fourth Avenue and Thirty-sixth Street. Generals Howe, Clinton, Cornwallis, and Tryon accepted the proffered hospitality ; and while they ate, drank, and jested over the repast,—studiously protracted by their hostess,—the American troops, by forced march over the western roads, escaped from their perilous position and joined Washington's army at Harlem Heights, where, on the following day, the British met with a cordial, but different, reception.

The residents of the district around Kip's Bay borrowed its name somewhat freely, and applied it indiscriminately to private estates and industrial establishments. We know of a "Kip's Bay Grocery," that was owned and kept for many years by a brother of Peter Cooper. To-day the passenger on any of the East River boats, though a stranger to the

DeVoor's Mill Stream

city, may easily identify the locality; for the name given to it nearly two hundred and fifty years ago stares him in the face, with all the emphasis that large letters and fresh paint can give, from the walls of a brewery.

In 1677, about the time that De Heere Graft disappeared and the great Wet Docks came into being, Sir Edmund Andros granted to David Duffore a tract of sixty acres, lying along the shores of the East River, between the present lines of Forty-first and Forty-eighth Streets. Deutal Bay indented the eastern edge, and a stream, which emptied into it near the foot of the Forty-seventh Street of to-day, ran through the northern part of the farm. On this stream the grantee built a grist-mill, but we have no record of any other improvements made during his occupancy. His name, however, remained associated with the property for many years after the latter passed from under his control, and the recorded deeds describe it successively as formerly belonging to "Deffore," "Devore," "Devoor," and DeVoor." The brook was known as DeVoor's Mill Stream when the estate, then called the Turtle Bay Farm, became the country-seat of Francis Bayard Winthrop. As a tiny rivulet, this brook rose among the rocks on high ground near Ninth Avenue and Seventy-second Street, and ran, southeasterly, in a narrow, stony channel, to Eighth Avenue and Sixty-fifth Street. Here it entered a wider valley, and its bed lay, for a considerable distance, through alluvial deposit. The banks were more or less boggy, and, just east of the point where the projections of Sixth Avenue and Sixty-third Street would cross, the stream formed a lake, about one hundred and fifty feet in diameter. Continuing in a general southeasterly course, the valley opened into a broad plain at Sixtieth Street, made swampy by the brook, which flowed through it sluggishly. (The pond near the Plaza, in Central Park, was formed by the excavation of this swamp.) The stream crossed Fifty-ninth Street between Fifth and Sixth Avenues, turned to the east, recrossed Fifty-ninth Street near Madison Avenue, and, at Fourth Avenue, curved again to the southeast, maintaining a fairly constant course to Second Avenue and Fifty-first Street, and then flowing south, parallel with Second Avenue, to Forty-eighth Street, where it turned sharply to the east until the line of First Avenue was reached. Here it swung again to the southeast, finding an outlet at Forty-seventh Street. In its course it received several tributaries, the most important being a brook which collected the flow from a number of small springs between Sixty-fourth and Sixty-ninth Streets and Fourth and Sixth Avenues. This feeder is

Turtle Bay

worthy of special mention, not on account of size or historic association, but because of the serious consequences which followed ill-planned attempts at suppression.

The Reverend Mr. Burnaby, whom we already know as an expert on Kissing Bridges, declares, in his diary, that another of these interesting structures spanned this stream "in the way . . . about three miles distant from New York, where you always pass over as you return," and he tells of it with evident satisfaction. It is interesting to speculate as to the probable train of reasoning which gave rise to the observance of this ancient custom. Did the ingenious youth of the day explain to the coy maiden that bridges and kisses are both conjunctions, and that there are times when the stream of conventional propriety may properly be spanned? However that may be, the bridge existed and probably it was well patronized, for Turtle Bay was a famous pleasure resort. Just above the bridge stood "Old Cato's Inn," famous for its dinners and suppers, and here large parties gathered for feasting and frolic. The social Mr. Burnaby enjoyed these occasions, and thus does he describe them:

"Thirty or forty gentlemen and ladies meet and dine together; drink tea in the afternoon; fish and amuse themselves till evening, and then return home in Italian chaises (the fashionable carriage in this and most parts of America,

Beekman Mansion

Virginia excepted, where they chiefly make use of coaches, and those commonly drawn by six horses), a gentleman and a lady in each chaise."

Just west of First Avenue and between Fifty-first and Fifty-second Streets, in a little rectangular area bounded on the east by the East River and Turtle Bay, and on the west and south by DeVoor's Mill Stream, stood the Beekman country-seat, a fine old mansion, which served as headquarters for Generals Howe and Clinton, and where Baroness Riedesel lived after the capture of her husband at Saratoga. Here, in consultation with the British officers, Major André passed the night before starting to meet the archtraitor Arnold. Here, in the greenhouse, was imprisoned Nathan Hale, and here Lord Howe sentenced to death that young martyr, whose only regret was that he had but one life to lay down for his country.

In later years, on the other side of the stream, near Third Avenue and Fifty-first Street, lay the Potter's Field, used after burial in Washington and Madison Squares had been prohibited. Near its northern boundary was a spring, yielding soft water of such reputed purity that it was carted into the city, where it readily sold for two cents a pail ; and the demand for it did not cease until some time after the Croton supply had been introduced.

The Yorkville District

In 1865, the natural drainage afforded by DeVoor's Mill Stream was interrupted by the embankments which were reared on the lines of advancing streets, and several squares along its course, in the neighborhood of Fifth Avenue and Fifty-seventh Street, were flooded and remained flooded for years. Gradually these, and similar ponds near Fifth Avenue and Sixty-fifth Street, were filled in and built upon, but without adequate drainage ; in consequence, the entire district, and the region north of it, became so notoriously unhealthful that the physicians of the city, in treating cases of intermittent, remittent, or typhoid fevers, usually inquired of the patient if he had been visiting in the vicinity of Yorkville or Harlem. Under the act of 1871, a suitable system of underground drainage has been constructed, and the former insalubrious conditions have disappeared. The old stream now finds an outlet through a sewer nine feet in diameter, which discharges into the East River at Forty-ninth Street.

To the east of Hamilton Square was a short and small water-course, which ran, southeast, from about Second Avenue and Sixty-fifth Street, across First Avenue between Sixty-fourth and Sixty-fifth Streets, and emptied into the river between Sixty-first and Sixty-second Streets. It collected a very limited

The Saw-Kill

amount of surface water, and in midsummer its bed was often dry.

From the rocky ridge which overlooked Bloomingdale Village, two rills flowed to the east. One of these rose near Ninth Avenue and Eighty-fifth Street, flowed in a southerly direction through Manhattan Square, where it spread into a little pond, and then turned to the east, crossing Central Park to Fifth Avenue near Seventy-fifth Street, and receiving three tributaries within its limits,—two from the north and one from the south. At Seventy-fifth Street near Third Avenue it was joined by the other stream, which rose in the vicinity of Eighth Avenue and Eighty-ninth Street, and flowed, in an easterly course, through the meadow afterward converted into the greater Croton Reservoir, to about the line of Sixth Avenue, where it curved to the southeast, crossing Fifth Avenue near Eighty-third Street, Madison Avenue near Seventy-ninth, and Fourth Avenue near Seventy-sixth Streets. Near its junction with the southern branch the old Boston Post Road crossed it; and from this point it ran, almost due east, to its outlet near the foot of Seventy-fifth Street. Near Avenue A, it received a short superficial tributary from the northwest.

This stream was known as the Saw-Kill, and on its banks, about 1680, John Robinson, a well-to-do merchant, bought a farm of

The Great Tidal Marsh

thirty-eight and a quarter acres, built a dam, erected a grist-mill, and did a thriving business in the manufacture and sale of flour.

Much of the eastern part of the district originally drained by this stream lay below the level of the city sewers, and in converting its fields and valleys into building-lots, the natural outlet was choked, and fifteen acres of land were flooded. Lots on Seventy-fourth Street, between Third and Fourth Avenues, were covered with from six to ten feet of water. Nearly every inhabitant of the surrounding region was stricken with malarial disorder, and many died, among them the contractor who was responsible for all the trouble. Between 1871 and 1878, about seven thousand feet of deep drains (apart from sewers) were constructed in this district, and these removed all excess of water from the soil, and, with it, malarial disease disappeared.

Two insignificant brooks rose between First and Second Avenues, flowed to the east and emptied into the river, the one near Eightieth Street, and the other near Ninetieth Street. Save for the narrow valleys in which their channels lay, the ground, even to the shore, was well elevated as far as Ninety-first Street. West of Third Avenue the land, though gradually sloping to the north from Ninety-sixth Street, remained high until One hundred and

The Harlem Flats

fourth Street was reached, where the descent to the Harlem flats was very abrupt—in places, precipitous. But the tract lying between Third Avenue and the shore, and Ninety-second and One hundred and fourth Streets, was an immense tidal marsh, intersected by numerous wide inlets, through which the East River made its way, even to the wall which, for several blocks, supported the eastern side of Third Avenue. A little stream, which led from a spring in Central Park, near the imaginary intersection of Sixth Avenue and Ninety-eighth Street, skirted the northern end of the high ground lying west of this marsh, and emptied into one of its inlets.

North of a diagonal line extending from Eighth Avenue and One hundred and twelfth Street to the East River at One hundredth Street, and east of Eighth Avenue, the character of the land changed completely. The rocky formation ended, and broad fertile meadows stretched to the Harlem River on the north and east. The Indians called the land "Muscoota"; the white man called it "The Flats." With the exception of a single hill, —now Mount Morris Park—which rose to an elevation of about one hundred feet, this region was low and level, covered with alluvial deposit and devoid of large trees. All indications make it seem highly probable that the entire district was originally submerged;

Nieuw Haarlem

and that the waters of the Hudson, pouring through the valley which cuts the rocky ridge on the west at Manhattanville, swept over its plains to mingle with those of the East River.

That these flats proved attractive to the early Dutch colonists is not surprising, for the topography was of the sort with which they were most familiar. As early as 1636 they came, and they stayed. It is a rather curious fact that the first white settler in the new district should have been a Frenchman, Henri de Forêt; but others followed so closely that, although he died about a year after his arrival, he had already been surrounded by Dutch neighbors. They built their homes on the site of an Indian village, at the foot of the isolated rocky hill, which they named *Slang Berge*, or Snake Hill, and which is known to us as Mount Morris. The settlement grew, and—like all new settlements—needed a name. Each Dutchman, with fond thoughts of home, wished it to bear the name of his native town. But, unfortunately, they came from many towns and could not agree. The wise old Governor, Peter Stuyvesant, undertook to solve the problem; and, after questioning each settler as to his former residence, and finding that *none* had come from Haarlem, he nipped in the bud all jealousy by christening the place Nieuw Haarlem.

Along the southern edge of The Flats ran a

Montanye's Rivulet

considerable creek, twenty feet deep and one hundred feet wide where it emptied into Hell Gate Bay, near the foot of One hundred and sixth Street. One of its branches rose in the rocks east of Bloomingdale, entered what is now Central Park near the line of One hundred and first Street, then curved northeast and east, and joined the main stream near where One hundred and ninth Street now enters Fifth Avenue. In its course, it flowed through McGowan's Pass, rapidly, but in nothing like so much of a hurry as the stream of redcoats which ran through it, pursued by Washington's troops, after the battle of Harlem Plains. From here to the mouth of Turtle Creek stretched a line of fortifications, never used; and to the east, upon Mount St. Vincent and a neighboring elevation, arose, at a later date, Fort Clinton and Fort Fish. This brook was long known as Montanye's Rivulet, and, in the development of Central Park, was used to feed the Pool, the Loch, and Harlem Lake.

The northern and larger branch of the stream collected the flow from a number of springs at the foot of the steep hills which flanked "Martje Davit's V'lei," or "The Hollow Way," at One hundred and twenty-fourth Street, where Manhattanville afterwards nestled. From this valley, which witnessed the rout of the British troops at the battle of Harlem, the stream

Benson's Creek

flowed placidly, between swampy banks, to a point west of where Fifth Avenue crosses One hundred and seventeenth Street. Then it swung towards the south, received the flow of its southern branch, and turned towards the east along the line of One hundred and sixth Street.

Soon after the settlement of Nieuw Haarlem, the enterprising Dutchmen organized an improvement company of a primitive sort. They determined to construct a dam and gristmill, and to erect a tavern. Probably they decided upon the tavern first. However this may be, they built the dam in 1667, a little west of the present Third Avenue line. The gristmill stood at its northern end. Two bridges crossed the stream ; one just below the dam, and the other, over which the post-road ran, at the head of the mill-pond, west of the present Fifth Avenue.

In 1730, Derick Benson, of Greenwich Village, bought the property. Thenceforth the pond and creek were called by his name, and the point on the shore, south of the creek, became Benson's Point (afterwards Rhinelander's Point). In 1738, the property was further improved by Samson Benson, brother of Derick ; and, at the time of the Revolution, it was occupied by the soldiery and the buildings were burned to the ground. After the war, Benjamin Benson built a stone farmhouse and a

Harlem River

wooden mill, three stories high, which remained until work was begun on the Harlem Canal, in 1827.

This latter enterprise was, for those days, a gigantic speculation. The scheme provided for a canal sixty feet wide, faced with stone, following the line of Harlem Creek, and extending through the Hollow Way to the Hudson. A street, fifty feet wide and three miles long, was to be laid out on each side of the canal. The estimated profits were large and the prospectus most tempting. As a bonus, forty houses and lots were to be distributed among the subscribers. Eleven thousand shares of stock, at fifty dollars each, were placed on the market, and, with great flourish of trumpets, work was begun at the eastern end. Solid walls of masonry arose, expensive locks were constructed, and the canal was completed almost to the Fifth Avenue line. But disaster overtook the enterprise and it was abandoned.

East and north of The Flats stretched the Harlem River, which the Indians called by the same name they gave to the meadows themselves,—Muscoota. Beyond it lay the lands of the Morris family, and near its mouth, half-hidden by trees, stood the home of that aristocrat and laborer, Gouverneur Morris,—framer of the Constitution and tiller of the soil,

Macomb's Dam

skilled alike in diplomacy and hay-making. Near by was the country-seat of Lewis Morris, one of the signers of the Declaration of Independence. Mill Brook babbled noisily through this fair estate. Beside it, a little to the east of the old Boston Road, and just north of the line of One hundred and fifty-ninth Street, stood the school-house where the children of the Morris family received their early education; and the family church, St. Ann's of Morrisania, guarded the remains of their dead.

Beyond the Harlem Bridge, to the northwest, the shores were low, and a considerable swamp, intersected with numerous inlets and streams, stretched along the southwestern side from One hundred and thirty-fifth to One hundred and fifty-first Streets. On the northeast emptied the Mott Haven Canal and Cromwell's Creek; and just above the latter General Macomb waged unsuccessful warfare with his neighbors of lower Westchester. Twice he built a dam across the Harlem River, and twice the countryfolk destroyed it. Central Bridge now crosses the spot, but to this day the name of Macomb's Dam clings to the locality.

Above One hundred and fifty-ninth Street, for a distance of two miles, the shores were high and the river received no tributaries save a few small rills which trickled from the steep slopes of Washington Heights. Sherman

King's Bridge

Creek, which collected the flow from several small streams, emptied into it nearly opposite Fordham Heights; and from its southern bank rose the hill, two hundred feet high, on which stood Fort George.

About a mile and a half farther north, the river curves towards the west, and here the first bridge to the mainland was constructed by Frederick Phillipse, early in 1693. It purported to be for the convenience of the public, but its chief function was to furnish revenue to its owner; for it was a toll-bridge, and the keeper of the gate collected three-pence from each traveller "passing over with a horse." For sixty-six years the Phillipse family enjoyed this monopoly; but in 1759, during the French and Indian war, Benjamin Palmer decided to build a parallel bridge which should be free to the public. Colonel Phillipse tried to kill both the project and the projector by causing Palmer to be drafted twice as a soldier; but the latter hired substitutes, paying five pounds for the first and twenty pounds for the second. So the bridge was built and opened, and the people expressed their satisfaction by a barbecue on Bowling Green. During the Revolution the British burned the free bridge and erected fortifications which controlled the other. Across the old King's Bridge marched Knyphausen and his Hessians, on their way to ravage Westchester; and close by, Lord

Howe, who seems always to have been blessed with an excellent appetite, ordered dinner for himself and his staff at the Blue Bell Tavern. Doubtless he enjoyed it, for this was a famous hostelry, Beyond it, on Vault Hill, which was the private burial-place of the Van Cortlandt family, were stored at this time the public records of New York, concealed by Augustus Van Cortlandt, the City Clerk. In 1781, Washington's army lay encamped upon and around this eminence, while Clinton's troops occupied the southern side of the creek. All night the British sentries, who expected an attack in the morning, watched the blaze of the American campfires ; but when the dawn broke, the place was empty, and Washington was far on his way to join Lafayette, Wayne, and De Grasse before Yorktown, and to fight the ten-days' battle which ended the war.

At King's Bridge the Harlem River ended and Spuyten Duyvil Creek began. The latter stream wound its inebriated course to the Hudson through broad marshy meadows, which so attracted the first Dutch colonists on their arrival that the settlement at the lower end of the island was not made without much debate. The Indians called it Schorakapok, or Spouting Spring, and Tibbett's Brook, which enters from the north, was the Mosholu to them. Here they gave battle to the crew of the *Half Moon*, anchored in its waters; and on its shores, after the fight was over, the sailors laid their dead to rest. It seems strange that the first possession of the white man upon the island should have been a grave.

From De Heere Graft to Spuyten Duyvil nearly all of the pleasant "Fontanels and Issues of running waters" have disappeared, or are fast disappearing. Here and there, in the upper part of the island, a ghost of a brook, like an old man in his dotage, babbles feebly of the days when it was lusty and strong, when the trout leaped in its waters and the bears drank from its pools.

We know that the island is no longer young; that the laughing streams and smiling valleys which once dimpled its face have given place to the countless hard wrinkles, called streets; but, in the heart of each faithful old lover of the land of the Manhatoes, the memory of its rippling waters is still an everflowing spring of pleasure.

Barnard College

343 MADISON AVENUE

COURSES IN AMERICAN HISTORY

For Undergraduates. General course, reading, recitations and lectures.—Three hours a week: H. A. Cushing, A.M.

For Graduates. Political History of the Colonies and of the American Revolution.—This investigation course, extending through two years, deals in the first year with the settlement of the Colonies and their development in the seventeenth century, and in the second year with the growth of the system of colonial administration, the conflict with the French, and the revolt of the Colonies. The work of the students consists chiefly in the study of topics from the original sources, with a formal account of the results of such study.—Two hours a week for two years: Professor Herbert L. Osgood, Ph.D.

These courses are open not only to candidates for degrees, but to special students who can show ability to read French and German, and can satisfy the Dean and Faculty of their general competence.

Half Moon Series

Published in the Interest of the New York City History Club.

VOLUME I. NUMBER XII.

THE BOWERY.

BY

EDWARD RINGWOOD HEWITT

AND

MARY ASHLEY HEWITT.

Origin of Bouwerie Lane

THERE was a time when the "Bowery" was a name both soberly derivative and pleasantly appropriate; but of those days when the lane running between the Dutch bouweries, (*boerderij,* farm) or farms, was inevitably Bouwerie Lane, two material things alone remain to these days when the Bowery is the Highway of the Confusion of Tongues. Of these, one is a branch of the patriarch pear-tree which survived from the orchard of Peter Stuyvesant, planted probably about 1664; it lived to see its surrounding gardens and green fields swallowed up in brick and mortar, and in the course of the city's growth it became a land-

Bouwerie Lane the only Entrance to New Amsterdam

mark, protected by a railing, at the corner of Third Avenue and Thirteenth Street. But neither dignity nor age availed it, for in November, 1867, a loaded truck broke it down, and aside from individual souvenirs all that speaks for it is the little branch labelled and preserved at Police Headquarters.

The other still stands and mutely speaks of ancient days. It is the mile-stone in the Bowery, opposite Rivington Street, on which, if it does not happen to be covered over with bills, one may still read the legend, "2 miles to City Hall." This stone has seen the rolling of the old mail-coaches and the measured marching of many feet. For it was through long years that the Bouwerie Lane was the only highway leading to the little town clustered about Fort Amsterdam. But for many years after the settlement of New Amsterdam highway is rather too large a name to apply to the wooded, wandering lane, whose sole use was to connect the outlying farms or bouweries with the town. The town was a trading-post; but very early in its settlement it became evident to the ruminating minds of the Dutch West India Company that the fur trade was good, but that farmers they must have. Now there were more Indians about than was soothing to a peace-loving mind, so that fair inducements were necessary; and the West India Company accordingly offered each farmer

Conditions Attending Grant of Bouwerie

free transportation over sea, together with his wife and family, and on his arrival the grant of a "bouwerie," or farm, of partly cleared land partly ready for the plow, a house, barn, farming implements, and tools, together with four horses, four cows, sheep and pigs in proportion (thus the records), the usufruct and enjoyment of which the husbandman should have during six years, and on the expiration thereof should return the number of cattle he received. The entire increase should remain with the farmer. The rent for the cleared lands and the bouweries was one hundred guilders annually, and eighty pounds of butter.

These inducements wrought upon the minds of the thrifty Dutch, and early in Governor Kieft's reign, 1637–1647, the island between Wall Street and Fourteenth (approximately) was divided into six bouweries. Two of these the outgoing governor, shifty Wouter Van Twiller, took, "boodled," to quote Mr. Janvier, unto himself. But the thick-witted and hot-headed policy of Governor Kieft soon plunged the settlers into a fierce war with the Indians, and the lonely bouweries were sacked and pillaged and destroyed, and the surviving settlers glad to take refuge in the fort.

Mr. Valentine recounts the next attempt in the settlement of a little elevation at about the junction of Chatham Street and the Bowery,

Promise of Prosperity

known to the natives as Werpoes, and supposed to be an Indian lookout. Here a giant negro, known as Emanuel de Groot, was allowed to form a settlement, together with ten other negroes and their wives, all superannuated slaves who were given their freedom. Each was to pay the town 22½ bushels of grain and one fat hog annually, and their children were to remain slaves. In the midst of the settlement was an enclosed clearing for the protection of the cattle of the burghers. And for the further protection of the live-stock which wandered at will through the forests, a clearing was ordered to be made from the Great Bouwerie at about the present Fourteenth Street to Emanuel the Negro's; and all who wished to pasture their cows therein for better protection against the Indians were required to appear and help to fence it in. Thus the site of the present Bowery was the first extensive clearing, outside the settlement, made on the Island of Manhattan.

It was not until the arrival of Peter Stuyvesant as governor, in 1647, that there was any promise of prosperity for the bouweries. In 1651, after four years of firm and vigorous fair-dealing had regained the friendship of the Indians, he caused to be bought for himself the Great Bouwerie, paying therefor 6400 guilders. This was an extensive property, embracing the land lying east of Orange Street, north

Stuyvesant's Great Bouwerie

of East Broadway, and extending about two miles along the East River. The other bouweries were known by the names of their tenants, rather than by their numbers, 1, 2, 3, 4, 5, 6, and were called Bylevelts, the Schouts, Wolferts, Van Corlaers, Leanderts, and the Pannebackers, but they changed owners, and it is not until after very many years that we find them bearing familiar and interesting names. The Great Bouwerie has an interest for us as the home of that testy old governor, truculent of temper and true of heart, where he lived in prosperous retirement, after New Amsterdam had become New York, and he had returned from Holland and his hard-won vindication before their High Mightinesses the States-General. Here, among his orchards and gardens sloping to the shore, Peter Stuyvesant lived, with Judith his wife, until he reached the ripe age of eighty years; then dying, he slept in his beloved Bouwerie Church. St. Mark's, on the corner of Second Avenue and Tenth Street, stands on the site of this old church of Stuyvesant, and there his gravestone may be seen.

To Stuyvesant and his bouwerie, Bouwerie Lane largely owes its permanence, for while he was still governor another outbreak of the Indians was occasioned by the thick-witted violence of a Dutch citizen, who shot a squaw whom he found stealing his peaches. The existence of the farms was threatened as be-

Bouwerie Village

fore, and Stuyvesant ordered all living in isolated places to come into the town, or else to bind themselves into villages. This was the origin of Bouwerie Village. Stuyvesant built the church, which together with the inn and the blacksmith-shop constituted the village. In the church on Sunday officiated with due solemnity Dominie Selyns, who during the less holy days of the week was the town schoolmaster, and to him succeeded Dominie Megapolensis, who remained pastor of the church to the end of his days. Stuyvesant contributed annually one hundred dollars ($100) to the support of this personage, and seems to have regarded the church as his personal property. Judith, his widow, bequeathed it in her will to the Dutch Reform denomination. Its use lapsed for many years, and its site at last, in 1795, became the site of the Church of St. Mark, as we know it now.

Most of the streets of New Amsterdam originated in paths that were the shortest way to some place of general use, and Bouwerie Village with its inn and church confirmed the incidental lane running between the farms into the beginnings of a thoroughfare. Stuyvesant is reported to have made a map of the town for their High Mightinesses, but I have not been able to find any copy of it; the earliest maps to be seen do not extend so far as the bouweries. But four years after the

English occupation it was ordered that the small villages without the walls construct a carriage-road to Haarlem, and for this the lane, which Stuyvesant had caused to be much improved, was used as the beginning. Thus began a new life for wooded Bouwerie Lane. Up to this time the frequenters of the lane had been those only whose immediate use or pleasure lay among the farms along it or in the Bouwerie Village. One of the many interesting maps which I have seen through the courtesy of Judge Daly, calls the lane the way "to the governor's that last was." Even as late as 1660, Mr. Valentine tells us of one Jansen who petitioned to be released from his tenancy of a bouwerie, on the ground that his ride to town was through two miles of dense forest. But now Bouwerie Lane was to become part of the only highroad leading to the town, destined thereby to be the scene of all the historic entries of the ensuing century.

Bouwerie Lane Becomes a Highroad

In 1673, this road, which had been ordered made, was fairly open, running along substantially the lines of Broadway to Park Row, Chatham Street, and the Bowery; continuing in the line of the Bowery until it met Broadway again at Fifteenth Street. Along this the post-rider began making his monthly journey, at much risk to life and limb, establishing the first postal connection between New York and Boston. Notice was given to

Post Boy Rides from New York to Boston

"those that be disposed to send letters, to bring them to the secretary's office, where in a locked box they shall bee preserved till the messenger calls for them, all persons paying the post before the bagg be sealed up." The dangers and difficulties of the way made the ride of the post-boy a serious matter, and the expense of the carriage caused the sending of a letter to be of weighty consideration ; fourpence (4*d.*) within sixty miles for a single sheet was not for cheap gossip.

With the opening and improving of this road, the Bowery Lane, as the English called it, grew into a new life. The little tavern of Bowery Village, which Jacob Leisler described as "a good neat house, about two miles from the city," made a delightful turning-place in a pleasure jaunt, and a safe refuge in time of scourge. Here the Commissioners from the New England States, declining to enter the town because of the violence of the prevailing small-pox, met with those of New York, in 1690, to discuss the invasion of Canada. It was the enterprising landlord of this inn, John Clapp, who published the first almanac of New York, in 1697, and it was the same lively gentleman who the year previous had introduced the first hackney-coach for hire. In the days of Dutch dominion, the water was the natural thoroughfare wherever possible, as more convenient to the Dutch mind. But Englishmen

Life in Bowery Lane

and Englishwomen brought English manners; so horses, races, cards, dice, and driving for pleasure began to change the face of things, and not least the green and sober Bowery blossomed into life. Madame Knight, a Boston lady, visiting New York in 1704, kept record of her experiences:

"Their Diversion in Winter is Riding in Sleys about three or four miles out of the town where they have a House of Entertainment at a place called Bowery; and some go to Friends Houses, who handsomely treat them. X—— gave us a handsome entertainment of five or six Dishes and choice Beer and metheglin, Cyder &c., all of which she said was the produce of her farm. I believe we mett 50 or 60 Sleys that day; they fly with great swiftness, and some are as furious that they 'll turn out for none except a Loaden Cart. Nor do they spare of any diversion the place affords, but are sociable to a degree theyre Tables being as free to theyre Naybours as to themselves."

Their tea-tables, good Madame Knight; but the dinner at eleven in the morning was in strict seclusion, which it was a social sin to disturb. So dwelt the Dutch along Bowery Lane, amid their trim and flourishing gardens, in their low-set houses. A thrifty folk, who rose at dawn, and routed idleness and dirt. The parlor was a room of solemn state, opened once a week for the devastation of cleaning that was the good Vrouw's creed, the floor covered anew with fine white sand, swept into intricate patterns by the skilful wife, and then closed as a sanctuary until another seven

Stuyvesant Houses

days rolled by. Funerals were rare and solemn enough to warrant the opening of this sacred door; weddings, too, were permitted to turn its low hinges, but I fancy the gayer sort crept back into the kindlier kitchen. The kitchen was the family-room, where around the great open fire there was spinning and drowsing and content. It was in Stuyvesant's house, standing near where the St. Mark's churchyard now is, that the terms of capitulation of New Amsterdam are said to have been signed.

This house is now believed to have stood near the corner of Third Avenue and Twelfth Street ; accounts differ as to its destruction, but it is generally accepted that it was burned on Saturday, October 24, 1778, at about two o'clock in the morning. There were two other Stuyvesant houses erected on the estate, one called Petersfield appears from maps to have been by the shore of the East River, between Fifteenth and Sixteenth Streets. A long lane winding from the Bowery past the pear-tree of later fame served as the approach. The other, known within the present century as the Bowery House, was the house of Nicholas Wm. Stuyvesant, situated between First and Second Avenues and Eighth and Ninth Streets, with entrance from the Bowery near Sixth Street. Other names of interest in connection with the bouweries are the Bayards, the Beekmans, the Roosevelts, the De Lanceys, the Depeysters. The Bayards were connected with the Stuyvesants by marriage, and were prominent and prosperous citizens. Their bouwerie embraced between one and two hundred acres, extending from the present Bayard to Prince Street. It was not an original bouwerie granted to the family, but had been gathered by August Heemans, interesting as perhaps the first real estate speculator of those early days. A large windmill on the Bayard bouwerie is noted in many of the early maps, and it appears to have been of great consideration, for when the Bowery was built upon beyond that point, way was still left to reach it. At the laying out of the streets, it was found that the mill came upon the eastern side of Elizabeth Street. It continued to stand for some time after the Revolution.

Beekman Bouwerie

The Beekman bouwerie was bought, in 1760, by William Beekman, who came to America in the same ship with Stuyvesant. The farm lay along the East River, near the town, his orchard being where Beekman Street now lies. He had five sons and one daughter, who married Nicholas Wm. Stuyvesant. He was for nine years Burgomaster of New Amsterdam, and held many positions of high trust. His descendants were men of distinction during the Revolution, and have served through all

De Lancey Bouwerie

the generations to maintain the traditions of the founder of the family.

The Roosevelts, who bought part of the Beekman bouwerie, were also a family of distinction, their names appearing in the important petitions and protests and official undertakings of the provincial period.

The De Lanceys' estate lay north of Division Street to an irregular boundary at about Stanton Street, and extended from the Bowery to the river. Just south of it lay the bouwerie of Mr. Rutgers, and north, that of Mr. Depeyster. James de Lancey was a conspicuous figure, destined by the irony of fate and the course of events to appear first as the ideal aristocrat and champion of conservatism, then as the people's leader. He died in his country-seat on the Bowery on July 30, 1790. He had been Chief-Justice, Lieutenant-Governor, and a man of conspicuous ability.

At the house of Mr. Rutgers, whose country-seat adjoined that of Mr. de Lancey, met the Assembly in 1731, driven from the city by the small-pox.

From the time of Stuyvesant the bouweries had gradually become the country-houses of substantial and influential citizens. Yet in the midst of these peaceful lives were the eternal jealousies and reprisals. Judith Stuyvesant, widow of the sturdy Peter, bequeathed certain properties to the children of her "El-

Negro Insurrection

dest Son, deceased, with the further Limitacon that the said Inheritance and Legacyes shall not in any way be mixed In with the rest of the Estate which then shall be belonging to my said Son, or be of any profitt or benefitt to his wife or his Relations."

On an old map of New York there is, between the open common where is now our City Hall Park and the Bowery, a little picture indicating on close inspection fagots and people burning. This is a curious reference to the tragic end of the hysterical outbreak known as the Negro Insurrection. The gibbet, pictured farther to the west was the regular place and mode of capital punishment, but New York never had the habit of burning criminals alive, as one might judge from this lively representation. The Negro Insurrection, as it was called, occurred in 1741, when the town numbered ten thousand inhabitants, of whom perhaps two thousand were negro slaves. There seems to have been some not unnatural dread of a rising among these negroes, and when mysterious fires, following the detection and punishment of negro thievery, destroyed first the Governor's house in the fort, and the houses and barns of many well-known citizens, the latent suspicion at once awoke and was especially directed against some negroes who had been taken from a Spanish prize then in harbor, and, after the thrifty way

Mary Burton's Accusations

of the time, sold into slavery. Some not unnatural murmurings had arisen among them at this treatment, and these were now construed into threats against life and property. They were thrown into prison; but the fires continuing, the belief spread that this was indeed the dreaded plot to burn the town, murder the whites, and set up a negro colony.

A reward of a hundred pounds was offered by the Common Council for the plot and the names of the conspirators. A negro serving-woman, in prison as concerned in the thieving spoken of, seizing the opportunity to free herself and set herself up in life, gravely told a long story of conversations overheard between negroes frequenting the inn of which she was a servant, in which she incorporated the rumors prevalent, and named as conspirators a number of known visitors of the inn, together with her master and mistress. The story of the accusing children of Salem repeats itself in the person of this serving-maid, who first rid herself of her master and mistress and those whom doubtless for reasons of her own she thought it well to do without, and then, pleased with her importance, she let her tongue run on from accusation to accusation until she overreached herself, and began to accuse "persons of quality." Then at last the strain of hysteria broke, and outraged common decency saw with horror the record of its folly.

Burning of the Negroes at the Five Points

From spring up to the middle of August, Mary Burton's accusations had caused the imprisonment of one hundred and fifty-four negroes and twenty-four white people. Of these four white people, one a clergyman, Ury, the schoolmaster, and eighteen negroes were hanged, seventy-one negroes were transported, and fourteen negroes were burned to death in the little hollow in the wood, which later achieved evil note as the Five Points.

This first association of the Five Points links itself not unnaturally with the violent reputation of those converging streets in the days but just outgrown, when all the evil passions made their playground there ; but the stately and beautiful Tombs prison (now in process of demolition), which was so often the receiving hall for the climax of life at the Five Points, stands on the site of one of the gay pleasure-grounds of old New York. Those most remarking gentlemen, the Labadists, note the beautiful "Fresh Water" as they turn into Bowery Lane. This Collect, or *Kolch*, was the only considerable body of pure water within easy reach of New York. The water in the town itself was so bad that the horses refused to drink it, so that the importance of the Collect Pond is easily estimated. It lay between the streets, as we know the locality, White, Bayard, Elm, Canal, and Pearl, and was one of the favorite far walks and pleasant

The Tea Water Spring

drives from the town. The Tea Water Spring, not far off, at the head of Roosevelt Street and the Bowery, gave a supply of fourteen to fifteen thousand gallons of water daily, and never fell below three feet in depth ; its water was the sole supply of the dainty in the town for table and tea, and was peddled from door to door by enterprising tradesmen, who paid at the spring three-pence per hogshead. In 1796, the lessee of this famous pump, there erected, advertises to deliver water, not only for drinking and tea, but for washing and family use, for four shillings per hogshead of one hundred and forty gallons. Wetherbotham wrote of it in 1690 as about a mile out of the city. Near by was the Tea Water Pump Garden, whither it was the fashion of the polite world to resort, and pass a pleasant hour in the brewing of punch and the exchange of civilities. The famous old pump of the Tea Water Spring was found and identified, it is said, not long ago, in a saloon at 126 Chatham Street, where its origin was, of course, unknown. The water of the Collect became, for a time, part of the city supply, and it is reported that, in 1789, in an after-dinner speech, it was suggested that the city buy the pond and the surrounding grounds for a future park and pleasure-ground for the city. Had this been acted upon, those who have studied the relation between crowding and

Trial of First Screw Propeller

crime, parks and peace, can suggest what would have been saved the city. Instead, the suggestion was the jest of the day, the city would never grow so far, and the pond lay shining in the sun, until the encroaching town and the neighboring tanneries corrupted it into a menace to the public health, and it was finally filled in, and became, in 1836, the site of the Tombs prison. One event of greater interest than the pleasuring and picnicking with which it is associated, is the trial there, in 1798, of the first steamboat with a screw propeller ; it was the invention of John Fitch, was a boat eighteen feet in length, six feet beam, with square stern, round bow, and seats. It circled several times around the pond, making, it was thought, six miles an hour. The trial was witnessed by several notable gentlemen, who were interested in the problems involved,—John Stevens, Nicholas Roosevelt, and Chancellor Livingston.

The tanneries, which were the chief source of the corruption of the water of this idyllic pond, were gradually locating themselves in what was known as Beekman's swamp, a portion of the bouwerie of the Beekman family, bought by Jacobus Roosevelt in 1732 for two hundred pounds. The leather trade of the city still centres there. What portion of it could two hundred pounds now buy?

Another point toward which those walking

Pleasant Mount

on pleasure bent turned through the Bowery Lane, was a hill on the bouwerie of the Bayard family, known for a time as Pleasant Mount. It reached a considerable height at the point, since become the corner of Mulberry and Grand Streets, so that from its summit a fair view was to be had of the Hudson River and the shining *Kolch.* It was one of the first places fortified at the outbreak of the Revolution, and seems thereafter to have kept its warlike character. In 1787, a duel was fought there at eleven o'clock at night, in which the Chevalier de Longchamps was killed, it was supposed, by a Captain Verdier, late of the American army ; and later it was the scene of many of those boys' battles between the Bowery boys and the Broadway boys, in which, with sticks and stones and fists, with much excitement and little damage, the warlike spirit of the time exhausted itself. The levelling of this centre of contention began in 1802.

Meanwhile, in 1732, the first stage began its regular trips to Boston, once a month, the journey taking fourteen days. So, with the blowing of horns and buckling of straps and general spirit of adventure with which the hazardous trip was undertaken, the life of Bowery Lane as an important highway began. It was no longer simply the fashionable drive of the city, but the connecting link with the

Stages to Boston

world outside, destined to witness the stirring marching of the troops of both armies during the Revolution. Bouwerie Lane became soon on English tongues Bowery Lane; and Bowery Lane, the Bowery Road, and the High Road to Boston seem to have been used interchangeably by many; but in general, in the maps of this period, the Bowery Lane or Road is used to indicate that portion of the highway below Grand Street, and above the open space which afterward became Chatham Street. Above Grand Street we have the Road to Boston, the Boston Post Road, and in one Revolutionary map, "Road to Kingsbridge, where the rebels mean to make a stand." It became "The Bowery" in 1807.

By the time of the Revolution, the Bowery, as far as Grand Street, was already largely built upon, judging from thirteen licensed liquor vendors being registered there; and during the Revolution the British troops were encamped about it, not, it is to be supposed, to the detriment of the licensed vendors. When the day came for the formal evacuation of the city by the British, General Washington and Governor Clinton rested with the troops of the Continental army at Harlem until the British troops should have left the town. At the request of Carleton, to prevent disorder, Knox and a small troop of soldiers followed the retreating British army as those encamped

Evacution Day on the Bowery Road

about the Bowery joined the withdrawing troops. They marched down the Bowery Road to the Fresh Water Pond, near which they rested until about one o'clock in the afternoon ; then, as the rearguard began to embark, they took possession of the fort, and Knox with a small guard galloped back to Washington at Harlem. As the worn troops with their shabby uniforms moved down the Bowery, so lately vacated by the well-provided and brilliantly accoutred British army, the thousands who eagerly pressed out from the city to meet the coming heroes may well have felt that they were witnessing a miracle. One little incident broke the strain of solemn thanksgiving for the moment, and called once more uppermost the joy of contention and conquest. On reaching the Battery it was found that the British flag was nailed, in parting defiance, to the flagstaff, the halliards were unreefed, the cleats knocked off, and the pole greased to prevent climbing. Some unconquered British spirit had left this last defiance. But a young sailor named John Van Arsdale nailed on cleats, sanded the pole, and succeeded in hauling down the British colors and placing the American flag before the British ships had left the lower bay. This little flurry of excitement over, Washington and his staff marched back along the Bowery to Bull's Head Tavern, situated on the present site of the Thalia Theatre, where they were greeted with "many and ardent addresses" by the returned exiles, those thorough-going patriots who could not remain in their town during the British occupation. With hats wreathed in laurel, and wearing cockades of black and white ribbon on the left breast, this hearty assembly assured Washington that "they looked up to him with unusual transports of gratitude and joy."

Washington at Bull's Head Tavern

The British army of occupation, which had encamped along the Bowery, seems to have been more effective in determining the fate of the street than on the country it was here to subdue. For drinking-shops and places of low amusement sprang up to minister to the appetite of a semi-idle soldiery, and though the army vanished it left its curse behind for Bowery Lane. Two factors aided in making the first descending steps easy. The fashion of the town had already set out Broadway, so that that influence failed to keep the beautiful broad Bowery the stately street for which it was fitted; and on the other side the narrow streets leading from the Bowery to the water-side were inevitably, with increasing commerce, filled with sailors' lodging-houses and the homes and shops of those who minister to Jack ashore. Through these narrow streets ran open sewers which backed up at high tide, rendering their neighborhood any-

Vauxhall Garden

thing but wholesome and pleasant. Thus, little by little, the Bowery became the outlet for this life, and by slow, invisible steps its doom settled upon it.

Still, the close of the Revolution saw it yet remaining the fashionable drive and main highway. In 1799, a Frenchman named Delacroix leased for a term of twenty-one years (21) from John Jacob Astor the gardens and greenhouses laid out by Jacob Sperry, a Swiss, extending from Astor Place to Fourth Street, and from the Bowery Road to Broadway. This was to be the new Vauxhall Garden, a pleasure garden for New York for half a century. Many New Yorkers still remember the high wooden fence, the large gate opening under a semicircular sign from the Bowery, the gorgeous saloon made by the greenhouse moved against the fence, and the amusing diversions of the place. Balloon ascensions were popular and were of daily occurrence from the garden ; frequently a large cat was fastened in the basket, and the ascension of Miss Pussiana was advertised as an attraction at Vauxhall. The garden was laid out with ornamental shrubs, trees, walks, and flowers, and seems to have been an attractive resort. In 1807, a theatre was built in the centre, where song and dance varied the regular dramatic performances. Later, it became the popular place for public meetings. It survived

Charlotte Temple

in great popularity until after the Astor Place riots, and finally disappeared in 1855.

There is a reputed connection, immediately arising from the British army's occupation of New York, between the Bowery and that pathetic figure which Mrs. Rowson's *True Tale* made for our grandmothers a household word to conjure pity: Charlotte Temple, abandoned, ill, despairing, repulsed from Walton House, found shelter at a low wooden house some distance from the city, at 24 Bowery Lane, and there died. This story is related with every evidence of conviction by writers earlier in the century, and is confirmed, as being current and received, by Judge Daly, who describes the house indicated to him as being near Astor Place. The stone in Trinity churchyard which bears this name was cut by the head stonecutter when Trinity was last rebuilt, and is authentic only in sentiment.

I have already spoken of Bull's Head Tavern which stood on the site of the Thalia Theatre. It appears to have been a conspicuous inn in the days of Bowery Lane, frequented largely by butchers and drovers in consequence of the slaughter-yards adjoining. In a newspaper of 1763 appears the advertisement, "The noted Inn and Tavern in the Bowery Lane at the sign of the Bull's Head (where the slaughter-house is now kept) lately kept by Caleb Hyatt, is now occupied by Thomas Bayeaux who is

Fore-stalling on the Bowery Road

well provided with all conveniences for travellers." A prosperous butcher, Richard Varian by name, was landlord of the inn from 1770, until the breaking out of the Revolution, and also superintendent of the public slaughter-house. After the evacuation a petition appears from him to the Common Council, wherein he states that he has been in exile during the war, having in fact been privateering until he was captured toward the end of the war, at the close of which he returned to find his wife in full and prosperous possession of the inn. He was the tenant of another not less interesting butcher in the Fly Market; Heinrich or Henry Ashdor, or Astor, as the name variously appears in the petitions and records of the times. Henry Astor arrived with the British troops, but seems even during the Revolution to have entered into the "Mystery and Art of Butchering," in an exceedingly small way, aided by his handsome and frugal wife.

But it is not as the industrious butcher, using the small hours of the morning in preparation for the chance profits of the day that Henry Astor is prominently an interesting figure of Bowery Lane; rather as the forerunner of the *trust* of to-day, in his business conception, execution, and the effect upon the public mind. Practically all the cattle coming into the town entered of necessity by way of Bowery Lane, and Henry Astor was wont to leave his stall in

Old Bowery Theatre

the Fly Market, to ride far out the highway, meet the incoming drovers, and bargain with them for their stock. Great was the indignation of his fellow-butchers, who were thus obliged to buy of him, at a profit, and many were the petitions sent up to the Common Council against his "pernicious practices." Forestalling was to the people of the day a flagrant evil, but Henry Astor waxed prosperous and content; in 1796, he owned and lived on a substantial country-seat on the Bowery Lane, north of Bull's Head, owning as well the inn and slaughter-yards themselves. It is pleasant to find recorded in approving terms in the *Market Book*, that his devotion to his handsome wife grew with his prosperity, and that it was his delight to declare, as he loaded her with presents, that his "Dolly was the pink of the Powery."

Bull's Head remained the meeting-place of the butchers and drovers until 1826, when the inn was pulled down, and the Old Bowery Theatre, at first called the New York Theatre, and for a year the American Theatre, was built in its place. This was a very grand structure, of the appearance of white marble outside, with lofty pillars and entablature. The house was to seat three thousand persons, and the stage, the largest up to that time, was the first stage lit by gas; the interior decorations were elaborate, and the house as a whole was the

Mme. Hutin Dances

pride of the town and the hope of its managers.

It was hoped that the substantial people still living in the seventh and tenth and fourteenth wards would insure a fashionable audience, and secure the prosperity of the venture.

The theatre opened on October 23, 1829, with *The Road to Ruin* and *Rousing the Mind*, under the management of Gilfert, with a stock company including Mr. and Mrs. Duff, Mr. and Mrs. Young, Mr. and Mrs. George Barrett, and Edwin Forrest. The prices were fifty cents for the boxes and pit and twenty-five cents for the gallery, but Ireland remarks, "to keep part free from the vulgar and unrefined" the price for boxes was raised to seventy-five cents, the pit reduced to thirty-seven and one half cents. High hopes were held for the future of art in this brilliant setting; the opening poetical address welcomes nature in art to her first home, saying, in reference to the old acting,

> Reason still rose in Fiction's painted fears
> And gave but sadness where she asked for tears.

They were to change all that, it seemed; and indeed the very next year an exhibition of nature in art convulsed the proprieties of the city. Mme. Hutin, the first ballet dancer in the modern costume, danced a *pas seul* before

Theatre Burned

which most of the audience blushingly retired. The affair was the talk and turmoil of the town to the extent that the famous French dancer was obliged for a time to dance in Turkish trousers.

An evil fate menaced the lively prospects of this venturesome house, for it was four times burned; in 1828, when it was rebuilt in ninety days, again in 1836, rebuilt in 1837, burned again in 1839, again in 1845, and finally rebuilt in 1846. But between these fiery ordeals, its stage saw play their several parts many actors and actresses whose interpretations are still potent with the profession, and whose names are still household words. Here Mme. Malibran was paid $600 for a single performance, an enormous sum in those days. Here the Vestris dancers appeared, and George Holland made his debut in seven different parts in one evening; here was the last appearance of Mrs. Charles Young, whose husband was killed in a duel by Gilfert the manager. Mrs. J. W. Wallace, Jr. (Mrs. Sifton), made her first appearance here, and Miss Clifton the first American actress to play in London; Miss Priscilla Cooper, later to play her part as lady of the White House during President Tyler's brief tenancy of the Executive Mansion, after her marriage with Mr. Tyler, his nephew. In 1836, Charlotte Cushman made here her first New York appearance as

Famous Actors at the Bowery Theatre

"Lady Macbeth"; here also appeared John Gilbert as "Sir Edward Mortimer," Mrs. Melinda Jones as "Bianca," John Drew as "Doctor O'Toole," and the original Mrs. Potter as "Juliet." The elder Booth and Lester Wallack were two of the great names connected with the glories of the old Bowery Theatre.

With the shifting of population and the upward movement of the house of fashion and of substance, the Bowery Theatre came to cater to the new population about it; from 1850 to 1860 it was essentially the people's theatre, where melodrama and tragedy prevailed; good plays, often, and well presented, depicting always a rush and tumult of emotion. In 1879, the population had changed again, and the Bowery Theatre became the German Thalia; so it is still called, but the plays are now presented in that curious Hebrew corruption, spoken by so many thousands of our east-side neighbors, Yiddish.

Edwin Forrest, for so many years a conspicuous and attractive figure connected with the Bowery Theatre, lost much of the love the people bore him, from his connection with the Astor Place riots. Forrest had already figured in a riot, trying, though ineffectually, to still the violence of the mob which attacked the Bowery Theatre, on the night of July 10, 1834. This riot was one of those arising from the violence of the antagonism toward the anti-

Riot at the Bowery Theatre

slavery agitators in the city, and the attack on the theatre was caused by one of those curious twists of unreason, supposed in calmer times to be the attribute of the feminine mind. William Lloyd Garrison, in England, had joined with some Englishman in a bitter rebuke of his country for tolerating slavery; the attack had but added fuel to the smouldering fire. The manager of the Bowery Theatre was an Englishman, and unpopular; that was sufficient for the mob, already excited and balked of its hoped-for victims, and the "Bowery Theatre" became the cry. Forrest was playing, and exerted his power over the people to restore order, but in vain; finally the police drove out the rioters, who rushed on exulting in fresh destruction to Lewis Tappan's house on Rose Street.

The Astor Place riots, however, were a very different and much more disgraceful affair. They were the outcome of the personal jealousy between Forrest and Macready, an English tragedian. In the spring of 1849, Macready came to the Astor Place Opera House to play a parting engagement. He billed *Macbeth* for his opening night, and Forrest, playing at the Broadway Theatre, billed the same play for the same night. When the doors of the Opera House were opened a motley throng poured in, evidently sent to stop the play; they did stop it, in spite of Macready's pluck, and the

Astor Place Riot

efforts of the police. The decent citizens of the town now urged Macready not to throw over his engagement, to such effect that he once more billed *Macbeth* for May 10. The house was filled with well-known people, tickets being given to such only as were vouched for. About two hundred police were distributed among the audience, wisely as it proved, for when the play began, a number of roughs appeared, determined to rush upon the stage and seize Macready. Instead they were seized and ejected or confined. But meanwhile the mob outside had grown more and more violent, stoning the house and attacking the police until the Seventh Regiment appeared, preceded by the National Guard Troop. The mob attacked them with paving stones and marble scrap, until at length Colonel Duryee threatened to withdraw his men unless the order was given to fire. It was given at last, and the mob realized that it was dealing not with show, but with stern intent. Cannon were sent for and part of a battery, before which the mob retired. In all this frightful violence more than two hundred people were killed or wounded. Many people believed Mr. Forrest to be directly instrumental in the beginning of the disturbance, and he was widely blamed for not exerting his influence, and publicly condemning violence done in his name.

The Fire Laddies

The Seventh Regiment, which then and on so many occasions stood surety to New York for peace in the face of turbulence and riot, had been the Twenty-seventh National Guard until 1847, when the Governor of the State ordered that it become known as the Seventh Regiment National Guard. Its armory was on the Bowery, on the east side just below Cooper Union.

Most of the excitement of this sort up to this time was made up from among the Irish and Irish-Americans who already claimed the Bowery as their own. Rough they were, rather than tough in the modern Bowery sense. Ready for a lark, eager for a spree, reckless of consequences and unreckoning of the future, they yet had a quality of loyalty, of chivalry if you like, that seems to us, when we hear of it on the western frontier, very like heroism. Of such stuff were the Bowery B'hoys made who "ran with the machine" in the days of the volunteer fire department. Keen for the excitement of fire and possible rescue, those who did not belong to the company made short work of appropriating a fire laddie's jacket, and from this indiscriminate joining of the ranks, the machine acquired in time the bad name which clings to its memory. But the Bowery Boy of those days was not as the heir to his name to-day. "Mose" was a dandy in apparel, with carefully tended

The Bowery Boys

hair, close cropped in the back, the long locks in front stiffened with bear's grease, and then rolled and polished till the soap locks shone like glass bottles. Mr. Dayton admiringly describes him: "His broad, massive face was closely shaven, as beards in any shape were considered effeminate, and so forbidden by their creed ; a black, straight, broad-brimmed hat, polished as highly as a hot iron could effect was worn at a pitch forward, with a slight inclination to one side, . . . a large shirt collar turned down and loosely fashioned, school-boy fashion, so as to expose the full proportions of a brawny neck ; a black frock-coat with skirts extending below the knee ; a flashy satin or velvet vest, cut so low as to display the entire bosom of a shirt often embroidered ; pantaloons tight to the knee, thence gradually swelling in size to the bottom, so as nearly to conceal a foot usually of the most ample dimensions." Much jewelry, a swaggering gait, a language of his own, and his lady friend as carefully gotten up as himself completed the picture. But when the general immigration set in, and all the nations of the earth planted colonies tributary to the Bowery, trouble in earnest began.

The Bowery Boy knew the use of his fists in argument, but the Italian understood nothing about it, and cut the knot of the enigma with his stiletto. Pistols answered, and the race war

Changed Conditions of the Bowery

waged merrily. Meanwhile the more pretentious shops were moving up-town away from the Bowery, and drinking shops multiplied. The Pig & Whistle, the Duck and Frying Pan, and other jolly homes of the Bowery Boy gave place too often to the dive and the panel-house where life, honor, and property were equally hazarded. The days of the shadow dances, in which someone was surely sandbagged and robbed, and all the other curious iniquity of crime held carnival, are too near us to be picturesque, and yet the days of their glory are departed forever. A new day is shedding a dull light on the Bowery. Still the gardens and saloons and the occasional pistol-shot at night ; still the museums and cheap amusements ; more and more frequent the three golden balls, and the shops offering the cheapest clothing in the world; and the 25-cent and 10-cent lodging-houses, with all they mean of homeless men ever increasing. But from it all the zest is vanishing, and the Bowery, first the home of simple, serious, contented dignity and prosperity, then the great processional road and home of plenty ; next the scene of vigorous, lusty youth in its frolic and madness, then the haunt of low-browed crime, is seeming to slumber before awakening to a new phase.

Cooper Union stands across the upper end of the Bowery. The first annual report of the trustees describes the object of its erection :

Cooper Union

"Peter Cooper, a mechanic and merchant of the City of New York, having become satisfied early in life that the working classes of this city required greater opportunities for instruction and rational recreation than were afforded by existing institutions, determined, if he could command the means, to found an institution designed especially to supply the needs of which he himself had been conscious."

The building was erected in 1854, and a deed was executed, in 1859, to the trustees without reservation upon a trust specified in the Act of the Legislature, ". . . that the above mentioned and described premises, together with the appurtenances and the rents, issues, incomes, and profits thereof shall be forever devoted to the instruction and improvement of the inhabitants of the United States in practical science and art." That Mr. Cooper was right in reading the needs of the people the history of the institute has shown. Its utmost capacity has been taxed from the first, and the waiting list of those whom it cannot accommodate is as long as the list of those whom it is possible to admit. Its capacity has been enlarged by gifts and bequests from Mr. Cooper's immediate family and connection, and its work has expanded always in the direction intended by its founder. Gifts from friends of the institution who realize its meaning in the community have also aided in carrying out its founder's large hopes.

His grand-daughters, the Misses Hewitt,

The Bowery a Barrier

have this spring opened to the public use in the Cooper Union building a Museum of Decorative Arts which it is hoped will render to the public a service similar to that of Les Arts Decoratifs, in Paris.

On May 28, 1897, there was unveiled in the little triangular park looking down the Bowery from the front of the Cooper Union, a statue of Peter Cooper, by Augustus St. Gaudens, once a pupil in the institute, now our best-beloved sculptor. As the venerable seated figure looks down the Bowery we hope that he sees the dim beginning of that better day he strove for, when evil contention shall grow less and less, in the content of a people prosperous from full development under fair conditions ; freedom to be themselves in childhood, in play, in the new parks and playgrounds that are opening; in youth to study under the direction of the New Education which strives to give every one full development and control of mind and body ; and in maturity to express that developed self in work.

But to most, the Bowery to-day is the half-humorous, half-dreaded portion of the city, strange and foreign ; a quarter to be visited, but never known ; seemingly a vast, insurmountable social barrier, shutting off intercourse not only between the northern and southern parts of the city, but between its own eastern and western tributaries, so that these

The Bowery a Barrier

people living so near each other, having the same vital interests and opportunities, are yet as separate as though the sea rolled between them.

Barnard College

343 MADISON AVENUE

COURSES IN AMERICAN HISTORY

For Undergraduates. General course, reading, recitations and lectures.—Three hours a week: H. A. Cushing, A.M.

For Graduates. Political History of the Colonies and of the American Revolution.—This investigation course, extending through two years, deals in the first year with the settlement of the Colonies and their development in the seventeenth century, and in the second year with the growth of the system of colonial administration, the conflict with the French, and the revolt of the Colonies. The work of the students consists chiefly in the study of topics from the original sources, with a formal account of the results of such study.—Two hours a week for two years: Professor Herbert L. Osgood, Ph.D.

These courses are open not only to candidates for degrees, but to special students who can show ability to read French and German, and can satisfy the Dean and Faculty of their general competence.

HALF MOON SERIES
PAPERS ON HISTORIC
NEW YORK

EDITED BY
MAUD WILDER GOODWIN
ALICE CARRINGTON ROYCE
RUTH PUTNAM

The Bowery

By

Edward Ringwood Hewitt

and

Mary Ashley Hewitt

ON SALE AT G. P. PUTNAM'S SONS AND AT BRENTANO'S WHERE SUBSCRIPTIONS WILL BE RECEIVED

ISSUED MONTHLY

Price Ten Cents
One Dollar a Year

The City History Club of New York

◆◆◆◆

The City History Club aims to awaken a general interest in the history and traditions of New York, believing that such interest is one of the surest guarantees of civic improvement. Its work is carried on through three channels :

1.—A Normal Class
2.—Popular Classes
3.—Public Lectures

For further information, conditions of membership, etc., address

SECRETARY CITY HISTORY CLUB,
11 West 50th Street,
New York.

The Half Moon Series

The Second Series of the Half Moon Papers will commence in January, 1898, with a paper on "Slavery in Old New York," by V. Edwin Morgan.

Among other subjects treated will be "Tammany Hall," by Talcott Williams; "Family Names and Their Origin," by Berthold Fernow; "Bowling Green," by Spencer Trask; "Old Prisons," by Elizabeth Dike Lewis; "Breukelin," by Harrington Putnam; "Old Taverns and Posting Inns," by Elizabeth Brown Cutting; "Early Schools," by Edith Putnam.

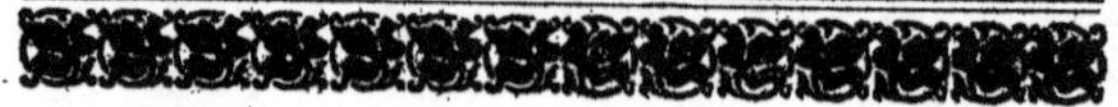

www.ingramcontent.com/pod-product-compliance
Lightning Source LLC
LaVergne TN
LVHW020551110826
845149LV00002B/232